Interest of

Love

(Thoughts)

Jeremy Tolbert

ISBN 978-1-0980-7367-1 (paperback)
ISBN 978-1-0980-9982-4 (hardcover)
ISBN 978-1-0980-7368-8 (digital)

Christian Faith Publishing
832 Park Avenue
Meadville, PA 16335
www.christianfaithpublishing.com

Printed in the United States of America

Contents

Introduction

Interest of Love is designed through the use of its divine inspiration to empower us to discover our true purpose. In order to do it, we must learn who we truly are, and it requires discovering our thoughts to be the first step! Thoughts will determine how we feel and how we view things. It is how we connect with the world around us and the people in it. The very first thought we have is the foundation of interest, and discovering what we think is the starting point of the *Interest of Love*. Interest is only an accumulation of thoughts. The more we think about one particular person or one particular thing, the more interested we become in them. The *Interest of Love* will explain why you will not think about something or someone you are not interested in, just like you cannot be interested in something or someone you've never think about.

Power of the Mind

Thoughts are the gateway to the mind! It is the one main element that controls our human behavior. A point of view is created purely through thoughts, and it is the sole communication we have between our mind and **everything that surrounds** us.

Our thoughts are what bridges the perception of how we think and **what** we **believe** together. Our collective thoughts are what accumulates to the way that we think. This is why, when new ideas are created inside of our minds, it can cause our opinions to change, and every time our opinions change, it is due to a development in a change of thoughts.

Our thoughts will determine how we interact and respond to any situation, and they are the predominant factor in controlling how we truly and honestly **feel.**

First Exercise:

Rate how your marriage is on a scale from 1 to 10, with 1.0 being the worst score and 10.0 being the highest, **or if you're not married, rate any relationship you have with someone that is important to you.**

Example: "I will rate my marriage, **or relationship with my father** a 7.5."

Question: **How would you rate your life in general** or at this very moment with using the same scale?

Example: "**I rate** my life over the course of **the last three years a** 6.2, or I rate my entire life at a 7.0."

Question: **What thoughts did you think of when you rated your relationship and life in this first exercise?**

Question: **Do you think your rate would have changed** if the thoughts you had were any different from the thoughts you were thinking at the time you answered these two questions?

Example: **Instead of thinking about a disagreement you had with your loved one, you think of something fun you both experienced together.**

Final Question: If your answer is "yes," explain to the best of your knowledge, why you think if you had different thoughts, it would cause your rate to these two questions to change?

If your mind were a computer, it would be the most dominative, innovative and expensive machine on the planet. And if this were so, your thoughts would be its software! Software is what controls how a computer operates, it is what brings its capabilities into existence, and it is ultimately what causes a computer to be able to function. Just like the brain uses our thoughts to carry out our requests and injunctions on its command, a computer uses software and other programs to enable it to operate.

Thoughts control how **our mind thinks, how it responds**, and **systematically** it **controls what** a **body does**. History has shown that when the brain loses its capability to think, as humans, we have lost our ability to act, our ability to respond, and even in the most severe cases, our ability to breathe on our own; have been lost, from the inability to think.

Studies show that the brain produces over 50 thoughts per minute and average around 3000 or more thoughts per hour. Our thoughts happen so quickly that our brain can translate massive amounts of data and send out various messages throughout the body simultaneously without our awareness. And it is all engineered through our ability to think. Our thoughts are so critical that we can be somewhere or doing something at a particular point in time and be unaware of what is going on at that very moment without the development of certain thoughts.

Even learning to do something different takes learning a new way of thinking, and a new way of thinking can only be developed by creating different thoughts. If it's a new job, a new schedule, a new workout regiment or just a different way of acting, none of these things can be performed without the brain's ability to evolve its way of thinking. And without the brain's ability to adjust, we would always be stuck in a behavior pattern that is consistently the same as we are at this very moment.

Example: **If I** just replace my old printer with a top-of-the-line printer with all the capabilities of the most superlative equipment on the market, **the machine cannot function** without first **downloading** the new software that goes with it.

Software is what gives the computer its instructions on what to do; it provides the network with its capabilities and establishes its programs to control the hardware operations. **Through the power of the mind, our thoughts do the same thing**.

Through the use of algorithms, the software processes a set of rules using its commands to problem solve and carry out operations according to its calculations.

Example: Like a flow chart, **software uses its** algorithms **to** tell its host to go left if this happens or go right if that happens; to stop if this is selected or to go forward if it is not selected.

A computer cannot operate new or old equipment without the installation of its programs, just like we cannot grow and mature without producing new thoughts.

You are what you do, and you do what you think; which means **we are identified by what we do, and** normally, you wouldn't find yourself doing anything without the thought of doing it first.

🍂 **Example: A funny person couldn't be funny without thinking of something that could make people laugh. A serious person could not be serious at a moment when their brain is effectuating humorous thoughts. And just like a depressed person's thoughts are** depressing, to be in that state of mind requires them to continuously produce depressing thoughts. Unless a depressing person has depressing thoughts, it would be impossible to be depressed or continue to stay that way!

🍂 *Question*: What score did you **rate** your marriage **or the relationship you chose with the person that is important in your life?**

🍂 **Question: What score did you rate** your life?

I've learned through experience that most people rate their marriage between a 5.0 for the low side and a 7.5 for the high side. The revealing part of it is according to the American standard grading scale, a score of 7.5 would put the typically highest rate for a marriage at a score of 75 percent. That's barely making a C!

According to how we rate our life, we typically score anywhere from a 3.0 for bad days and all the way up to a 9.0 when things are going well. The only problem with this is, that it leaves a spread of 6 points from the lowest number to the highest number typically given. With life giving us so many ups and downs, and with so many twists and turns, our life typically stays somewhere in the middle of these two rates. That averages out to a 6! This means many of us typically spend most of our lives unstable and at an average rate of 60 percent of possibly our fullest potential!

Thoughts give awareness and to think sheds light on the things not seen or thought of before. We can be living what we feel is an ordinary life, never realizing what life could be like if we knew how to access the power of our minds.

Think very carefully to every detail and remind yourself again of the thoughts that went through your mind right before you rated your life and the relationship you chose in the first exercise in this book.

🍂 *Question*: What were your thoughts?

You only know what you know, and **everything** you know can only be identified **by** what you think. This means, through the power of the mind, your individual thoughts about anyone or anything is conformed to the entirety of what you thought of and of what you subconsciously think! **That's why gossiping is frowned so heavily upon by God. It takes a person's thoughts of what they think about a person away and causes them to think the same way as the gossiper.** Our reality comes solely from what we know, and through the process of what we think, it gives knowledge of everything that we **believe**.

If we can gain control over this resource and use it effectively, it can not only turn our marriages around, but it also has the capability to change your whole world and the life you have **in it** into something better!

Thoughts are not just limited to what if, how come, or why is; they are more than just questions, answers, or suggestions inside of our minds. Thoughts are also the ideas you have, the decisions you make, and the determination that drives you. Our thoughts are definitely one of the major parts of what makes us as a species human, and how we think will be the one single determination of what makes us humane.

Animals are limited in their thoughts, which causes them to rely more on their animal instinct to get through life. Their intelligence is classified based on how they think and how they respond in certain situations. The frequency of the thought patterns of a more cerebral animal is distinctively different from an animal of lesser intelligence. Thoughts are the primary source of what separates the more intelligent species from the more primitive ones.

The body is controlled by the mind, and the mind is programmed through thoughts. Any action the body performs without thinking is only a mere reaction. That's why thoughts are considered the most powerful factor of humanity; it is what establishes what you do, it is what creates your spirituality, and it is what makes you, *you*.

In this book, we will answer many of the questions that are in**side** of our minds; and we will go through these teachings to uncover **and identify** many of the different thoughts that are so common to us. We will learn the effects that these thoughts have on our lives and **how they affect** the many different relationships we have with other people. Through the power of **choice**, **your** thoughts will **be** the key to **a better life**, and through the power of the teachings in this book, you will be able to access a greater volume of integrity, **happiness, and true self-worth**!

By placing the power of thoughts back into the hands of the beholder, where it belongs, it will give you the ability to have the power to control your mind. **Through the power of the mind,** you **will gain back the** power **you were destined** to have, ever since the beginning **of creation**, and it will give you back the purpose each and every one of us was born with, dating all the way back to when God first made man!

The Power of Choice

A choice is the act of selecting or the ability to make a decision when you have more than one possibility. In actuality, the mere knowledge of having a choice creates a wide range of possibilities that can alter or completely change our course of actions. With having the power of choice, you don't have to be what people limit you to or do the things that you are pressured to believe you have to do. You don't have to confine yourself to a certain space and you certainly don't have to accept what the majority of people want you to think.

Through choice, we have the power to break the cycles of distress and discomfort rotating in and out of our lives and we have the power to bring ourselves out of the ruts we find ourselves in. As a matter of fact, it is proven that only through the power of choice, can you become something greater than anything that was ever expected of you. And through the teachings in this book, you will be presented with the knowledge of many choices that can be made that will change your life forever! The knowledge taught through these teachings will allow you to be able to decide anything your mind can imagine. Most importantly, through the teachings in this book, you will be able to know the reason as to why a choice is chosen and also why a choice is not taken.

🖋 Question: Did you know that the power to choose is the most powerful ability known to humankind?

Every human being is given the power of choice! The power to choose is **what gives us authority over our lives. And** having a choice is what gives us the power to obtain the things desirable and put away the things that are undesirable. It can distinguish the difference between us **giving up** to us **overcoming and rising above**. It is what separates success from failure, **wrong** from **right**, good from bad, **and even life from death.** The power to choose is what separates and distinguishes us as human beings from **every** other living creation on the face of this planet.

God has given each and every one of us the power of choice, and because we possess this power, we possess the power to utilize this gift to maintain control over how we think and what we do. **Also, by possessing** this level of control, we have the ability to govern ourselves in the midst of this wonderful but troubled world. The ability to decide what we eat, what we drink, how we live, how we behave or how we react towards one another, whom to like or dislike and whom we serve are all examples of the many decisions we make every single day in each of our lives. Everything which is in your power to consciously do, knowingly or unknowingly of the outcome, is all done because we all have the ability to make a choice.

A choice to be happy or a choice to be unhappy, a choice to be loving or a choice to be unloving; **a choice** to be more caring or a choice not to care as much; a **choice** to be a good example; and, above all, the opportunity to be who you truly want to be are all parts of making a choice.

Question: What are some important choices you've made throughout your life?

Question: Have you ever made an important decision that you've **regretted? And if so, if you were given the chance, would you change or take back the decision you made?**

Every **decision** a person makes is entirely **based solely** on what that person knows **or thought of at the time that the choice was made.** This limits our possibilities to be contained only to the things that we recognize. That is why a lack of knowledge gives opportunities to make mistakes, but the regret of these mistakes gives us a knowledge that opens up the possibility to make better choices following every mistake we make.

Genesis 2:19

19 And out of the ground the LORD God formed every beast of the field and every fowl of the air; and brought them unto Adam to see what he would call them: and whatsoever Adam called every living creature, that was the name thereof. (Genesis 2:19)

When God created humankind, He gave them the power to choose, **and that power was demonstrated when Adam executed his ability to name all the animals that God created. The Heavenly Father not only gave man the ability to name the animals, but He also gave humanity the ability to decide how we as individuals will be identified. And it gives us a choice to decide how we should live in correspondence to the possibilities that we face.**

Example: Hating the world for what it has done to you can make you a hateful person but choosing to dedicate your life to making the world better than what it has shown you, can make both you and the world, better.

Through the power of thoughts anything is possible, and you can monopolize that power to become whatever type of person you want to be. And what you become will only be done through the act of making a choice.

Quote: "You are what you do, and what you choose to do, solely comes from the thoughts you think."

With being offered a choice, there are bad decisions, good decisions, and even better decisions with every opportunity we decide to take.

And with every choice, no matter how big or how small, it has **rewards and** consequences **attached to every single decision we make.**

Deuteronomy 30:19

19 I call heaven and earth to record this day against you, that I have set before you life and death, blessing and cursing: therefore choose life, that both thou and thy seed may live. (Deuteronomy 30:19)

Every choice we make will have a direct effect on **our lives, and with every decision we've made, it has changed the way we choose to live our lives from the exact moment.**

Proverbs 6:6-11

6 Go to the ant, thou sluggard; consider her ways, and be wise:

7 Which having no guide, overseer, or ruler,

8 Provideth her meat in the summer, and gathereth her food in the harvest.

9 How long wilt thou sleep, O sluggard? when wilt thou arise out of thy sleep?

10 Yet a little sleep, a little slumber, a little folding of the hands to sleep:

11 So shall thy poverty come as one that travelleth, and thy want as an armed man. (Proverbs 6:6-11)

With every choice we have, there is a perception attached that comes from the way we think. Even if the reward comes later in life, a good choice will always be worth the payment or reward no matter how hard the decision may be, and a bad choice's benefits will never equal its cost. By definition, a bad choice that is done knowingly or unknowingly, will eventually always cause remorse, hardship, and regret in due time.

Genesis 3:1-6

3 Now the serpent was more subtil than any beast of the field which the LORD God had made. And he said unto the woman, Yea, hath God said, Ye shall not eat of every tree of the garden?

2 And the woman said unto the serpent, We may eat of the fruit of the trees of the garden:

3 But of the fruit of the tree which is in the midst of the garden, God hath said, Ye shall not eat of it, neither shall ye touch it, lest ye die.

4 And the serpent said unto the woman, Ye shall not surely die:

5 For God doth know that in the day ye eat thereof, then your eyes shall be opened, and ye shall be as gods, knowing good and evil.

6 And when the woman saw that the tree was good for food, and that it was pleasant to the eyes, and a tree to be desired to make one wise, she took of the fruit thereof, and did eat, and gave also unto her husband with her; and he did eat. (Genesis 3:1-6)

Question: What would cause someone to choose to throw their lives away?

Question: What would cause someone not to care or give up trying?

Final Question: What would cause someone to sin against God?

Thoughts are everything. It is what we think, it is what we know, and it is what gives a perception to everything that we imagine. What we see comes from our thoughts, and **how we see will determine the perception of our understanding.** Satan caused Eve to doubt God through ideas, and her doubt, created by her thoughts, led her directly into choosing to sin against God. When Adam was faced with the choice not to sin and possibly lose Eve forever, he ate the fruit also, and they both became sinners.

Studies have shown that, staggeringly, on average, we make less than 30 percent of our own choices in life. These studies have also shown that majority of our decisions have been made through influences, situations, and thoughts harvested through our subconscious mind. If we do what we do because "that is all we know," or in a reaction to, then our power of choice will begin to fade away and we will become similar to a more primitive species. Life fills itself up with new choices every day, and the choices we make will be a contributor to what our lives are acceptable to. But no matter how bad life gets, each day will always present you with a choice to make your life better.

Question: Are you where you want to be in life right now, with no regrets?

Question: Have you done all you can to have the best relationship with the people that are most important in your life?

Question: Are you how you want to be and who you want to be right now?

Final Question: If you said "no" to any of these questions, why haven't you decided to change it?

This book will show you through the examples, questions, and exercises how making the right choices can dramatically change your life and how you feel about everything imaginable! And through this knowledge, you will know the benefits of making certain choices and the disadvantages of making specific decisions.

Question: What grade did you give when you **were asked to rate your life and your relationship** in Exercise #1 located in the previous chapter of this book?

🍂 *Question*: **Were you satisfied with your score, or** if you could, **would you** choose to **take the necessary steps to increase the** rating you gave?

The way we think is the primary source that directs the decisions that we make and the actions that we take. It is what has control over us, and it has been doing just that ever since we formed our very first thought! One right decision, no matter how small, leads to a better life, and one good thought increases your chances of making that right choice.

Struggling to make a choice is solely based on having a mixture of thoughts. According to the power of choice, if you know what to do, all you have to do is do it, and in order to do it requires thinking of doing it first!

If you are struggling to make the right choice, it is because you either don't know what to do or you are in between different thoughts **on what decisions to make** next. This will cause you not to know what to do. Wisdom comes from knowledge, and knowledge only comes from what we know. Understanding the effects of our thoughts and the consequences of our choices in life can clearly give you the insight of knowing what steps you need to take next.

🍂 Exercise: #2

Close your eyes and erase all thoughts from your mind. Once your mind is clear, open your eyes again and continue on reading:

Place the thoughts into your mind as listed: "I am hopeless." "I would only make things worse." "My life isn't worth fixing." "My marriage is over."

"There are better things I can be doing than reading this book." "This book is a waste of my time!"

🍂 *Question*: What do these thoughts make you want to do?

🍂 *Question*: How does this affect the way you feel about reading this book?

After you've answered these two questions, close your eyes and erase all the last thoughts entirely out of your mind once again, and when your head is clear, continue with the *Exercise*.

Place the thoughts into your mind as listed: "This book sounds really great." "The content so far has been truly **inspirational**." "My marriage isn't over just yet!" "I still have time to turn my life around." "I believe reading this book will be well worth my time!"

🍂 *Question*: What do these thoughts inspire you to do?

🍂 *Question*: How does it change the way you feel about reading this book?

This exercise was taken to **reveal an example of how the power of thoughts works. If you found these thoughts to be less convincing, it is only because you didn't convince yourself of what you were thinking. We only know what we know, and if our thoughts are contradictory or if it's causing us to second guess how we think, it will make what we know to be indecisive or perceived through blurred lines. This exercise** can also be used to show proof as to how your thoughts can control the way you feel and significantly influence the decisions you make.

In the next chapter of this book, we will proceed to go deeper inside the mind to reveal what we truly think. These teachings will reveal to you that mind control is just that; it's merely having control over the mind. By controlling your thoughts, you will gain back control over your mind and possess the power to regain back control over your life. By putting you back in the driver's seat, where you belong, you will be able to consciously decide where life is going to take you next. And it all begins with realizing what you already know!

Take action now! (Turn to pages #243 through #265 for recommended fasts and exercises.)

Realization of Thoughts

Realization is the act of becoming fully aware, and it is the acknowledgment of accepting something as being true. It is the outcome developed through the perception of why; and it is also the comprehension of the knowledge obtained, that transforms the recognition of our understanding. We **only** know what we know, and through the power of our thoughts, realization is the pathway to bringing everything that we know into reality as we know it.

Example: Every time you learn something new, you realize something that you didn't think of or know before. And that something you didn't know existed before, just got brought into reality by the realization of your thoughts.

That's the power of realization, and even at this very moment, without **its awareness**, you wouldn't be able to fully understand the enlightenment of what you are reading in this book!

The mind knows what it knows, and our thoughts are everything that we know. The realization of our thoughts is what separates a mistake from being a deliberate choice, and it is the difference between the knowing and unknowing.

Example: Everyone knows that having sex before marriage has a risk of contracting a sexually transmitted disease or caus-

ing an unplanned pregnancy. Premarital sex comes at even a far greater risk when it is done without using protection. Yet, many of us knowing the risks, will still engage in sexual activities before marriage. Typically, it is only when a person has just contracted a disease or found out they are pregnant when they would really know or actually realize the risk they were taking by having premarital sex.

Realization is one of the essential attributes of life because it is the creation of knowledge. It is what gives an understanding of what we do and who we are at that moment. In its absence is the nature of ignorance. And by the lack thereof, is the cause of something or someone being disregarded, ignored, or overlooked.

Question: Have you ever been in a conversation or listening to someone and "zoned out"?

In life, focus is key! Focus allows us to concentrate, it enables us to be determined, and it **gives us** the ability to **be able to understand what is being done or said at that moment**. It is the ability to pay **closer** attention **to something or someone by allowing you to block out distracting thoughts that cause a lack of focus, which can potentially cause someone to be ignored**.

When the mind wanders off, **it causes us to think differently from what the mind should be focusing on at that moment**. While having a conversation, it produces a reaction more than a response, and it encourages us to fill in the gaps of what we missed with preconceived notions that often cause us to jump to conclusions.

Question: If the rarest, most beautiful flower grew in the middle of the forest miles and miles away from civilization and no one was around to see, would it cause that flower not to exist or be the **rarest most beautiful** flower in the world?

Answer: No, the flower will still exist, but you just wouldn't see it to be able to realize it was there!

Many relationships grow dry and distant because the people in them don't realize the importance of their correlation, nor do they recognize each other's value. Many people live redundant lives with no **real** meaning or no **practical** purpose because they fall short of realizing what is **truly** important to them. We get so consumed in gadgets and social media that the best thing in your life could be standing right in front of you, and **still be out of your reach.** If you don't have the power to break away from being so consumed, you **can** miss out on the most important thing to you and not even realize it!

Through the power of thoughts, it is impossible to realize anything new without processing new thoughts; and **without creating new thoughts, it will be impossible for you to know anything more than what you know right now.**

Realization releases not only knowledge of the present; it also preserves the knowledge of the past. To change how you would think in the future, you must realize something you never thought of before that moment. And if you have to correct the incorrect thinking you had before, you must recognize the wrong ideas you had in the past!

Thoughts are not only what we think; they are also what we know, and it is the absolute **comprehension** of all existence. Our thoughts link what is going on outside of ourselves to what is going on inside of our minds, and it is the instrument that transforms our perception into reality as we know it!

🍃 *Question*: What is the best thing to ever happen to you?

🍃 *Question*: How did it make you feel when you realized the best thing that ever happened to you happened?

That's the importance of realization; it inspires improvement, and it is the acceptance of truth. Through its thoughts, it develops into what causes things to become important to us, and it can reveal to us the things we thought were vital to us but really are not. Realization is the act of bringing everything we know and feel into existence. It is the creator of true discernment, and without realization, what gives life true purpose can be standing right outside, and you will not realize it!

Revelation 3:20

20 Behold, I stand at the door, and knock: if any man hear my voice, and open the door, I will come in to him, and will sup with him, and he with me. (Revelation 3:20)

Question: Who intentionally wants to do something wrong or desire for something bad to happen to them?

Question: If your answer is no one, **then I ask** why so often that so many of us when we are given a choice between good and bad, we choose bad; and when given an opportunity to do what's right, we choose the wrong things to do?

Final Question: Why do so many people hate correction when correction is the only thing that can take something that is wrong and make it right?

Knowledge leads to wisdom, and knowing truth is the **gateway of** distinguishing facts from fiction. **Not** acknowledging the truth when it is presented is like turning your back to wisdom when it presents itself.

Proverbs 1:20-22

20 Wisdom crieth without; she uttereth her voice in the streets:

21 She crieth in the chief place of concourse, in the openings of the gates: in the city she uttereth her words, saying,

22 How long, ye simple ones, will ye love simplicity? and the scorners delight in their scorning, and fools hate knowledge? (Proverbs 1:20–22)

There are many people in this world who are miserable because they are forced to live with regrets of making wrong choices in their lives. Some may **have** even made bad decisions intentionally, knowing very well the choices that they were making were wrong. **Maybe wrong choices were** committed without thinking, **which is why m**any times, if you were to ask them to give you a reason why they made the wrong choice, they could not give you a **reason as to why. Thoughts provide us with knowledge, and knowledge is knowing; not thinking of what you do is the same as not knowing what you do or what you've done.**

>**Proverbs 1:23-28**
>**23** Turn you at my reproof: behold, I will pour out my spirit unto you, I will make known my words unto you.
>
>**24** Because I have called, and ye refused; I have stretched out my hand, and no man regarded;
>
>**25** But ye have set at nought all my counsel, and would none of my reproof:
>
>**26** I also will laugh at your calamity; I will mock when your fear cometh;
>
>**27** When your fear cometh as desolation, and your destruction cometh as a whirlwind; when distress and anguish cometh upon you.
>
>**28** Then shall they call upon me, but I will not answer; they shall seek me early, but they shall not find me. (Proverbs 1:23–28)

All it takes to make a mistake or make the wrong choice is to have the wrong thoughts in mind.

Realization of thoughts is knowing, and in wisdom we find truth. Once we begin to make unwise choices in life, it can tend to become a part of **who we are.** And the wisdom we once had not to do the things we now do, leaves us, and we are left stuck with living uncomfortably in our own sins and thinking, "It's just a way of life."

🍃 *Question*: Have you ever done something foolish, and as soon as it was done, you come to realize it and say, "Now, why did I do that?"

Realization is awareness. It is insight, and if anything is to come between you and knowing the right thing to do, it will be because of the perception you have created through your very own thoughts. Through your thoughts, your understanding can change. And according to perception, some things could have always been looked at as being wrong, but now, be thought of as right.

🍃 *Question*: Have you ever referred to yourself in the second person or referenced yourself as "we" while you were reflecting on something or making a decision?

🍃 *Example*: If I had done something wrong, I would generally think to myself, "Now why did I do that?" or "What was I thinking?" Normally, I would never refer to myself as *"you,"* by my first name or in plural form without consciously thinking about it first.

As humans, we typically think to ourselves in the first person or maybe even in the third person; but to think of yourself in the second person without making a conscious decision to do so would usually signify some sort of mental breakdown or a medical condition such as being bi-polar. What we don't realize is, there is another reason why we can have a conversation with ourselves in the second person.

The term *second person* means to be addressed by someone other than oneself. By definition, this means making a notion or suggestion that is in "second person," it usually requires there to be more than one person involved.

Revelation 12:7-9

7 And there was war in heaven: Michael and his angels fought against the dragon; and the dragon fought and his angels,

8 And prevailed not; neither was their place found any more in heaven.

9 And the great dragon was cast out, that old serpent, called the Devil, and Satan, which deceiveth the whole world: he was cast out into the earth, and his angels were cast out with him. (Revelation 12:7–9)

Mainly throughout the entire Bible, there haven't been any instances of someone having had direct contact with Satan on earth outside of Eve in the Garden of Eden or Jesus when He came down as the Son of Man. But there have been countless instances where his deceptions caused many people to fall.

Question: How can a person be deceived by someone they've never seen or talked to, directly or indirectly, before?

The most intimate conversation you can have with someone is through their thoughts, as opposed to communicating with them only through words. Words are only meant to spark a thought in the hearer's mind, and nothing less or nothing more.

Quote: *"Pay close attention."*

Prayer is communication with the Most High, but to have a conversation with God while having your thoughts on something else is like being on a date with someone **who is constantly on their phone** the entire night. God's most effective way of communicating with us is through our thoughts, and if our mind is thinking of something else, it will be as if He **wasn't talking at all! Realization is so powerful; in its absence, it can cause our thoughts to create a reality where it seems as if even God Himself doesn't exist!**

Quote: "I didn't think about that."

Our thoughts have a significant role in our beliefs, and it also has a vital role in our awareness. Our thoughts have everything to do with what we are conscious of, and it absolutely makes up the entirety of what we think. To make an absolute conscious choice, we must be fully aware and understand what is taking place, and to have an effective conversation **requires the** acknowledgment of what is being said. Often, to be fully aware of what is **being** said, it sometimes takes knowing who is doing the talking!

🍂 *Question*: Have you ever seen a situation on tv where two fictional characters were giving advice to the same person, at the same time?

🍂 Example: A cartoon where there is an angel talking in one ear and a devil talking in the other ear of a person, trying to convince them to take their advice.

🍂 *Question*: What if I told you those **fictional characters aren't so** fictional at all?

Some people teach that it is your conscience that talks to you, or you may be addressed inside of your mind by some other kind of inherent existence. And all of this might be true, and many may even refer to it as a "conscious way of thinking," but try **doing** this exercise and see if you realize something more.

🍂 Exercise: #3

Think of a difficult choice you've been avoiding to make. Once you've thought of a choice, try to make a decision by brainstorming the pros and cons of the different choices you can make.

🍃 Question: Did you have any thoughts that you haven't thought of before, or did you come to realize something you didn't previously think of?

🍃 Question: While thinking of all the different options you have; did you ever reference yourself as you or we?

🍃 Example: "I know that I'm taking a chance." "I think we should do this." "You should just call things off and walk away."

🍃 Question: Did you have any thoughts that **suddenly** came out of nowhere and come against what you were thinking **of at the** time your thoughts were causing you to decide **to do what you thought was best for you?**

🍃 Example: I think I should go back to school. Furthering my education can give me something positive to do, while at the same time, I can make more money or get a better job. But **you are** too old to go back to school. When **you** step into that class, everyone is going to turn around and think, what are **you** doing here. No, that's not true! There are a lot of people my age that are going back to school. But those people are smarter than you, and they have more money. Well, maybe school is not for me, and I should've gone to school a long time ago, and now I think it's too late.

🍃 **Question:** If these thoughts have a similar pattern to something you've experienced before, why would you think of something negative while in the middle of brainstorming the benefits of making a decision **unless you had doubt?** And more importantly, why would you address yourself as you, instead of I or me?

🍃 Example: The conversation should have gone more this way if you were thinking about going back to school:

I think I should go back to school. Furthering my education can give me something positive to do, while at the same time, I can make more money or get a better job. But what if **I am** too old? I feel like if I step into that classroom, everyone is going to turn around and stare at me. Maybe, I need a little more time to think about it.

(Thoughts outside of yourself can also play a positive role in your life.)

🍂 Example: Thinking to yourself, you can do something and begin to develop doubt. And it **later causes you now to think, *No, I can't*. And as soon as you were about to give up, thoughts suddenly come out of nowhere into mind and say, "*You can do it*" and to,** *"Just keep trying and give it all you got!"* But what if I fail? *"It doesn't matter, as long as you tried, that's all that counts."*

A person overhearing what was being said will normally think two people were having a conversation. **While o**nly the person who is having the conversation will **normally** think **that nothing was odd and that** they were **only just talking to** themselves.

🍂 Question: So, how far do these thoughts go?

> Ephesians 6:12
> 12 For we wrestle not against flesh and blood, but against principalities, against powers, against the rulers of the darkness of this world, against spiritual wickedness in high places. (Ephesians 6:12)

🍂 Question: If **the thoughts you are having are all your own thoughts during these particular instances when you are having a conversation with yourself,** why would your first reaction be to question what you just thought and began to talk in the second person?

🍂 **Question: How can you disagree with yourself and then turn around and agree and again disagree without developing new**

thoughts or without consciously realizing something that you didn't think about before?

🍃 **Question:** What if a horribly inaccurate thought comes to mind?

🍃 Example: "If you do this, it will make all your problems go away."

🍃 Question: "What if that thought led you to use drugs or something worse like suicide?"

🍃 Final *Question*: If it was only your conscience, how can your conscience tell you to do something that will hurt you or that you are fully aware is wrong **to do**?

🍃 **Quote: "I say this in good conscience."**

Usually, when someone is consciously telling themselves to do something, it is always something that they truly feel is right. Your conscience can't tell you to do something you don't believe, and it certainly can't tell you to do something that you feel is wrong! The only way something can tell you to do something that is good or bad outside of what you already believe is if that something is truly something other than yourself.

> **Matthew 16:22-23**
> **22** Then Peter took him, and began to rebuke him, saying, Be it far from thee, Lord: this shall not be unto thee.
> **23** But he turned, and said unto Peter, Get thee behind me, Satan: thou art an offence unto me: for thou savourest not the things that be of God, but those that be of men. (Matthew 16:22–23)

The greatest deception Satan has ever committed was to convince everyone that he doesn't exist. If he can persuade you to think that his thoughts are your very own, it will create a perception in your mind that this is who you truly are, and *"making yourself your own worst enemy."*

Thoughts can cause family members to fight; **it can cause loved ones to hate one another**, it can cause friends to become **each other's** worst enemies, **and it can cause you to be significantly misled by your very own perception.**

It can cause someone to be depressed and stay that way; it can make an addiction out of a habit and cause many people to give up **on their dreams and on life itself!** Your thoughts can create a rift between friends and allies, and it can cause separation between **a** husband and wife.

If Satan can influence one spouse to think of things one way and the other spouse to think of the same situation **in a totally** different **way, he can cause** a small situation to become much more serious than what it was before. And by doing so, it will take someone from being fairly compromising, to thinking in a way that is destructive **and otherwise overwhelming. Being misunderstood** will cause a discord inside any relationship, which means it will even create a rift between the Creator and you!

> Quote: "Pride comes from thoughts, and if you are too proud **for correction**, your pride will cause you to live in ignorance, not because you have to, but because you choose too!"

Question: Have you ever been led to get help when you needed it the most or come to the front of a church for prayer and thoughts were created inside of your head that changed your mind?

Question: If you said, "Yes," to this question, when you were being *thought* out of doing something you wanted to do, were the thoughts you were having in first person or second person?

Thoughts can change the decision we want to make, by putting the idea of what someone else might be thinking into our mind.

🌿 Example: If you get help, it's admitting to everyone there's something wrong or that you are weak.

Thoughts can cause you to make bad decisions in life because it causes you to think, "You are trying too hard to be perfect," or maybe, "You must think you're better than everyone else." Or maybe thoughts can make you feel like being different is bad or respecting yourself is thinking that you're better than everyone else. Perhaps the wrong thoughts can even cause you to hate an entire race of people, many of whom you've never met before. Your thoughts that say, "They all are the same" or "They all only want one thing," can lead to not only being thoughts but being the way that you think.

Negative thoughts have negative effects, and it is the sole cause of making anything you don't like or any person that you detest unlikable. Many times, you will only see what you think, and having negative thoughts about someone or something will almost always cause you to see them in a negative way. Anytime you notice a person or think of someone, an impression is applied to how you think of that person. Creating a feeling toward a person due to the thoughts or memories you have of them doesn't happen intentionally but automatically due to perception. If a new thought is generated, a new feeling will also be created, causing your opinion to change and adjust, just like your thoughts.

Ever since humankind sinned, we've been given the knowledge of good and evil; and for that reason, we also have the knowledge of wrong and right. For many reasons, people have made the wrong decisions throughout our history. And personally, there are many reasons we make bad decisions throughout our life. To know that making a bad decision will absolutely only make things worse, and by understanding the power of choice we are given, we can come to realize that bad things don't always have to stay that way.

We can correct our mistakes and start to improve our lives, starting today. **But, in order to do so,** we must first realize the difference between our **thoughts and whose thoughts are doing the talking**!

Take action now! (Turn to pages #243 through #265 for recommended fasts and exercises.)

Introduction

🍃 **Exercise: #4 (Think carefully.)**

🍃 *Question*: **When was the last time you felt really good about something?**

🍃 *Question*: What type of thoughts were you experiencing **at that** time?

🍃 *Question*: During **this** time of enjoyment, **did you experience** any thoughts of discouragement, or were you thinking of anything **negative, or that** would cause you to get upset or feel hopeless?

🍃 *Question:* **If your answer is "yes," what kind of effect did it have on you?**

And if your answer is "no," what do you think would have happened to the way that you felt if those thoughts did occur?

🍃 *Question*: **When was the last time you felt happy while having discouraging thoughts; or felt worried or bad while having encouraging thoughts?**

How we think **is** how we feel, **which makes what we think and what we feel both** one and the same. You will never feel sad from thinking happy thoughts, just like you can never be happy when producing negative thoughts. **That's** why it is virtually imperative at the time of enjoyment that our thoughts during **those** times are complementary to the way that we feel **while we are in that** moment. If our thoughts are contrary to the way that we feel, it will absolutely reduce or quite possibly change the way we feel altogether.

🍃 *Example:* **Imagine you were enjoying a** date night with your spouse **or loved one,** and you want to top it off by going to see

34

a really good movie together. But the whole time, while you are at the movies, **all your loved ones can think of** is how they can't believe how much they charge for popcorn these days.

📝 **Question: Do you think those thoughts would have any effect on how much that person enjoyed being with you on a date night? And if so, give some examples of what kind of effects you think these thoughts would have?**

📝 *Question:* **If you've possessed these same negative thoughts, how do you think these thoughts would've affected you?**

Typically, it is impossible to think contrary to positive thinking while truly experiencing a positive moment; or **to think of disappointing thoughts continuously** while truly feeling blessed.

📝 *Example:* Dreams are merely virtual images developed in the mind that are created through thoughts. Although **dreams** are not real, it will be next to impossible to wake up from a good dream and be in a foul mood. If you find yourself in a bad mood after a good dream, it is usually the thoughts you have **developed** after you wake up **from the dream** that causes **there to be a** change **in** the way **that** you **feel.**

📝 *Question:* If you are still in doubt, **I ask,** when was the last time you felt good about something while having disgruntled thoughts or when was the last time you felt depressed or angry while thinking positively?

Thinking Positive

Positive thinking is the act of creating positive thoughts, and **it is in** these thoughts **that we** view the presence rather than the absence of certain **substances**, conditions, or **features**. It **generates improvement and** holds **an** account for creating a good perception rather than having a constant negative point of view, **which is common among many of us living in the world today.** Thinking positive creates confidence instead of insecurities. It encourages **growth** instead of discourag**ing potential. And** it **projects emphasis** on making things better instead of focus**ing** on **thoughts that** affects causes things to get worse.

> **Genesis 2:7**
> **And the LORD God formed man of the dust of the ground, and breathed into his nostrils the breath of life, and man became a living soul. (Genesis 2:7)**

Positive energy promotes positiv**ity** and moves forward while negative energy promotes negativity **and** retracts backward. **Producing negative thoughts can cause us to look back in the past, creating an opportunity to generate a feeling of regret and despair, but positive thinking allows us to grow from our past, and in doing so, it allows us to build hope for a better tomorrow.**

It is **thought of by many** that **energy was used to form humanity, and if that is true, it will also be what makes the use of that same energy be the source that continues to bring life to every living creature on the face of the earth.**

> **Quote: "Like the flow of water through a river, positive thinking brings on positive changes and gives life to everything it touches."**

Energy is the physical property that must be transferred to a recipient in order for the receiver to produce **movement** or generate **growth**.

Many **scientists** believe energy cannot be created nor destroyed, but **that it has to** be absorbed or channeled through specific acts **to be transferred from one place to another.** Positive energy is generated by positive thinking, and **positive thinking induces** movement in **a positive direction.** This progression is what causes us to move and grow as we are designed to. And by moving as we are intended to, it will form a vacuum effect that creates an urge for us to also move into our purpose.

Question: Have you ever realized that happy people **hardly ever** complain **or worry**?

The presumption **for** some people is that happy people don't complain **or worry as much as others do** because there is nothing **really bad that ever happens to** them, for them to worry nor complain about. **Although,** if you think about it, **even for the wealthiest of people,** there is very little to nothing in life that is perfect, **and that will always** leave room for **an opportunity to always have cause to worry or complain. Unfortunately, living in a world that is transformed by an opinionated society has led to an increase in extreme political views and negative commentaries around the world. With so much political correctness and inequality spread throughout the country, it is popular to be biased and show favoritism. And not to mention with sickness, self-doubt, and relation-**

ships falling apart every day, it leaves everyone to have something to worry and complain about and a reason to be unhappy.

Question: So is it, that **some people are** happy **because they have nothing to worry or complain about**, or is it **the** people who do the least **amount of** complaining **or worrying** are **the people** who are the happiest?

> **Galatians 6:7**
> 7 Be not deceived; God is not mocked: for whatsoever a man soweth, that shall he also reap. (Galatians 6:7)

Positive influences give off positive energy, and positive energy comes from positive thinking.

Negative thoughts are the creator of all negative things, and these negative things are what cause suffering to come upon every single one of us. Negativity can negatively consume you completely. No matter how powerful the negativity is around you, it will have absolutely no negative effect on you without your submission or acceptance to not think positive.

Positive **thoughts have positive** attributes that typically **include cheerfulness, generosity, and optimism. And above all, any thoughts that are considered to be positive must have the ability to cause someone's happiness or** success **in life.**

Example: **A customer asked a disgruntled worker at a restaurant if they were having a good day. The cashier answered in a sarcastic tone of voice, "I sure am!" The customer replied by asking, "How can you be having a good day when you are clearly unhappy?" The cashier didn't answer, so the customer began to explain to the cashier, "You are how you feel, and you feel how you think." A happy person will have happy thoughts, and an angry person will have angry thoughts. If an angry person had the thoughts of a happy person, they would no longer be angry but feel as they think. If you want** to change the way your day is going and genuinely have a good day, you must first change the way that you think.

Quote: "Remember, every day may not be good, but it is good in every day."

Question: Do you believe in good luck?

It cannot be scientifically proven that a form of good luck can be channeled into a particular object or form. It also can't be proven that a series of good luck has the ability to be distributed through specific act**s**. However, possessing a **good luck** charm or believing in any other superstitious aspect of good luck will produce positive thinking. In return, positive thinking will create a positive action that will absolutely result in a better or more positive outcome.

Quote: "What we know is what transforms into how we think, but it is the attitude of how we think, that will create a mindset for the way we act."

A positive mindset is a mindset that consumes your thoughts and changes the way you think into a pattern that complements its meaning. It expels an energy that is positively driven and is motivating to everyone in its grasp. There are tons of motivational quotes, self-motivational books, and programs out there just to teach **us** how to be positive. But it is important for us to learn that **in order to be positive, we must first learn how to think** positive thoughts. By simply changing a "no" into a "yes," an "I can't" into an "I can" or a "it will never happen" into an "anything is possible" can lead to making more positive choices and performing more positive actions in life.

Opportunities present choices, and either choosing to think positively or negatively will lead to the kind of choices that we make.

Example: **Household problems will either cause people living in them to work together to fix the problem or cause them to**

**become accustomed to the issues as they grow further apart.
Difficulties in a job or at school can cause a person to want
to quit and give up on trying, or it can challenge them to use
every resource they have to rise above their hurdles and create
a stronger effort to achieve success. Problems in life can cause
someone to fall and it can even cause them to want to take
their own life, but by thinking positively, it will lead them to
know that giving up on life and neglecting to fight is the last
thing they want to do.**

Positivity possesses the attributes of being certain, and it is the
surety of believing in who you are and what you stand for. A show of
confidence is the ideal way of thinking positive, and it is in that belief
that will allow you to move **decisively** in your purpose.

Matthew 5:13-16

13 Ye are the salt of the earth: but if the salt
have lost his savor, wherewith shall it be salted?
it is thenceforth good for nothing, but to be cast
out, and to be trodden under foot of men.

14 Ye are the light of the world. A city that
is set on an hill cannot be hid.

15 Neither do men light a candle, and put
it under a bushel, but on a candlestick; and it
giveth light unto all that are in the house.

16 Let your light so shine before men,
that they may see your good works, and glorify your Father which is in heaven. (Matthew
5:13–16)

*Quote: "Either doubt and uncertainties of not
knowing who you truly are will dim your light or
the light that you have in your life will shine and
light up the world you live in."*

Believing in yourself and realizing you have the power over your life **is essential to making a positive change.** Encouragement causes hope, and through that hope, **there comes** a belief that something is possible. Positive **energy** generates new life to whoever accepts it. And having a positive conversation with someone can alter your thoughts, just by the act of exchanging information.

🍃 Example: Communicating positively with your spouse will always move your relationship forward, and it can definitely bring your marriage closer to becoming an *"A+"* marriage.

Thinking positive **creates a feeling that anything is possible,** and it builds a confidence in you **that encourages you to go after your dreams. Believing** in yourself will **always** help you to keep going, **and it** will bring you closer to obtaining bigger and greater things. **Appreciation creates gratitude,** and making a **sacrifice builds a life** worth living!

> *Quote: "If you are persistent in your goals, you will get it. If you are consistent with the way you achieved your goals, you will keep it."*

Your perception comes from your thoughts, and the way we see things comes from the way we look at them. You can change your perception simply by changing your thoughts. If you choose not to change the way you view things, the way you see the world and everyone in it will always stay the same. Life is not always fair, and a marriage is not always perfect, but seeing things through a positive light will make the way you view any situation look a little better.

Ephesians 5:25-27
   25 Husbands, love your wives, even as Christ also loved the church, and gave himself for it;
   26 That he might sanctify and cleanse it with the washing of water by the word,

27 That he might present it to himself a glorious church, not having spot, or wrinkle, or any such thing; but that it should be holy and without blemish. (Ephesians 5:25–27)

Question: How can you see anyone, including yourself, any different from what you think?

Studies show that the more positive attributes we notice about our spouse, the more enjoyable our marriage will become. Thinking negatively about something or someone will only lessen the desire we have. **You only know what you know and o**nly through the power of thoughts can you create a perfect marriage **that involves** imperfect people.

> *Quote: "We can complain because roses have thorns, or we can rejoice because thorns have roses."*

Genesis 3:21-23

21 Unto Adam also and to his wife did the LORD God make coats of skins, and clothed them.

22 And the LORD God said, Behold, the man is become as one of us, to know good and evil: and now, lest he put forth his hand, and take also of the tree of life, and eat, and live for ever:

23 Therefore the LORD God sent him forth from the garden of Eden, to till the ground from whence he was taken. (Genesis 3:21–23)

We are made to produce, and if we are not productive in any "way, shape, or form," it will lead us to having no purpose, and we will become meaningless. Humanity is a creation of positive energy, and that energy illustrates effectiveness, **loving-kindness**, and Godliness. Negativity only is good if it is used toward negative things, and if we are negative towards how we are meant to be, it will only take away from **us** serving our real purpose.

Quote: "If every day were good, no day would be."

📎 **Question: Does your life consist of more bad days than good days or more good days than bad days?**

Yin and yang is a Chinese philosophy that teaches how seemingly opposite forces are complementary to **one** another. It is likened **to these same** teaching**s that** God **will show you** through the *Interest of Love,* how thoughts, negative and **positive,** are necessary to give the perception **of a reality where both actually exist and also have a purpose.**

📎 *Example:* If every day is good, **it will make no day be; because every day would be the same.** Not knowing **the difference between good and bad will leave us with no realization of what is good or bad, and only knowing one without the other will cause you to have no appreciation for having the good or hope when you are experiencing the bad. So by experiencing bad days will always give an opportunity for good days to exist as well.**

Quote: *"What doesn't kill you will not only make you stronger, it will also make you wiser."*

Everything in life is a learning experience. Therefore, if everything were done right, life wouldn't present an opportunity for growth, and without a struggle, it would be impossible to become stronger than what we are right now. Adversities build character, and pleasure brings gratification and thankfulness. **Unwanted things are needed so that preferred things can exist. If you take away one, you will take away the other. Also experiencing one negative moment will bring a positive effect to life as long as your mind is developing a constructive way of thinking.**

🍂 **Example: Experiencing the heartache of finishing in last place can cause you to be humbler the next time you finish in first place.**

> Quote: *"True value comes solely from the thoughts that you feel, which means the thoughts that you have will solely create the feeling that it generates."*

1 Thessalonians 5:16-18
> **16 Rejoice evermore.**
> **17 Pray without ceasing.**
> **18 In every thing give thanks: for this is the will of God in Christ Jesus concerning you. (1 Thessalonians 5:16–18)**

🍂 **Question: How can we generate happiness from the things we don't appreciate, and how can we appreciate something when we are not thankful?**

A real appreciation for something comes from fully understanding and recognizing the good qualities of someone or in something. One of the ways we can create an appreciation for what we have is to have the understanding that things can and eventually always will change.

> Quote: *"Without appreciation, it is impossible to be thankful; and without being thankful, it is impossible to be happy!"*

🍂 *Example:* A poor child who has very little can be happier than a rich child who can have anything they want, as long as the poor child avoids taking into consideration their happiness according to the things that the rich child has.

> **Quote: "Always look at the brighter side of things."**

The more dominant your thoughts are, the more impactful their influences will become. Negative thoughts will create negative results, and thinking positively, even though it may not change something all the way from bad to good, will always create a more positive outcome even in the worst of situations. If you were to generate the same thoughts, and in the same way you did when you first thought of something, you would produce the same effects, thus causing the same reactions, and possibly for many years to come!

Matthew 7:17-20
> **17** Even so every good tree bringeth forth good fruit; but a corrupt tree bringeth forth evil fruit.
> **18 A** good tree cannot bring forth evil fruit, neither can a corrupt tree bring forth good fruit.
> **19** Every tree that bringeth not forth good fruit is hewn down, and cast into the fire.
> **20** Wherefore by their fruits ye shall know them. (Matthew 7:17–20)

Quote: "It's *not the hand you are dealt, but how the hand you are dealt is played.*"

Positivity is beneficial and pragmatic; it encourages growth and promotes increase, which is attractive to most. You will know if your thoughts are positive or negative by the way it makes you feel. You will never feel good about having negative thoughts unless you are a negative person, and you will never feel bad about doing something positive unless being positive was the farthest thing from your mind.

Quote: "Through the power of thoughts, anything negative can be thought of as positive, and anything positive can be thought of as negative. The only way to actually know how

something is, is to realize the effects of what that something has on you."

No set situation and no particular person can change **the effects of being** positive **nor change the consequences of negative thinking. Therefore, no one can take the impact of something** negative **and make it into something positive.** It is impossible to change their effects, and **in doing so,** it is impossible to change the results of having negative thoughts or thinking positive. However, by choice, and through the purpose of God, we can make the whole outcome of any situation into becoming something positive!

🍂 Example: A person who gets fired from their job for something they didn't do can cause a tremendous amount of suffering and resentment and result in them becoming ill-willed. It can also bring an opportunity to look for work doing something else the next day. If that person finds a job that either pays more or has a more preferred job description, it doesn't change the fact that they got fired from their last job, but it can change them from becoming ill-willed into becoming grateful. By it working out better for them in due course, it makes the whole outcome of what was thought of as something negative into something positive. However, no matter the outcome, the negative effects of getting fired from their last job will always be there if they never let go of the resentment they feel for being fired from their last job. And that resentment is even great enough to take away the positive outcome of having a better job and cause something that should have been celebrated into being unappreciated and less enjoyed.

You are what you do, and you do what you think, and also, how you do things will rest on the way that you think. Bad is bad, and good is good. Thinking negatively toward **any**thing will create a **negative** result because that negative thought by its design will take away the thoughts and actions of something being **positive. And doing something positive, even in the worst situations, will make**

what is done, be done in a good way. But be careful because you might think you're doing something positive, and if it's done in a negative way, it will cause a negative result.

It can be extremely hard for a person to stay positive and live in a negative society, which makes it extremely challenging to work in public service without being affected by the negativities of this world. Many of these workers have to tackle dealing with disorderly people way too often without having any concern or sympathy given to them by the general public. It causes what these public service workers have to go through to do their jobs even harder. And to do their jobs in a positive-way while feeling resentment coming from the people they serve, can even seem impossible to achieve due to the failure of us noticing the challenges they have to go through.

🍃 Example: Having to deal with a disruptive student in a class can be hard, but having to communicate disciplinary actions to a parent that is more "unruly" than the student can be incomprehensible. A police officer's job is challenging, but trying to keep the peace in a situation that is "out of control" and with people that are difficult to deal with, while trying to keep their cool, can be overwhelming as well.

The expectation of things to only be done right, without ever making any mistakes or errors, can place a bigger impact on the fallacies of these service workers when they do make mistakes. Negative is negative, and positive is positive, which can make the way we do things to be contradictory to what we do.

🍃 Example: Doing something positive with a negative attitude can make our positive actions be viewed in a negative way.

Without thinking positively, it can be close to impossible to go through some of the challenges of working with negative people without being affected in a negative way. If staying away from thinking negative thoughts becomes too overwhelming, it can cause our good works to actually not be good anymore.

🍂 Question: A teacher's job is to teach and encourage their students, but what will happen if a teacher discourages their students, rather than encouraging them? And what will happen if they start to teach things that are untrue or teach lessons that gives an excuse for hatred?

🍂 Question: A law enforcement officer's duty is to serve and protect, but what will happen when a law enforcement officer stops displaying the characteristics of someone who should be respected or expected to keep order and uphold the law? Or what will happen if law enforcement is called, and instead of deescalating a problem, they make the problem worse?

You are what you do, and you do what you think, but you also are how you think. So, if you start thinking negative, then negative is what you will become.

🍂 Example: When a teacher is discouraging rather than encouraging or teaches that evil things done in our history is okay or is just plain history and nothing else, it can cause them to change from being the person we should be listening to, and instead, make them a person that needs to be ignored. And when law enforcement is breaking the laws they are sworn to uphold, it can take them from being the person who protects us from harm, and instead, it can turn them into the persons who we need to be protected from!

Life is full of ups and downs **and** staying positive will help you get through the lows and rejoice in the highs. Appreciate all that life has to offer, the good and the bad, and always remember to be positive and stay encouraged. Pay close attention to your thoughts because when you might be thinking you are **creating** positive thoughts, it can actually be a negative way of thinking!

Take Action Now! (Turn to pages #243 through #265 for recommended fasts and exercises)

Introduction

🍂 Exercise: #5 (Think Closely)

🍂 *Question:* When was the last time you felt bad or angry while thinking positive towards something or someone?

🍂 *Question:* When was the last time you felt peace while worrying, or encouraged by thinking of what could possibly go wrong?

🍂 *Question:* What type of thoughts were produced the last time you experienced something awful or **at a** time **when** nothing seemed to go right?

Usually the type of thoughts you have comes from the kind of experiences you are **going through** at that moment. However, there are many times when your experiences are dependent upon the type of thoughts **that** are produced. **And if through your perception of thinking, you can only see one thing a certain way, there is nothing anyone could do unless they are able to change the way you think!**

🍂 *Question*: During your last time of disparity, were your thoughts positive and encouraging, or did you get consumed into your circumstances **by** producing negative thoughts that created a feeling of hopeless**ness and** depression?

> *Quote: "It is impossible to feel hopelessly defeated while being optimistic, and it is virtually intolerable to stay negative while thinking positive."*

Thoughts are everything; it is how we think, how we feel, and what we perceive. In life, with everything that is going on around us, it is virtually impossible to think positive or feel happy living with a negative state of mind.

Negative Thoughts

 *Question:* Do you feel like you're not important, or do you think that your value is less than others?

 *Question:* Are you subconsciously diminishing your loved one or spouse's importance in the relationship you have with them?

 **Question:** Do you hate the way that you look or the way you feel about your life?

If you've answered "yes" to any of these questions, it may be due to the consequences of negative thoughts!

 *Question:* What are negative thoughts?

Negativity is the act of being viewed in or being characterized by the absence or the wrong, rather than taking notice to the present or the good of distinguishing features. Your thoughts are who you are, and if your thoughts are only negative, everything you see, everything you feel, and everything you think will only be negative. And that will absolutely have a negative impact on you and in your life!

 *Example:* A perfectionist is a person who spends their entire lives mostly correcting what is wrong much more than enjoying what

is right. Picture having something almost perfect but giving most of your attention to the things that keep it from being perfect. You can imagine it will cause you more misery when one thing may be wrong than gratification when everything is right.

Negative thoughts can affect your level of intelligence, and they can interrupt your ability to think. It's because negative thinking weakens the effectiveness of neurons in the brain, which causes us to have a lack of reasoning that is known to cause a negative attitude or a negative perception of thoughts.

Example: When two people are angry, they are more likely to keep fighting than they are to start compromising.

Dichotomous thinkers only see "black and white," and people having two different thoughts or two different ideas or two concepts divided into two extreme parts will eliminate any "gray area," leading to conductive reasoning. A lack of reasoning can cause instability in our emotions and our decision-making, which can affect our relationships with others and possibly worsen everything in our entire lives due to the negative effects of being irrational. And it could lead to having many personality disorders caused by having an unstable and unbalanced lifestyle.

Example: Starting the day in a good mood will typically be accompanied by thinking positive, but if or when those thoughts change and become negative, it will cause the way you think, along with your perception and mood, to change also.

Negativity can contribute to worrying because it can cause you to assume that something is worse than what it is. Negative thinking can lead to a weakened immune system due to it producing abnormal levels of cortisol in the bloodstream. Things such as obsessively complaining, being difficult to deal with, being disagreeable, having a pessimistic attitude, being judgmental, being unenthusiastic about doing things, being uninterested in your spouse and being depressed all stem from having negative thoughts.

Depression is a mood disorder believed to be caused by low serotonin levels between the nerve cells in the brain. These neurotransmitters are also believed to be chemically imbalanced often due to a rise in stress levels caused by anxiety. The symptoms of depression can and will affect how you feel, think, eat, sleep, and carry out your daily activities. Time and time again, these effects are often ignored while becoming a normal state of mind, which also often routinely become viewed by others as just a part of who you are.

Romans 8:28

28 And we know that all things work together for good to them that love God, to them who are the called according to his purpose. (Romans 8:28)

There are literally millions of unfortunate and awful things that could possibly happen to us, and there are some dreadful and bad things that actually do. Even though every experience we have is never quite the same, and although some of those experiences are far worse than others, they all share one common factor, they all create negative thoughts.

Fortunately, the bad things that happen to us, in most cases, doesn't have to be that bad at all. If we neglect to formulate into negative thinking and stay positive, through the power of thoughts, it will take away the power and control of the negative energy produced by the things that happened.

Question: The last time something bad happened to you or something got you upset, what thoughts were you thinking at that moment?

Normally, it's the thoughts that are created from the things that happen to us that make what happens to us bad or good.

🍃 **Example: Being asked by your boss to do something at work can cause you to get upset merely from the thought of feeling like you don't want to do the task at hand. But it also can generate happiness and value merely from the thought of feeling needed for fulfilling the duties you were asked to do.**

🍃 *Question:* **If the thoughts you were thinking at the time you got upset were opposite of the ones you were having at that moment, would that have made a difference in the way you felt? And if you placed a positive thought to what caused you misery, would that thought cause what got you upset, to not be so bad after all?**

Thinking positive not only makes a good thing better, but it can also make something that's horrible less terrible.

🍃 *Example:* Thinking of how good it is that you are getting some much-needed rest even though you are at home sick in bed.

🍃 *Question:* Why is it, if we get sick **and think it came from something we ate,** we never want to eat that particular food again?

Reason being, if food is linked to why you became sick, that thought can be enough to change the way you feel about eating that particular food again. Your thoughts are your reality, which means it doesn't matter if it was the food itself, if it was the way it was prepared, or if it was something **outside of eating the food entirely** that caused you to become sick. As long as those thoughts of how you felt are linked to that particular food, it will affect the way you think or feel about eating that specific food forever.

🍃 **Question: What happens when these negative thoughts are attached to the people and things that are around us?**

Unlike positive thoughts that cause forward progress, a negative thought causes separation and influences us to move backwards. Negative thoughts can cause you to give up on trying, it can create disruption within your marriage, and it can even cause you to hate the people that you are supposed to love. The thought of what someone has done wrong, or the thought of what is perceived of what someone is trying to do can change the way you see them. By changing the way you see someone, it will often change the way you treat them also.

Question: What happens when someone gets back at someone for getting back at them?

Negative thoughts are only good for one thing and that is to identify harmful and dangerous situations, because it causes separation and avoidance from the person or thing that is identified as bad. Negative thoughts, if used correctly, can encourage correction and fairness when things are seen as being wrong or unfair. Using it unfairly or for entertainment purposes through such things as gossiping or venting with friends with no course for resolution will only cause hurt, pain, misery, and even an unwilling hatred toward other people.

Example: Someone telling you something bad about a person can leave you afflicted and confused about how you feel now about the person you once liked.

1 Corinthians 15:33
33 Be not deceived: evil communications corrupt good manners. (1 Corinthians 15:33)

Negative thoughts are meant to tear down, to bring disrepute, and to identify what is wrong. It is the thought that goes against everything that you think is good, and it is the act to withdraw or take away from anything in its present state. If we view our spouse by everything they do wrong and nothing they do right, it will seem to us as if everything they do is wrong.

Ephesians 4:29
29 Let no corrupt communication proceed out of your mouth, but that which is good to the

use of edifying, that it may minister grace unto
the hearers. (Ephesians 4:29)

Thoughts are the reality we live in, and it **causes** the decisions
that we make. Through the power of the mind, we have the ability to
change anything negative into something hopeful and positive.

> *Quote: "The only way to fight evil is with good,
> and the only way to reverse negativity is by doing
> something positive."*

Our behavior towards one another is controlled by what we think.
Thoughts are attached to everything you do and everyone you meet,
and it does this automatically. When you see someone you know, there's
a thought attached to that person of an experience or a synopsis of many
experiences you had with that person to identify their character and who
they are to you. If there aren't any thoughts attached or if you've totally
forgotten the thoughts that were previously attached, there would be no
way of knowing who that person is or how you know them.

Example: If you were to meet someone you've known in the past
but can't remember **the association of how you know them**, you
would feel a need to jog a remembrance of why you know this person so that your conscious mind can put a thought with that person. Without associating a thought to identify a person, it will leave
you unknowing of how to **classify your behavior towards them**.

Our character is often distinguished by our actions, but there
are times when our actions are misunderstood and cause our character to be misrepresented. Misunderstandings are usually caused by
miscommunication, and a miscommunication will frequently lead to
a fluctuation of negative thoughts.

Example: Not communicating to your spouse that lately you've
been working late to catch up on some of the family's expenses
can cause your spouse to think that you are just somewhere being

carefree. And it may lead them to feel like you're irresponsible with your duties at home. If it's not addressed, it can also lead to your spouse feeling neglected and thinking that you are selfish.

Communication is the conveyance and disclosure of information, and it takes an open line of communication to send and receive the information presented. A relationship full of miscommunication is a relationship full of misunderstandings, and those misunderstandings may be the cause of a relationship not working if the problem isn't fixed. You are what you do, and what a person does, doesn't always have to necessarily change who they are to you; it may just mean what they are to you may be done a little differently. Remember that thinking negative toward someone will always cause you to act negative toward them. It can change relationships between parents and children, friends and family, co-workers and associates, and also husbands and wives.

Luke 6:37
37 Judge not, and ye shall not be judged: condemn not, and ye shall not be condemned: forgive, and ye shall be forgiven. (Luke 6:37)

Studies show that the more negative qualities you notice about a person, the less enjoyable your relationship will become. Even thinking negatively toward yourself can create depression, a lack of confidence, and insensitivity when it comes to taking care of your own needs. A sure sign of negative thoughts is when we identify ourselves or others by our wrongdoings or what hasn't been done, instead of what has been done or what we do right.

Question: Has someone ever accused you of always bringing up what they did wrong in the past and never mentioning what they ever do right, right now?

Negative thoughts will cause you to act negatively, which will ultimately cause you to be negative.

Question: Have you ever met a person who always talks to everybody about what is wrong with almost everything imaginable?

If they are not talking about what is wrong, somehow they will find a way to talk about what could go wrong. Worrying comes from negative thinking, and it can lead to things like insomnia, hypochondria, and cause an increase in aging. Remember, thoughts are everything; it is who we are, what we know, and what we will become!

2 Timothy 1:7
7 For God hath not given us the spirit of fear; but of power, and of love, and of a sound mind. (2 Timothy 1:7)

You do and act according to how you feel, but most times as human beings, the way we feel is affected by how we think. Whether you're watching a movie that makes you scared, a movie that makes you laugh, or a movie that makes you cry, it all has to do with thoughts. None of the things happened **in real life,** but the idea of it is enough to control your every emotion. If it's choosing to speak or not to speak, to be polite or impolite, or to be cordial or disrespectful to someone, our feelings toward one another will always come from our thoughts. And it will always have an effect on how we treat **other people.**

Negative thoughts will never have positive results, especially when these negative thoughts cause who you are to change for the worse. Bad things that happen usually aren't all that bad, but it is the thoughts that are created from what is bad that causes the most harm.

Example: One unfortunate event can cause a fluctuation of negative thoughts to occur, and the more you think about these things, the worse it will actually make you feel. It is when negative thoughts start to diminish, is when things that were very bad at first don't seem that bad anymore.

Quote: "*You are what you do, and you feel how you think.*"

Negative thoughts always shine a light on what is wrong in a relationship. It gives a harmful perspective that will affect everything you see. It causes doubt and is the creator of regret. It gives no thought to change or promise, but is cemented in its own self. If you're not careful, negativity can consume you, destroying your marriage and your relationships with everyone around you.

Example: Think back at every bad thing you went through in the past month or in the past week or even in the past few days to realize how much negative thoughts played an important role in your uncertainties and sorrow.

Satan places negative thoughts in our minds through whispers to distance us from who we are and from what purpose God has for us.

Genesis 3:4-5
4 And the serpent said unto the woman, Ye shall not surely die:
5 For God doth know that in the day ye eat thereof, then your eyes shall be opened, and ye shall be as gods, knowing good and evil. (Genesis 3:4–5)

Satan spoke to Eve to cause her to question God and sin against Him, and it worked! What the majority of us fail to realize is, that Satan is still speaking to us the same way he talked to Eve, but he does it now by placing thoughts in our minds that cause us to make horrible choices in life. Negative thoughts will always produce negative results, and if we attach a negative thought onto something that is positive, its effects are strong enough to change a person's good character into something unimaginable.

Example: Being picked on for being smart will cause someone smart to think that maybe it is wrong to be who they are. A person who tries to keep their innocence may feel as if things will be better if they just let go of their pureness and be like everyone else. And a person who hangs out with the wrong crowd may think that it's wrong to be kind and considerate of others and begin to be just like the people that they hang around.

Proverbs 22:24-25
   24 Make no friendship with an angry man;
and with a furious man thou shalt not go:
   25 Lest thou learn his ways, and get a snare
to thy soul. (Proverbs 22:24–25)

Question: What encourages us to be mean towards each other, when being mean towards someone doesn't make our lives or the relationships we have with anyone any better?

Question: Who gave someone the idea that using drugs is a good idea?

No matter what someone is going through, doing drugs doesn't make any situation any better, it only makes everything worse.

Question: Why do so many people choose to live negative lives when being negative takes any real joy you may have in your life away?

Negativity has a negative effect on both the thinker and the things or persons being thought of. Negative thoughts will affect the way we think and the way we feel about everything, and it can also eventually cause you to be in a marriage full of hatred. Negative thoughts are different from sadness, which generates compassion and sympathy. Instead, it creates a home for misery and hate toward everything and every person in which it applies. Thoughts are everything. It is what we know; it **is what controls** how we act and **how we react.** It is **how the** brain interprets anything around us, and **it is our perception of** everything that happens to us. Without thoughts, we will be unknowingly present without the realization of anything that **is going on around** us.

Philippians 4:8-9

8 Finally, brethren, whatsoever things are true, whatsoever things are honest, whatsoever things are just, whatsoever things are pure, whatsoever things are lovely, whatsoever things are of good report; if there be any virtue, and if there be any praise, think on these things.

9 Those things, which ye have both learned, and received, and heard, and seen in me, do: and the God of peace shall be with you. (Philippians 4:8–9)

A way of counter-attacking negative thoughts is to try and understand both sides of the issue. Instead of placing blame on the other person, try placing compassion on them. Talk with your spouse instead of talking at them. Every situation is an opportunity to learn. Be inquisitive and ask as many questions as you like, to get the understanding you need to stay positive.

Quote: "Negativity always leads to uncertainty, and uncertainty always leads to doubt."

Understanding that with only negative thoughts, it will always reveal a negative reality without a desire to makes things better. Recognizing the power of our thoughts will allow you to consciously choose which reality you decide to live. Knowing **why someone** thinks **the way they do** will only cause you to understand them more. And realizing that the power of choice will always give you the power to choose will allow you at all times the opportunity to change anything negative into something positive.

Take action now! (Turn to pages #243 through #265 for recommended fasts and exercises.)

Predetermined Thoughts

To predetermine means to establish or decide in advance. In most cases, thoughts that are predetermined are accompanied by being **closed-minded** and non-negotiable. Persons of this frame of mind are commonly not subject to compromise and known to often jump to assumptions. These presumptions can prove problematic due to the fact that assumptions are thoughts of things that are accepted as true or certain before it actually happens or exists. And it is thought of, without possessing adequate evidence or proof.

Example: The taste of one sour grape may lead to the assumption that every grape is bitter.

Question: What could have been done more to better assure that the whole bunch of grapes is bitter?

Predetermined thoughts may cause you to stereotype someone based on who they are or how they look. No matter if it's good or bad, labeling someone without possessing adequate evidence is judgmental and can cause you to be misled about that particular person.

Example: Thinking a certain group of people is smarter than others based on their origins can cause you to unfairly overestimate someone while **at the same time** underestimating the other.

Bias acts are a result of judgmental thoughts, and through their assumptions, it will create a closed-minded opinion of someone or something. If these thoughts are shared with others, it may influence them to think the same way as the influencer. It can also diminish the hope and potential for that person or the persons targeted.

Assumptions are supposed thoughts of a thing that is accepted as true or as certain to happen, which often occurs without proof. Assumptions can and will lead to frustration, disappointments, and feeling disconnected from a person when the thoughts you have are inaccurate or misunderstood. Through a personal experience or through the thoughts and influences of others, assumptions that are created through predetermined thinking lack the qualifications of being absolutely accurate.

Another danger of predetermined thoughts is that it is the thought of certainty, which can leave you blindsided without a backup plan. Many times in life, having options is what makes all the difference.

📝 Example: "*I assumed you were going to pick up the check.*"

Keeping an open mind will eliminate some of the chances **of** assuming something, and it will keep your mind available to make different choices in life. Predetermined thoughts have a large effect on the relationships we have with the people around us. It puts expectations on the unexpected and creates a feeling in the present based on the actions in the future **or** the actions that have happened in the past.

📝 *Example:* Someone who always lends you money when you need it is usually thought of as being very nice for the first few times, and after that, it is expected of them. If and when that some-one says no to the act that made them nicer and different from everyone else, will be the absence of doing that same act, or the lack thereof, that will make them be thought of as worse than everybody else once they fail to do it.

Supposing the unexpected makes it no longer unexpected but rather a requirement. Once something is expected, it will no longer bring excitement or joy when it is performed but will only bring sorrow and disappointment when it's not done. These measures are unfair to you, and it is unfair to every person it involves because it takes away the possibility of the happiness we feel when something is done, and it set unreachable expectations on anyone else.

Example: If someone compliments your spouse's actions or behavior, and your response is, "That is what they are supposed to do," is a notion of a predetermined thought.

The truth of the matter is that good is good, bad is bad, and it doesn't matter how many times something is done or not done. It still doesn't lose its meaning; we just tend to stop noticing it as much. Signs of predetermined thoughts are, but not limited to **is**, failure to listen throughout the whole conversation, assuming to know what is going to be said next, expecting something not asked for, **to** assuming what role a person should perform without having a conversation about it first.

"On the other hand," sometimes predetermined thoughts can overestimate someone, causing you to think they are going to change or rise to your expectations. To a certain degree, when we expect a person to just be who they are, it gives a reasonable expectation of the actions they take, while at the same time, it promotes you to properly address the concerns you have instead of being hopeful that things will change **without them making any real changes to the way they think**.

Exercise: #6

Your spouse has never remembered your anniversary, and for years, forgetting it made a night that should have been celebrated into a night full of disappointment and questioning the relationship you have with that person. On the fifth anniversary, they also forgot, and it sparked a huge argument between the two of you. In fact, it was so upsetting that your spouse made a secret vow to themselves to make it up by doing something big on the next year's anniversary. So they secretly saved money each month, and by the time of the sixth anniversary, they surprised you with a dream vacation to Hawaii!

🍃 *Question:* Would you be overjoyed with appreciation, that this year they got it right, or would you respond by saying, "This should have been done last year?"

One reaction brings a joy that encourages the spouse while the other action hinders the joy felt while at the same time demoralizing the person's efforts, and causing separation within the marriage.

🍃 *Question:* Do you think the spouse showed signs of not being the type of person who commemorates anniversaries before getting married?

Imagine doing something for the first time and all the while feeling excited by the thought of the other person's reaction. And when that moment comes, you only find more disappointment and criticism. Proper communication will resolve the issue of living with the effects of predetermined thoughts. Knowing what your spouse is expecting out of the marriage will bring clarity to the relationship. Understanding and knowing each other will build a strong bond that cannot be broken.

In life, we expect things to go a certain way. This can be very misleading and even heartbreaking at times, which may cause you to isolate yourself from the rest of the world. Know that being isolated from everyone else is never God's purpose for you, but sometimes through assumptions, it may seem like the most logical thing to do.

> *Quote: "Life is only what you make of it, and even though you are dealt a bad hand at times, know that it is not the end of the game."*

Predetermined thoughts can be positive, which produces encouragement or negative, which causes discouragement. It can lead to a better life because it creates hope and confidence, or it can cause doubt and insecurity that leads to suffering.

The mind is the most powerful instrument known to human-kind. In fact, it is through it's power that makes predetermined thoughts the leading cause of someone losing their faith in God today! Since our perception of God is much larger than it is with man, our expectations are much higher also. But believing God to do something not in His will to do is unjust and can even be detrimental to your salvation. Most atheists once believed in God, but due to some tragic event happening or something not happening, it caused them to think negatively toward God, which created a change in trust and perception.

Question: If something tragic happened to someone and that person never believed in God from the start, will that have prevented that tragic thing from really happening?

Predetermined thoughts build up expectations, and it doesn't matter if that expectation is fair or not. If it's not met, the expectation we have can cause us to lose trust or belief in anyone, including God. Not knowing what God's purpose is and replacing it with predetermined thinking will be very harmful to our relationship with Him. When things don't happen the way we presumed it should, can cause you to question the intention of our Creator, and thus, causing us to put flaws on an otherwise flawless God.

Job 38:1-18 New King James Version (NKJV)

38 Then the LORD answered Job out of the
   whirlwind, and said:
2 "Who *is* this who darkens counsel
By words without knowledge?
3 Now prepare yourself like a man;
I will question you, and you shall answer Me.
4 "Where were you when I laid the foundations
   of the earth?
Tell *Me,* if you have understanding.

5 Who determined its measurements?
Surely you know!
Or who stretched the line upon it?
6 To what were its foundations fastened?
Or who laid its cornerstone,
7 When the morning stars sang together,
And all the sons of God shouted for joy?
8 "Or *who* shut in the sea with doors,
When it burst forth *and* issued from the womb;
9 When I made the clouds its garment,
And thick darkness its swaddling band;
10 When I fixed My limit for it,
1253 And set bars and doors;
11 When I said,
'This far you may come, but no farther,
And here your proud waves must stop!'
12 "Have you commanded the morning since
your days *began,*
And caused the dawn to know its place,
13 That it might take hold of the ends of the
earth,
And the wicked be shaken out of it?
14 It takes on form like clay *under* a seal,
And stands out like a garment.
15 From the wicked their light is withheld,
And the upraised arm is broken.
16 "Have you entered the springs of the sea?
Or have you walked in search of the depths?
17 Have the gates of death been revealed to you?
Or have you seen the doors of the shadow of
death?
18 Have you comprehended the breadth of the
earth?
Tell *Me,* if you know all this.
(Job 38:1–18, New King James Version—NKJV)

It is very important that we know that the knowledge of God is like nothing we have ever known. And to find peace, we must understand that only through the power of choice are we connected to the most important element pertaining to the purpose of why we were created. Knowing this is the first step to give reason to why you are here and the ability to utilize our power of choice gives meaning to the existence of humanity. Knowledge gives fairness to the unfairness, but it doesn't make the unfairness of this world any more fair. Unfortunately for that reason, many often suffer and fall short of salvation due to the repercussions of sins committed by other people; but know that we have a choice to submit to the evilness of this world or to stand against it.

> *Quote: "The important things that happen to us are not the things that happen, but what is important is how the important things that happen to us affect the choices that we make."*

Know that the choices that are easily decided are decisions that are not hard to make. For that reason, many people who are wealthy question the love of the people who love them because it is sometimes unclear if the people who love them, truly love them just for being them, or only because their wealth makes their lives easier.

Matthew 4:5-7
 5 Then the devil taketh him up into the holy city, and setteth him on a pinnacle of the temple,
 6 And saith unto him, If thou be the Son of God, cast thyself down: for it is written, He shall give his angels charge concerning thee: and in their hands they shall bear thee up, lest at any time thou dash thy foot against a stone.
 7 Jesus said unto him, It is written again, Thou shalt not tempt the Lord thy God. (Matthew 4:5–7)

Predetermined thoughts will always lead to second-guessing, and sometimes it will cause us to question the unquestionable. Satan can put thoughts in your head that doesn't match the thoughts of the other person that it involves leaving one person feeling misunderstood while the other may feel unappreciated. Thoughts are everything, and if they are predetermined, it is as if these thoughts are foretelling the future!

Completion of this book will bring a much greater understanding of the things less understood and will create a much clearer purpose for the things that are unclear in your life.

Basing your thoughts and feelings on what you think a person ought to be will put in jeopardy the thoughts and the feelings you have of who they are right now! Assuming the actions of someone that is not fulfilled, *even if it's out of their character,* will in almost every case lead to the feeling of being let down and that can eventually lead to experiencing a moment of regret. In many cases, even if expectations are met, you will suffer a lack of joy because in your mind, that person only did what was already expected of them to do and nothing more.

Predetermining thoughts can put confusion inside of the relationship and be the cause of mistrust and doubt when unfulfilled expectations are not met. This can be the cause of frustration in the relationship that may lead to a fluctuation of negative thoughts to occur.

Cutting down confusion and misunderstandings by having a conversation; or preventing to be misled by having a healthy and effective view of reality can be a giant step in creating a happier life. It can also preserve your relationships with others and be the next step in creating an "A+" marriage!

Take action now! (Turn to pages #243 through #265 for recommended fasts and exercises)

Open-Minded Hope

🪶 *Question:* Do you consider yourself an open-minded person or a closed-minded person?

An open-minded person is one who is unbiased, nonpartisan, and exceptive to criticism. Being open-minded allows you to view things freely without judgment or limitation. A closed-minded person is typically one who is not willing to consider different ideas or the opinions of others. A closed-minded person is also a conventional thinker, restricted from diversity, and intolerant to making a change. There is a time and a reason for everything under the sun. There is also a specific time and a specific reason to be closed-minded, and there is also a specific purpose to have an open mind.

To be open-minded means you can talk to anyone! It is the ability to consider more than one choice. This will open up many new possibilities and many more opportunities in life. The thought of possibilities is what creates hope, and hope is absolutely what brings aspiration to making a choice.

> *Quote: "A good relationship takes trust, but to have a great relationship also takes consideration and compromise."*

Studies show that people who are more acceptable to change live happier and healthier lives, and that change is what causes a relationship to evolve. Without a change taking place, a relationship has no choice but to stay the same, even when it becomes predictable and dormant.

Example: Darwinism is the theory of evolution proposed by an English naturalist, geologist, and biologist, who went by the name of Charles Darwin. He is best known for his contributions to the science of the transmutation of species in order to increase their ability to survive, compete and reproduce. His theories states that organisms arise and develop through evolution by adapting to their environment through the act of evolving.

It is believed that a difference in the environment left some species on the verge of extinction due to the fact that they weren't accustomed to change. Many marriages **also are on the verge of extinction** due to "growing apart" **from their environment and the person they are married to.** The fact of the matter is, as humans, continuing to grow and continuing to learn is a natural part of living. Change is a way of life, and if we find ourselves growing apart, it may have a lot to do with the inability to adapt.

Being narrow-minded can cause your spouse to think of you as being unreasonable and intolerant. Relationships are designed to bring people closer together, and it is often when we are not getting closer, we are growing apart due to a lack of growth. Redundancy is always doing things the same way, and by the adaptive nature of us being human, it will cause the interaction we have with things that never change to be often the things that are overlooked and underappreciated.

Proverbs 13:12
12 Hope deferred maketh the heart sick:
but when the desire cometh, it is a tree of life.
(Proverbs 13:12)

Hope is a feeling of an expectation or desire for something to happen. Being closed-minded in a marriage and in life can create a feeling of hopelessness. Being open-minded is being receptive to improvement, and with that receptiveness to change, it gives opportunities for **accomplishing something greater. Having a choice to change is what gives hope, and fulfilling that choice is what creates happiness. H**ope brings joy, and joy gives life to those who hold on to it. And if the hope you once had is fading away, you might find yourself one day waking up in a dried-up marriage or in a depressed life wishing you had an option to choose to escape.

Too many of our young adults today are falling victim to their environment. Many young people are joining gangs and are involved in illegal activity due to the influences that are surrounding them.

Question: If living on one side of a particular city makes you enemies with another side of that same city, what happens if you are forced to move to your enemy's side of the city? And would that make your enemies now **become** your friends?

Question: If not, why?

Question: What if you moved to a whole different state; would it make a difference which side of town you stayed on in the last city you lived?

Question: If not, why do we put our life on the line based on a zip code?

When things look difficult or hopeless, sometimes what it takes to be different from your surroundings is to think differently from everybody that's around you.

Quote: *"Think outside of the box."*

Every invention ever invented came from inventors who thought differently than anyone else had before. Many times, these inventors were thought of as being bizarre or uncanny to the people who were like-minded and thought particularly the same way. Some of our most inspirational leaders and most creative inventors all came from people who were thought of as different. Through adversity, they had to be determined to look past the intermediate and straight through every obstacle that got in their way. Believing strongly in something means you have to be closed-minded to doubt; it means you cannot accept failure or take no for an answer. At times when you cannot see a clear path, it takes a person with a mind strong enough to be open to seeing what others cannot.

> Quote: "Change is good when it is a change for the better."

Being closed-minded is like being in a constant loop where everything stays the same. When people are closed-minded, they become outraged at the idea of someone looking at things differently. Unexpected things are usually annoying to them, and they are perfectly fine with living a predictable and customary life. Many of us live our lives contained in the imprisonment of our own minds. We build our environment around and accept only the opinions of those who think and look just like us and affiliation often takes precedence over truth.

Where there isn't some form of open-mindedness, there can't be any form of compromise, and without compromise, negotiation can never exist. The ability to negotiate is what makes this country so great! Taking into consideration the ideas and opinions of others gives a different insight on solutions to the similar problems that we all share. Negotiating is the act of bringing about a discussion; a discussion to work things out, to find a common ground, and finally to come together to come to an agreement. Compromise is the glue that holds two or more people together, and it is the gray area between the differences in any organization, **group**, or government party.

> Quote: "Division amongst us is division against us."

Political parties, social media, the entertainment industry, and even our daily news, all capitalize off of our differences. Through our sinful nature, highlighting our differences and promoting hatred is what sells. And because we are given a choice, our desire is sometimes for that choice to be to work against people instead of working with them.

🍃 *Question:* What do you get when two similarly equal, but opposite forces collide? Or what will happen if these two opposite forces pull something in the opposite direction, without restraint?

Government officials who are fighting amongst themselves to have power over the other party, will lead the whole country and everyone in it, to argue and fight against one another the exact same way. The hard truth is, with everyone fighting to be right and no one wanting to compromise, it may leave a country no longer existing to be right about.

Proverbs 16:18-19

18 Pride goeth before destruction, and an haughty spirit before a fall.

19 Better it is to be of an humble spirit with the lowly, than to divide the spoil with the proud. (Proverbs 16:18–19)

Two lines drawn in the sand cancels out any gray area from being created, and without the glue of compromise, a country will be torn apart. Through our purpose, we are given the power of choice, and it is through that power of choice a decision is made. Since the beginning of time, God gave man the right to choose; and ever since that right has been given, there has been a spiritual warfare between good and evil for the rights to give or take that choice away. Being closed-minded takes away your power of choice, leaving you captive and enslaved by your own way of thinking.

🍃 *Example:* Look at this country today. We are more divided by media influence than we are through the example, Christ gave to do what's right and fair to others.

Question: If given a choice to completely trust in God or trust in man, which would you choose?

Question: If your answer is God, then why are so many people putting their complete trust in the government more than they are the teachings of our Savior?

To completely decide on something wholeheartedly is to trust in what you chose entirely. If you believe in something or someone entirely, it will take away the option to choose something or someone else that is best suited for the job. And also, if you trust in someone that is untrustworthy, not only will that give a closed-minded opinion with no regard to anything else, it may also leave you confused and committed to a purpose that doesn't serve you the best way.

Question: If a certain group of people is determined to vote for a certain government party, no matter if they are representing their values or not, why would that party continue to fight for a vote that has already been given?

There are times where being closed-minded serves a necessary purpose, and there are times when it does not. Life is too precious to compromise, and if you negotiate what should not be negotiated, the outcome will never measure up to its sacrifice.

> *Quote: "Gambling is a game of winners or losers, and if your loss outweighs your gain, you have already lost before the game has even started!"*

Mark 8:36-38
36 For what shall it profit a man, if he shall gain the whole world, and lose his own soul?

37 Or what shall a man give in exchange for his soul?

38 Whosoever therefore shall be ashamed of me and of my words in this adulterous and sin-

ful generation; of him also shall the Son of man
be ashamed, when he cometh in the glory of his
Father with the holy angels. (Mark 8:36–38)

Some things should be optional when others should not.
Knowing what to be open to and what to be closed-minded to takes
wisdom and understanding what is at stake. To compromise the
things that should be uncompromisable, or to put a price on the
priceless, means you have to either not know what that something is
worth, or you don't understand or trust what you should know.

📝 Question: What do you do when your life is not enough?

Some people find comfort in consistency, and there is nothing
wrong with that, but staying open to improvement will always give
opportunities to improve. There is comfort in not taking a risk, but
when the comforts of life are not comfortable anymore, is when it is
time for our consistencies to become inconsistent and to utilize our
choice to make a change.

📝 Example: Communicating your thoughts and your desires with
your spouse open-mindedly and deciding to take action, could
be your key to a good relationship and a great step toward creating an "*A+*" marriage!

To completely devote yourself to something means giving up
the right to make any other choice. We are made to choose, and by
choice, we decide whom we choose to be and whom we choose to
follow. Who we are and what we stand for is the most important
choices we will ever make. So choose wisely in everything you decide
and always pray to the Most High, Omniscient God for wisdom,
understanding, **and guidance into** making the right **choices.**

Take action now! (Turn to pages #243 through #265 for recommended fasts and exercises.)

A Point of View

 Question: Do you see a glass half empty or half full?

The answer to this question is a test to reveal if you are an optimist or a pessimist. An optimist is a person who is hopeful and looks forward to the future, while a pessimist is a person who tends to see the bad and is unenthusiastic about upcoming events. Pessimists tend to live sheltered lives, expecting the worst to happen, while optimists typically live life more freely and imagine the best outcome to happen. It doesn't matter if you see the glass half empty or half full; either way, we all have good and bad thoughts about everything and everyone around us. How we see things will reveal the way we truly think, and how we think will determine our point of view.

 *Example:* Your spouse spends the money in the savings account for a surprise family trip. The way you react will reveal your point of view.

 *Question:* Will you only see them being irresponsible in spending money and think they should have saved the money to use for emergencies only, or would you see the good in your spouse's efforts for wanting to take the family on a much needed vacation?

Either way, you can make a good argument for both points, but if the people involved are not listening to each other, there really isn't a real purpose to argue **or debate**. It is important to know that a point of view is not purposed to create judgment or criticism; it is only designed to show how someone truly feels.

In a marriage or in any relationship, a person's point of view shouldn't be looked at as simply right or wrong. If the thoughts we have are only to prove that someone is right or wrong, it will do just that and nothing more. As a people and as a society, we must try more to understand what a person is thinking instead of just trying to prove them wrong. And by doing so, it will build bridges instead of tearing them down. Proving someone wrong doesn't solve the problem; it just proves you were right. By talking and addressing the issue openly, and by compromising, it can possibly change the way someone thinks and **also** give **everyone as a whole** a better understanding of each other.

If you can change a person's thoughts, you will be able to change the way they feel; and by changing **their** feelings, you will create in them a new point of view.

A point of view is what is considered to be the outcome of a matter; it is the perception created, and the opinions formed based on the thoughts that we have. Many people form their opinions based on the way they feel instead of the facts that are presented to them. This can seem biased due to the fact that our feelings are mostly based on our emotional state. This will make your point of view conditional and cause you to see the world based on how you mentally feel.

Example: Most people's opinions on a controversial foul called in the championship game will usually be solely based on which team the foul is called on. And wanting one team to win over another, can cause what you see, to be determined by how you feel.

Two people who normally think differently will often find themselves with two different points of view. Even though you may tend not to see eye to eye at times, remember, keeping an open mind and not solely basing your perception on how you feel is a key to sustaining a fair and understanding line of communication. Listening to the other person's point of view and opinion on certain things will also give you more options with handling the difficulties and complexities of everyday life all on your own. This will give you a better chance at success and overcoming the obstacles that keep you from achieving your goals and dreams.

A point of view is the act of taking something under consideration, and unfortunately, many people are drawn to notice the negative things happening in life and take less into consideration of the good things that are often happening in the same time span. This will cause a negative way of thinking, and the appearance we have of life will be full of misery and drama. To change your perception, you would have to change the way you think; and to change the way you think starts **first by** changing one thought.

Having a positive perception can change a negative point of view into a pragmatic, rewarding lifestyle. If the negative outweighs the positive, the outcome as a whole will be negative. If the positive outweighs the negative thoughts, the outcome will be positive. And no matter how complex your life is, **if** you give **more of** an account to the fewer negative things **that happen to you** than you do the greater positive, you will **never live or view** your life in a positive way.

🍂 Exercise: #7

Waking up in the morning, you are greeted with a hug **and** a kiss by your spouse, and them surprising you by making you breakfast in bed. As you are leaving out of your house to start your day, you are greeted with an array of sunshine and the song of birds chirping in the background. On the way to your job, the radio plays three of your favorite songs of all time, and every traffic light is green throughout almost the entire drive to work! The last light you get **to,** turns yellow, and instead of the car in front of you slowing down, they abruptly stop. And as you are jamming to one of your favorite songs playing on the radio, you almost ram **into** the **rear of the** car that stopped. During your day at work, your boss comes by the office and tells you that you've been doing a wonderful job, and for that, you're receiving a promotion that is going to cause you to work on one Saturday out of each month, but you are being rewarded with a 20 percent raise in return!

Your friends at work all decide to celebrate your promotion by taking you out for lunch. The waitress at the restaurant is very rude and causes a small altercation, but later apologizes. On top of that, the cook forgets that you ordered the fish and instead gives you chicken. **When the waitress realizes the mistake and offers to take the chicken back, she says she is going to throw it away so that she can give you the fish you ordered. You decide to keep the chicken instead of the fish because you don't want the food to be wasted. The chicken was okay, but** the rest of the food was some of the best side **dishes** and desserts you have **eaten** in a long time. Shortly after, you are presented with a bill charging you more than what it was supposed to be because the **fish** was entered **in** instead of the **chicken**.

🍃 Question: In your opinion, if you could only say one word, would you say the experience during lunch was good or bad?

As you are rushing home after work to get home and tell your spouse how your day went, you get a call from your previous realtor to tell you that the dream house you wanted and couldn't afford is back on the market at a reduced price. **As you realize the price drop plus the raise you just got will put you in a good position to buy the home of your dreams,** a car **all of a sudden out of nowhere** drives in front of you, almost running you off the road and into a ditch. Instead of apologizing, the person in the other car rolls down the window and vulgarly curses at you and speeds off.

🍃 *Question:* When you arrive home and your spouse asks, "How was your day?" what would be the order of the events you will tell them, starting from first to last?

🍃 **Question: How would you have reacted if these things actually happened to you?**

(Think specifically about what your actions would be. And answer in detail what you would tell your spouse or loved one concerning how your day went.)

🍃 *Question:* Just focusing on the lunch portion of the story, how would you determine your experience there?

🍃 *Question:* Without going back and rereading the story, how much of it can you recall in detail?

🍃 *Question:* Do you think more negative things happened or more positive things happened during that day?

Now reread the story to check and see if your answer is correct. Check and see if there is something you missed or forgot. And point out **and outline** anything you added to make the story complete.

You feel how you think, and at most times in our lives, our experiences will only be based on the things that we remember and think of. The fact of the matter is most of us would only give thought to the **car** incident coming home **before telling our spouse about the dream home coming back on the market.** Most of the negative aspects of the day **will usually be remembered** while forgetting some of the details about the good things that happened. Chances are, no one will ever forget to mention about the incident on the way to work, even though it was one of the first things that happened that day.

Most of the things we've added **will** show **the type of things we put more emphasis on, and the places where we added our acuity will show the type of behavior we identify ourselves with.** We might think that the car incident would stand out more because of the time it happened, but what if we changed the story so that the car incident happened on the way to lunch instead of on the way home?

🍃 *Question:* Do you think that difference in timeframe will change you from the surety of telling that portion of the story to your spouse **or loved one** first?

As humans, we are naturally drawn to sin; therefore, we often focus on the negative more than we do the positive. If untrained, our mind will go through life, observing the negative attributes to life far more than we do the positive. By recognizing more of the negative and less of the positive, you can cause your own suffering and possibly cause yourself not to care or appreciate all the good that is happening all around you as much as you should. Thinking negatively can possibly control how you view your entire life, and according to how you see things, it can cause your life to be far less enjoyable; unless something comes along and changes your point of view.

🍃 *Question:* Did you notice that the story never said who was at fault in the incident on the way home?

🍃 **Question: Who do you think was at fault for the accident that almost happened on the commute to work and the incident that happened on the way back home?**

Our opinions show our point of view. The way we see things doesn't always have to match up to what really happened to be what we think happened, in our own reality. Things don't have to be true in order for us to perceive that it's true. All you have to do is think it, and that will determine your perception of things.

The truth of the matter is, with you dancing to your favorite songs on the way to work, and because of the excitement created from the news of the "dream home" coming back on the market traveling from work, it would be more than likely that you would be the party at fault, due to being a distracted driver. This demonstrates how others can easily become the one blamed solely through a different point of view.

A sure sign of having a negative point of view is when we often blame others for our mistakes. By doing so, it protects the thinker by causing the blame to be on someone else. No matter who is at fault, the only thing you can control is you, and by controlling you, you can control the way you choose to see things. Remember, negativity moves you a step backward while positive thinking always moves you a distance forward.

🍃 *Question:* How do you see yourself?

Some of the most beautiful people to ever walk this earth have battled with having low self-esteem **in some moments of their lives**. There is nothing anyone can say or do to make someone see how beautiful they are if they refuse to recognize it. The only way to change the way you see yourself is to change the way you think **about yourself**. And all it takes to change your perception of thinking, is for you to look at things in a different way.

> **Psalm 139:13-14**
> **13** For thou hast possessed my reins: thou hast covered me in my mother's womb.
> **14** I will praise thee; for I am fearfully and wonderfully made: marvellous are thy works; and that my soul knoweth right well. (Psalm 139:13–14)

Know that typically the person that you married and the people who love you are your friends and not your enemy. They are for you and not against you. By understanding this, you will know that the decision they make and the perception that they have in their minds is not usually meant to hurt you but is an attempt to make things better, for both you and them. This doesn't mean every choice someone makes will show the love that they have for you, but it does open up an opportunity to have a conversation about the decisions people make and the thoughts behind those choices.

Quote: "It's the thought that counts."

🍃 *Question:* If negative thoughts are consistently being attached to your spouse, how can you view them as being anything other than what you think?

Taking notice of everything your spouse does wrong and nothing they do right is unfair, and these negative thoughts will soon consume your marriage, making it unbearable to reside in due to these thoughts. Thoughts are how you view the world and everything and everyone in it. And if **these negative thoughts are** not constrained, one day you may find yourself sleeping with the enemy.

Often couples may see things differently, and oftentimes individuals subconsciously view oppositions as a means of an attack. Understanding your loved one's position rather than viewing them as the opposition can allow you to view them in a more truthful and respectful light. Life is not always painted in black and white, and your thoughts are not always going to be the same as everyone else's. But know that just because sometimes people are not thinking just like you, doesn't mean that they are against you. It may just mean that **they** have **a** different way of looking at things.

Looking at things one way can make your life seem unbearable or that things will never change. It can even seem as if you are a mistake, or it can go as far as causing you to think that God doesn't love you. Looking at things only through one point of view is just like buying a book and only reading one-half of the story.

Seeing things as an opportunity rather than an obstacle can instantly change your point of view into creating something positive instead of conforming to a negative state of mind. You are what you do, and you do what you think. Things don't always have to be negative or impossible. Where there is an option to change your mind, there is hope; and where there is hope, there is always a possibility.

Changing your thoughts to knowing that a glass is not always half empty can take the strain and irritation out of the complexities of life and in our relationships. Sometimes you will see that the person you don't see eye to eye with doesn't mean you both don't have the same ambitions. If we can know and understand what the other person is thinking, we can find out we are trying to get to the same place, but just have a different way of getting there. Even though at times you may see things differently than your spouse and the other people around you, viewing others fairly can be the very key to making your relationship and your life go from no more than a 7.5 into a very rewarding and enjoyable life!

Take action now! (Turn to pages #243 through #265 for recommended fasts and exercises.)

Reality

🍃 *Question:* What is reality?

By definition, reality is the state of actual or absolute truth, but what does that mean for us? Reality comes in many different forms of existence, which **can be subjective or objective. Subjective, which is the most common form,** allows us to view reality in our very own individual way. Even the life and the death of Christ were told by four different truths. Reality doesn't mean that one person was any more truthful than the next; however, it does mean that majority of the state of our very own existence comes from the thoughts that we produce. And these thoughts **create** what we see, **what we hear,** and what we think we know.

Subjective and objective realities are separated by facts **and** beliefs. Subjectivity describes a reality based on influence or opinion rather than what can be proven. **It is subject to a** person's emotions, feelings, and thoughts; **and** can play an important role **in causing a conditional reality.** An objective reality **determines a reality based solely on evidence** and is clear from all opinions, influences, and partisanships. By definition, it is neutral, unbiased, and unopinionated.

In the true nature of reality, something **that** will appear real to some **may** not **seem** real to others, **and in some realities, things can be perceived as true to some and untrue to others. This** cognizance of reality alters based on **evidence, perception, and** the desire to believe in something that is beneficial to oneself. **Reality** conforms to how a person thinks, **and it is created from the experiences that we go through**.

Being subjective to something usually consists of using phrases such as "I feel." "In my opinion." or often end with a phrase such as, "It doesn't matter what no one else thinks." or "I don't care what they say." **While in an objective reality, it may contain phrases such as "Take a look for yourself." "The proof is right in front of you." or "It is evident." Objective reality is based more on facts rather than beliefs, which causes it to disregard things that are suspected but cannot be proven.**

Example: A highly successful person with a higher level of education or knowledge than some will say to those who are less successful **than they are, studies show that** going back to school **and hard** work **leads** to success. An unsuccessful person with the same level of education and knowledge as the highly successful person would say to gain a high level of success not only takes education and hard work, but it **also is based on** who you know **and will take a bit of luck as well**.

Question: Does the existence of God fall under a subjective reality or an objective reality?

> Luke 7:19
> 19 And John calling unto him two of his disciples sent them to Jesus, saying, Art thou he that should come? or look we for another? (Luke 7:19)

Everything that we know in its entirety only exists within our very own thoughts, and the thoughts that we hold on to will create the reality in which we live. **We only know what we know, and anything that is forgotten or outside of what we know will not become a part of the reality that we live in and understand. Our individual reality solely comes from what we are knowledgeable** about, which means that a reality that we are not familiar with can only be brought into existence through the realization of our thoughts. Knowledge is knowing, and it is derived through thoughts. Only through thoughts can something be acknowledged or continue to exist, and it is only through thoughts or the lack thereof that things can be neglected, misleading or forgotten. True existence dictates an objective reality, but in a subjective reality, things that don't exist can be created, and the things that actually exist can be overlooked.

Example: A person who looks for the bad things **in life** and the wrong in people **instead of looking for the good in people and the decent things in life** will always find it. And it can create an unnecessary reality of fear and hate.

Realization is the act of becoming aware, and it is through this process we consider something to be true. Reality comes from what we are conscious of; it is how we perceive everything, and it is even what defines who **we are and** what exists within our beliefs. Perception comes from thoughts, and the thoughts we have are commonly linked to the **most common things around us**. That's why, unfortunately, the evilness of this world is getting larger due to the fact that it is something that we are growing more and more accustomed to every day. And the things that would be thought of as being upsetting will just be part of the reality that we live in.

Example: With so many killings and hate crimes reported every day, a person can easily grow accustomed to the sins of this world and never give the people who are devastated by it a second thought.

Matthew 6:22–23
22 The light of the body is the eye: if therefore thine eye be single, thy whole body shall be full of light.

23 But if thine eye be evil, thy whole body
shall be full of darkness. If therefore the light that
is in thee be darkness, how great is that darkness!
(Matthew 6:22–23)

Quote: "They only see what they want to see."

What we take away from any situation can be altered by what
resonates with us. By its effects, it can cause you to see certain things
only **a certain** way, and you can **find yourself** blinded by **a subjective** reality **due to the** perceptions of your mind.

What you see is what you think, and your thoughts can quickly
alter the reality surrounding your existence.

Example: Many of us live in the reality that was taught to us
growing up. Being born into a family that doesn't believe in God
will often customarily cause you to also not believe in Him. In
your reality as a child growing up, there was no God, and that
nonexistent reality is something you will have to overcome to
keep from living in that same reality today.

Matthew 10:32–33
32 Whosoever therefore shall confess me
before men, him will I confess also before my
Father which is in heaven.
33 But whosoever shall deny me before men,
him will I also deny before my Father which is in
heaven. (Matthew 10:32–33)

Example: When watching the big game, everyone is a referee.
There are usually debates and arguments going back and forth
about what's right and what's wrong in every sport **known to
man. Ever since the creation of** instant replay, many people
have been proven wrong by the replay of footage that shows what
actually happened **as** opposed to what **people think they saw or
what they thought might** have happened.

With reviews in place, people who once completely thought one way were forced to be face-to-face with what actually happened. As soon as the realization hit that what they thought they saw or what they think happened didn't go exactly as they had thought or even hoped, **they were now faced with making the choice of rather they want to accept the truth or keep living in their own reality.** A perception of reality cannot change actuality, and because of that, many people are naive or living **in a** neglect**ful world**, causing **them to exist in a false reality different from everyone else.**

🍃 *Question:* What **reality do you live in?**

People that are brought up in poverty or living in broken homes can be familiar with a reality that is disturbing to most people. Many people living in these types of environments can be accustomed to some of the difficulties and challenges **in everyday life** that would usually never be considered a normal way to live. Every day, these environments are destroying our young people's potential because the reality that they live in doesn't allow much room for hope to exist, and even for some, not much food **or adequate shelter either.** That in itself can be the cause of creating a hopeless reality.

For some people, money is thought of as just being something readily available if they need it, while for others, it is a source of security. For some people, food is abundant and endless, while for others, it is a matter of life or death. For some people, clothes are **only meant for fashion** and are only **bought** if it **falls** in line with popular opinion while for others, it is a necessary tool for survival.

A greater part of our reality comes from perception, and if what you perceive is **to neglect or not acknowledge the people that are in need**, it can cause you to be living in existence different from **the existence of** a large number of other people living in **the** same world **as you.**

> Quote: *"Some people say that people, who are in need, need to work while others say that the people who have don't really have to work."*

🍃 *Question:* **Does wasteful spending bring happiness?**

And if so, how?

Many people say money makes you happy, but recent studies show that money only brings happiness to the point of sustain**ability,** after that, it becomes irrelevant and self-absorbent. **Spending money irresponsibly not only throws away a required resource many people don't have, but it also becomes harmful to that person and to everyone around them if it's done wastefully.**

🍃 **Example: Profligately spending can make someone spoiled, arrogant, and unappreciative of what they have. It can also influence other people on the outside looking in, to desire to spend money the same way. Due to a lack of sacrifice, it causes a lack of appreciation, and what would normally cause someone to be happy, is now overlooked and disregarded.**

🍃 **Question: If getting things makes people happy, why aren't there more people happier from having too much?**

It comes to my recognition that no one usually gets more happiness from having too much of one thing. It **instead makes them less happy from having too much after** their needs are sufficiently met. Having more of something after you've gotten enough is by definition, the example of having too much. **Too much of something, often** only causes you to be more unappreciative of what you do have **by causing you not to recognize the importance of what you have.** It **happens due to the thought of** if **something valuable** is **lost or** taken away, it can easily be replaced; and causing the something that you value to be less important than it would be if it could not be replaced.

> **Quote: "What one person desires another person takes for granted and what one person wants is what another person neglects."**

Reality is what summarizes our way of life **and** it is also what separates us from living as individuals. Your reality may not be the same as others or even as most, which is why your life is unique and special. **However, w**hat you've taken from life is what you will give to it, and what you contribute to life will also be credited to what defines you.

> Luke 13:6–7
> 6 He spake also this parable; A certain man had a fig tree planted in his vineyard; and he came and sought fruit thereon, and found none.
> 7 Then said he unto the dresser of his vineyard, Behold, these three years I come seeking fruit on this fig tree, and find none: cut it down; why cumbereth it the ground? (Luke 13:6–7)

Question: If you lived thinking one way and reality hits you and you find out that things are different outside of the reality that you know, would you **have the power to be brave enough** to **help** change reality **as we know it**?

By creating your reality, you are making sense out of your environment and the things that are in it. **If you can't make sense out of what you do or in the environment where you live, it's up to you to change it.** It takes far less effort to stay in a reality we are familiar with than to venture out into a reality that is unknown. That's why many people lack the ability to get out of reality or situation that is controlling or even dangerous **when they have the knowledge** or the means to escape. For that reason alone, many abused victims return to their abusers because of the reality that they live in. Once they leave, it is different from the reality that they've known and grown accustomed to. Many people who lived in destructive environments for a long-time often take that same destruction with them when they leave that environment, and often it is done voluntarily.

Abuse can come in many different forms, including mental, spiritual, and physical abuse. A narcissist is a person who has a mental disorder that causes them to have a misrepresentation of reality. They have to live in a controlled environment, typically exploiting others with guilt or shame to maintain a high sense of importance, entitlement, or admiration. This exploitation will be dangerous for many people who are subject to these types of environments because it can create a reality around them that can be clinically classified as traumatizing. **Those victims can be tortured for an extensive period of time without them knowing it, which often makes it a normal part of their life.**

A reality created out of opposing control over others is a defective and false reality that people are forced to live. **The only way out for many is to get help from a professional. The only way to help the ones affected by these types of situations is to get them to think differently from how they think. And hopefully that would be enough to cause them to not want to continue to be subject to the flawed reality that they live.**

Dreams are only figments of our imaginations created through thoughts inside of our minds. Even though what's **imagined isn't** real, it still can increase **your** heart rate, **affect your** emotions, **and even** cause **your body functions to react.** Hallucinations are images **that are also** experienced **from the** perceptions of things that seem apparent but truly are not **there. A**nd even though, in actuality, they don't exist, they still have the power to influence your thoughts. And through the power of your thoughts, it still possesses the same effects as if those things really do exist.

Quote: *"Take it under consideration."*

Consideration is the act of contemplating the facts when trying to determine what reality is. It is how we separate truth from fiction. And what we give our attention to will determine what we will let go of and what we will hold dear.

Question: If and when the majority of us believe that God **doesn't** exist, **in today's world**, will it cause His Word to be outdated or His presence to not be felt?

Reality is **a concept of** how we understand everything. It gives definition to the things and people in the world around us. It is what connects our environment to our meaning, **and it is a key element** that gives us the reason as to why we are here.

🌿 *Question:* Do you believe Jesus lived and died for you?

🌿 *Question:* If your answer is "no," how do we obtain salvation?

🌿 *Question:* If you **say you** don't believe in salvation, then why were you created?

Creation cannot create itself, and just because we procreate doesn't mean we aren't created by design. The reality of life is that we all were created to serve a purpose, and in that purpose, we have reason and that reason gives meaning to **every single one of us!** If you have no purpose, you have no meaning; and if you have no meaning, you have no reason for living. **If you find yourself in a reality where there is no meaning, realize you can change it by changing the way you think. The** reality **of it is**, thoughts are everything! It is what lifts you up; it is what motivates you and gives you hope.

The Spirit of God **is the compass that leads to** purpose, and only **through** your thoughts, will **it** give you a reason to live. If **you** are living in a reality absent from **your** purpose, it must be you're living in a reality absent from God's purpose. **Living** in a reality outside of **our Creator's** design is a depressing thought. **T**o be in a reality spent on living a life full of good or bad without any repercussions or rewards and no **accountability** for doing the things that we do **will put you in a world where anything is okay. If we live** a life with no real meaning until one day we just become no more and return into the ground from where we came from is a reality without a promise, which also makes it a reality without hope. **And without hope, there is no real reason for making a choice.**

🌿 *Question:* If we were formed only from dirt, how can only mere dirt create what is staring back at you when you look in**to a** mirror?

Believing in something brings real hope. It is hope that gives you purpose, and **in that purpose,** it will give you **actual** meaning even when you feel as if you don't have any real meaning at all.

Quote: "*Reality comes from the eyes of the beholder.*"

Reality is how two **children** growing up **in the exact same household** can form two totally different opinions of how **it was like being** raised **by the same parents.** It is how two people that are married can live in two different **worlds and view** their marriage **differently from one another. It** is how a person gives reason to why they are the way they are **and live the way that they live.**

Reality is a canvas, and what we sometimes need to do to coexist in harmony with others and within ourselves is to find a reality that exists only by design. **There is a reason for every situation we've been in and a purpose for all that we go through.**

Living in a reality that goes beyond our own selfish needs **and gives us a reason to inspire to become better than what we are today will serve as a purpose** to bridge together lives that are worlds apart.

Quote: "*Take a walk in my shoes.*"

A perception of reality is what separates us, and it is also what binds us together as a people. It is what can make us, as a human race, move past our differences and progress forward as one people. You can change the reality you live in simply by changing **the** perceptions that you've developed **in life.** It's okay to live in your own reality when no one is **affected by it,** but when other people **are depending on you** and **when salvation is** at stake, it's when it is time to reconsider your perception of reality and base your truth on things that actually exist!

Take action now! (Turn to pages #243 through #265 for recommended fasts and exercises)

10

Trust Issues

Trust is the firm belief in the reliability put into **something** or **in someone**. It is the glue that holds any relationship together, and it is the bridge that leads to love. It's a feeling of security, making it one of the most critical elements to **happiness and gaining** a happy marriage. I**ts bond is what strengthens all relationships,** and it gives the assurance and comfort that creates a confidence inside of whomever or whatever it is placed. Losing the trust you have in someone will create doubt, **and** that **doubt will alter** the way you feel about that person. T**rust is so powerful that even the** feeling of not being trusted can have you questioning if your loved one truly loves you.

When a trust is broken, it will typically create a feeling of betrayal, neglect, and disappointment. Negative feelings come from negative thoughts, which will have a negative effect on our spirituality, our emotional connections, and our physical well-being. That's why it's so important to remedy broken trust caused by a loved one; because a mixture of loving someone and never trusting them will lead to a life of confusion, doubt, and sorrow.

Understanding why someone did something instead of what they did can give **more** clarity to any situation. Taking out the guesswork of knowing what a person's intentions are, will cut down a lot of the time spent on frustration **and aggravation, which** allows you **more time** to get to **the** solution of problems a whole lot faster. **In regard to having a relationship with someone, b**eing clear on expectations will create a clearer and more accurate path to what steps should be taken next even if the path should be to end the relationship completely.

Communication is key! An open-minded form of communication will allow opportunities to develop to discuss your thoughts and feelings **with** the people that you **trust**. Being truthful to the people you **care about** not only will make your relationships more sincere, but it will also give the people you trust an opportunity to trust you too.

Question: What do you trust?

To answer this question, you must first be very truthful and honest with yourself. What you trust will give you a feeling of comfort, having it will make you feel secure, and just the thought of losing it can strike fear through your heart. Trust takes multiple thoughts to create, and ironically enough, it typically requires only one thought to entirely take that trust away.

Question: What will happen if the person you trust **doesn't** agree with **you or what you are thinking, but instead,** have a difference of opinion?

Question: Does this make the person you once trusted, now untrustworthy?

As humans, we all have to trust in something, and typically, all it takes for us to give our trust is for something to fall right in line with what we already believe. Also, many of us trust in the traditional sense, where trust is mostly given to those who support us and sees things the same way as we do. This transfer of trust can make it easy for someone that may not have the best intentions to come in and win over our trust; because all it takes to **gain** most of our trust is to listen and agree with everything we say.

To have trust doesn't mean you always have to agree with someone, and what you trust in doesn't always have to be with good intentions. It doesn't mean you have to give someone more credit than they deserve, and it doesn't mean the things and people that you trust have to be trustworthy or good. Unfortunately, all **you have to do to establish trust** is to be somewhat aware of how you truly feel, and once that's done, the only thing left is to choose to believe that what you think and feel is true.

🖋 **Question: What happens to those who put their trust in things and people who are untrustworthy?**

> Matthew 7:15-20
> **15** Beware of false prophets, which come to you in sheep's clothing, but inwardly they are ravening wolves.
> **16** Ye shall know them by their fruits. Do men gather grapes of thorns, or figs of thistles?
> **17** Even so every good tree bringeth forth good fruit; but a corrupt tree bringeth forth evil fruit.
> **18** A good tree cannot bring forth evil fruit, neither can a corrupt tree bring forth good fruit.
> **19** Every tree that bringeth not forth good fruit is hewn down, and cast into the fire.
> **20** Wherefore by their fruits ye shall know them. (Matthew 7:15–20)

Trust is a form of belief, and it is where our confidence is found. It is important to know that what we put our trust in is usually what we will put our confidence in, and it is where our belief will also be. Often in life, we put our confidence into what we believe, but if that belief is questionable, it not only will make our trust questionable, but it will also make what we find our confidence in questionable also.

Belief is the act of feeling like something is true; it is where our reliance is placed, and for it to exist, it will take the power of thoughts to form and the power of choice to decide. Belief comes in three main forms, and these forms are trust, faith, and hope. Faith is trust in the absence of evidence or proof, and hope is the belief that something is possible. When evidence presents itself, we can put our trust in that the evidence is true, but if that source of evidence is unknown, it will take faith in order to believe.

> Hebrews 11:1
> **11** Now faith is the substance of things hoped for, the evidence of things not seen. (Hebrews 11:1)

As Christians, our faith should **absolutely** not be implemented into conditional things. Having faith in conditional things is the total definition of having conditional faith. The true form of faith means that getting a job, getting a promotion, the ability to pay bills, receiving healing, and even saving your marriage should be prayed for through hope and having faith that God can do it and not that He should do it.

> 2 Samuel 12:16-20
> **16** David therefore besought God for the child; and David fasted, and went in, and lay all night upon the earth.
> **17** And the elders of his house arose, and went to him, to raise him up from the earth: but he would not, neither did he eat bread with them.
> **18** And it came to pass on the seventh day, that the child died. And the servants of David feared to tell him that the child was dead: for they said, Behold, while the child was yet alive, we spake unto him, and he would not hearken unto our voice: how will he then vex himself, if we tell him that the child is dead?
> **19** But when David saw that his servants whispered, David perceived that the child was dead: therefore David said unto his servants, Is the child dead? And they said, He is dead.

20 Then David arose from the earth, and washed, and anointed himself, and changed his apparel, and came into the house of the LORD, and worshipped: then he came to his own house; and when he required, they set bread before him, and he did eat. 2 (Samuel 12:16–20)

Question: When King David fasted for his child, did he have hope or faith that God would heal his son?

Could and *would* have very important differences. *Would* **being used in the past tense of will** states that something will definitely take place, while *could* put confidence in the ability to do something. Fasting is **the act of paying homage to or giving honor to, but in the sense of making a request, fasting is** like submitting in **an** offer or making a proposal. **T**his act through belief allows God to see the faith and trust that we have in Him**; And through faith and belief, it brings a hope that shines its' light even in the darkest places. If a person is depressed or hopeless, it is due to a lack of faith. A person who lacks faith and belief in God is a person who will never be able to trust in Him!**

When **David's** child never received healing, to everyone's surprise, David was able to move pasts his child's death because his faith in God **was** never compromised.

Proverbs 3:5-6
5 Trust in the LORD with all thine heart; and lean not unto thine own understanding.
6 In all thy ways acknowledge him, and he shall direct thy paths. (Proverbs 3:5-6)

Question: How can someone not trust in the God who created them?

Believing in the existence of God and trusting in Him are two totally different things. When we believe in God and that He will perform a certain act, we put this into our reality. And when

our reality doesn't equal what we think it should be, it is where we lose our trust and eventually our faith in Him!

When praying to our Heavenly Father, God will sometimes answer our prayers in a different way than what we **were** expect**ing of Him**. Believing that God, in His entirety, is every essence of good, and that He is always in control, allows you to trust in Him even when things don't go the way you had hoped they would. God is all-knowing, He is in full control, and sometimes He has the same goals for us as we do, but just a different way of getting there!

Example: It is God's will that nothing bad ever happens to us, but it is also His will that He create in us a feeling of empathy and a show of compassion for one another. For many of us, if we go through something, it will make that same something that we've been through something that we can relate to when other people or going through the same thing.

Question: Many people question God for allowing us to go through difficult times, but have anyone ever questioned how humanity would be if we never suffered?

> Quote: "Not going through hard times can often make someone arrogant, vain, and self-righteous, but humility and humbleness is created through the destruction of pride."

Trust is the absolute belief or confidence in someone or something, that it is or will be just as you thought. That's why it is so important not to put your trust in predetermined thoughts because it encourages the surrender of choice and gives power to circumstance. And that circumstance has to be just like we'd expected in order for us to maintain our definition of **who or what we** trust. If this happens, you would no longer be trusting in what or how something is or even who **someone** really is; because they cannot truly be themselves without losing your trust. And if they cannot be themselves around you, the person you thought you trusted, in **actuality,** will cause you to be trusting in a lie.

It is hurtful to put **your** faith into something that doesn't happen or something that is false because it leaves **you** with the realization that the thing that **you** once believed, may be something that actually was not true.

🍃 *Example:* Atheism is created through acts of believing in things that are not true and putting faith in the things that are **subjective**, which ultimately generates doubt.

Doubt is a feeling of uncertainty, suspicion, or is a lack of conviction that can cause hesitation or the inability to make a decision. Trust and doubt are total opposites, so much in fact that **both of them could never co-exist together in the same moment**.

🍃 *Example:* When Lucifer tempted Eve in the Garden of Eden, he used doubt to cancel out her trust in God. It is my interpretation that as he tempted Eve, He used more than just words. I believe that as he spoke (and being already condemned), he plucked the fruit off the tree and held it in his hand. And as **Eve** witnessed him still standing and not falling dead as **he touched the forbidden fruit as** she had **thought** would happen, that was when Eve began to doubt. The scripture says that "the woman saw that the tree was good for food and that it was pleasant to the eyes." It is my interpretation that Eve stood and watched Satan take a bite out of the fruit that he was holding, and as the juice from the fruit rolled down his face, it was when Eve **concealed her doubt, and her** trust in God was broken!

🍃 *Question:* What else could explain why Eve would have doubted the God who created her over someone she **didn't** know?

> Quote: "Doubt creates denial, and denial produces the act of disobedience."

Doubt comes into play when we see signs of things coming into existence we thought didn't exist or wasn't possible. Choice is the most powerful factor of human existence, and to create any form of trust, can't be forced. To be real, trust in someone or something can only be given, **and to be given can only be done through choice**.

> Quote: "You can't truly live if you are truly living in fear."

Fear is created from negative thoughts, and negative thoughts are often produced from **having** doubts. Not only do doubts make you second-guess your choices, it can also make you second-guess yourself. Doubt creates a feeling of insecurity, and if that insecurity is felt toward the things and people you care about, it will cause you to worry. That worrying can grow into a fear for the things and people that you care about.

Worrying is a sign of a lack of trust, and if you don't trust in anything that is important, it will also cause you to lose your faith in the things that matter the most. It gives many people and atheists comfort not to have faith in anyone outside of themselves, but with that lack of faith, it will also cause you not to trust anyone. A trust leads to love, and if you are the only one you have trust in, you will also be the only one you will truly love.

As Christians, it is very important that we don't put our faith in what God does but in what God is. If we put faith in the what, it will put our requests before His purpose, and our faith will quickly become contingent on what God is doing for us instead of what He has already done. Applying your trust, faith, and hope in the right context will create a stronger feeling of appreciation when things hoped for are granted rather than creating a feeling of resentment when it is not. A marriage that has trust is a strong marriage, and a relationship with God that is built on faith cannot be broken!

Take action now! (Turn to pages #243 through #265 for recommended fasts and exercises.)

Emotional Thoughts

Ecclesiastes 3:1-8

1 To every thing there is a season, and a time to every purpose under the heaven:

2 A time to be born, and a time to die; a time to plant, and a time to pluck up that which is planted;

3 A time to kill, and a time to heal; a time to break down, and a time to build up;

4 A time to weep, and a time to laugh; a time to mourn, and a time to dance;

5 A time to cast away stones, and a time to gather stones together; a time to embrace, and a time to refrain from embracing;

6 A time to get, and a time to lose; a time to keep, and a time to cast away;

7 A time to rend, and a time to sew; a time to keep silence, and a time to speak;

8 A time to love, and a time to hate; a time of war, and a time of peace. (Ecclesiastes 3:1–8)

There is a **time for every** purpose in this world, and **there is also a purpose for every** emotion **felt.** There is a thought developed to employ the understandings of every instance that occurs, and these thoughts are also designed to trigger every emotion we feel. The way we think and the way that we feel are very similar to one another. Both of them can initiate an action or reaction to any situation, and they both are used to describe what we are.

That's why you can explain the way you feel by saying what you think, and you can describe what you are thinking by expressing how you feel. A reaction is the only act we can do without thinking, and every reaction we do is only triggered through emotional thoughts.

Emotions are a naturally instinctive state of mind that is developed through thoughts that are created from the circumstances and situations we've experienced. Our most common emotions display a description of our natural state of mind. And that natural state of mind has been developed in each and every one of us throughout the course of our lives, in correlation with our feelings and the power of our thoughts.

Example: People who are always upset are upset because they are consistently emotionally angry. Being mean to people because someone has made you mad can not only cause you not to feel good, but through the power of thoughts, it can also make you become a mean and hateful person. By being nice to people despite how you are feeling at that moment comes from choosing to think positive.

And being positive will keep you from ever becoming mean or hateful.

Question: What kind of person are you?

You are what you do, and at most times, you do how you feel. Therefore, how most people feel is how most people conduct themselves. You wouldn't usually see a happy person sad, and you usually certainly wouldn't see a depressed person happy. If a person who normally feels sad is happy, it is only because they've thought of something that made them happy. And if how a person behaves makes them sad, it has everything to do with the thoughts behind their actions.

If a person who is normally sad feels happy, they will no longer be sad; and if a happy person feels sad, they will no longer be happy, at least for the moments while they are thinking the way they feel. But once their thoughts change, their feelings will go right along with it!

Ephesians 4:31–32
    31 Let all bitterness, and wrath, and anger, and clamour, and evil speaking, be put away from you, with all malice:
    32 And be ye kind one to another, tenderhearted, forgiving one another, even as God for Christ's sake hath forgiven you. (Ephesians 4:31–32)

Quote: "Take control over what you do by not letting your emotions take control over you."

Example: Getting upset with an authority figure can cause you to get locked up in jail or in another horrifying situation that you would never deliberately decide to be in. And although sometimes our emotions get the best of us, knowing how what you are feeling is influencing what you do can give you the knowledge to make the choice to reduce your emotions and make a decision that will benefit you more!

How we think affects the way we feel, but the way that we feel also affects the way that we think. If our emotions change the way we think, the way we think will also change what we do, which gives our emotions authority over our lives. Through the power of choice, we can prevent the emotions we feel from controlling how we think. And by maintaining control over the way we think, we will manage to have control over everything that we do.

🍂 **Example: Quitting a job for not getting paid more will leave you temporarily making no money instead of less money than you think you deserve. If you were to replace your emotions with your thoughts, your decision will be more likely to either be patient or to immediately start looking for another job while staying employed. A choice to make no money rather than less money will most likely make a situation worse before it gets better. Our emotions are linked to the way we feel just like our thoughts are linked to the way we think. And remember, our thoughts and feelings are often interchangeable, which means, the feelings we feel can easily take presidency over the way that we think. But if we take control over the way that we think, it will give us a certain amount of control over the way that we feel and authority over our emotions as well.**

> **Ephesians 4:26–27**
> **26** Be ye angry, and sin not: let not the sun go down upon your wrath:
> **27** Neither give place to the devil. (Ephesians 4:26–27)

🍂 Question: How good could you sleep after being in a horrible argument with your spouse right before bed?

Many couples make the mistake of designating time right before bed to talk about bills or other controversial topics that often result in a difference in opinion. Waking up the next morning from a rough night of sleep caused by an argument or speaking hurtful things to each other can distance the relationship you have. Also, being upset can cause you to emotionally say things to a loved one that you don't actually think. The scriptures used in the Bible never suggest staying up all night until you resolve your issues, but it may suggest that you refrain from bringing any issues to bed with you that can cause distress at all!

A healthy couple gives space throughout the day, when their minds are fresh, to discuss important issues, and uses God's designated time for rest to relax, unwind, and enjoy each other's company. Through time, learning to live with anger can lead an emotional thought to becoming a decision, which can cause a setback or even destroy the relationship entirely.

Question: Would it be unusual for a person brought up in a different environment to be the same as you, or is it more common for that person to be less like you due to their environment?

All humankind, all over the world, have very similar characteristics. However, there are times when we think what we would do or won't do might be different from what other people do. But the fact of the matter is that the things that we would do would be exactly the same thing as other people who we think are different from us do, if we thought the same way those people feel.

> **Quote: "If I thought the exact same way as you, I would be exactly like you and feel the same way as you do."**

Being placed in a different environment, you may find that it is much easier to be like everyone else than it is to be yourself; but if you are not yourself, you are not being who you truly are. Commonly, we act the way we feel, and we feel the way we think. Emotions reveal the way we feel, and even though sometimes we don't understand why emotions develop, it doesn't change the fact that emotions reflect how we presently think.

A sad person will have depressing thoughts, and a mean person will have angry thoughts. A happy person will have happy thoughts, and a silly person's head will be full of humorous thoughts. An angry person will never get happy over having upsetting thoughts, and a cheerful person would never get sad over having happy thoughts. Someone usually wouldn't laugh

from devastating thoughts, and a person hardly will ever weep from happy thoughts unless they're tears of joy.

There are times when a person will act differently than the way they feel, but the way they feel will still reveal how they honestly think. So often as adults and many times as young adults, we try to alter our emotions to try and fit in with everyone else. So, we change the way we think, to change the way we act, but the way we act will often change the way we feel, and it will also construct a change in who we are. "You are what you do," and sometimes we eventually will end up not being ourselves, just so that we can be like everyone else.

Quote: *"The only person you should try to be like is* ***being*** *yourself."*

It is important to be truthful with yourself. If you are not honest with the way you feel, your feelings will eventually build-up, and without **being** released, it will create an emotionally unbalanced life. A misuse or a disproportionate display of emotions can make you seem as if you are uncaring. Misuse of these same emotions can also cause you to appear overbearing, such as being overly dramatic. This unbalanced show of emotions can be prevented with the ability to control your thoughts, **and it will** cause **you to have better control over** your lifestyle **and** the relationships you have with others as well.

Philippians 4:8

8 **Finally, brethren, whatsoever things are true, whatsoever things are honest, whatsoever things are just, whatsoever things are pure, whatsoever things are lovely, whatsoever things are of good report; if there be any virtue, and if there be any praise, think on these things.** (Philippians 4:8)

For every emotion you have, there is a thought attached, **and for every way you feel towards something or someone, it is due to**

the way that you think! Some emotions at times may have the ability to influence your thoughts, but your thoughts will always have the ability to influence any and every one of your emotions.

🖉 *Example:* People often **don't immediately know how to feel** from the initial reaction of someone dying, but often the mere thought of never being able to speak to a particular person again **or spend time with them is enough to** cause **a person** to weep.

Once we get over the initial **shock** of someone dying, every thought after that will influence the way we remember that person and how those memories **make us** feel. Changing your state of mind from thinking about your loss to appreciating the special times you shared with your loved one may be enough to pick up your spirits. And from the feeling of being grateful, it could change the sad and depressed tears you have into glad and joyful tears just from thinking of having a chance to be in that special someone's life. Emotions are like seasons: They are not meant to last more than what is naturally intended, **and if they do last more than their natural design, it will create unnatural circumstances**.

🖉 *Example:* Forcing or allowing yourself to be sad for an extended period of time will always lead to some form of depression or worse. **Sadness is not designed to last for a lengthy period of time. And if we are saddened for longer than what we are naturally designed to, it can cause health problems, rapid aging, and many other complications.**

True love is a positive energy that flows through us. It is not measured by how long we mourn for someone, but is measure by the amount of positive influence it has in our lives. To feel sad or depressed is a direct reflection of negative thoughts; and remember, negative thoughts will always produce some form of negative results; **but k**eep in mind; everything has a season, and **in those seasons,** there is a reason for every emotion **felt**.

Example: Being happy all the time can cause you to not be emotionally intact with the people and situations that surround you, **and being sad all the time can cause you to be self-centered and unenthusiastic**.

Knowing the reason for each of our emotions and understanding its purpose will allow you to live a more balanced and stable life. It will also enhance the life you live. Emotions can cause our lives to be significantly more gratifying. Your emotional thoughts will intensify the process it takes to accumulate thoughts into interest. And that interest is great enough to turn any ordinary instance into a moment full of promise and value!

With every emotion, there is a reaction; and with every reaction, there is a thought or feeling that caused it. By keeping our emotions in check, we can assure that we will act appropriately in every situation. Keep in mind, in life, we can not only have power over the things that we do; but through the power of the mind, we can have the authority over every emotion that we feel. And that control will give us more control over our lives, even when it's a time to lose control and let our emotions show!

Take action now! (Turn to pages #243 through #265 for recommended fasts and exercises.)

Mistakes

A mistake is an act of doing something accidentally or unknowingly. These actions are often taken without much thought or being fully aware of the consequences to come. Mistakes are a result of our imperfections, and even though they are not done purposefully, in fairness, mistakes are something in life, that we should expect to happen.

Like mistakes, spills are **things unintendedly done by accident.** If time passes, the stain will set, making it more problematic **when it comes to addressing these situations**. A mistake brings attention to our insecurities by revealing our imperfections. Through pride, mistakes are hidden or covered up, and through time, when they are revealed, they are not so easy to wipe away. Spills are not always in liquid form. A spill can be a mistake we sometimes make that can leave a stain, **and that stain can have an effect on our relationships with other people**. I've spilled many things in my life, literally and figuratively. One thing that both have in common is, a spill is much easier to clean up, if it's addressed in a timely matter.

Mistakes show that we are not perfect, but often, it also gives us the opportunity to correct the results of our imperfections. Making mistakes is a part of being human, and not accepting that we all make mistakes can be the cause of our miscommunication with other people. Miscommunication is a failure to communicate adequately. Inadequately communicating with someone **through a** misunderstanding **or through predetermined thoughts can create negative thoughts. And these negative thoughts** can **create a perception that mistakes only happen because someone is careless or just does not care. And it would cause the people that you trust not to be trusted.**

Example: Making one mistake can lead to assuming that if given a chance, there will be many more to come.

People often **give excuses or** get defensive when being accused of making a mistake. **But excuses can be perceived as only justifying a mistake, instead of using it as a learning experience or an opportunity to take on responsibility.** Owning up to our mistakes and simply issuing an honest apology can take away something that can be held against us and make it **into being** something that moves **our** relationships forward **in the right direction. And that takes away the negativity of a misfortunate event and turns it into a deliberate act to make a situation and ourselves better.**

Remember that negative thoughts are the creation of insecurities and doubts. Focusing on the cause of a mistake rather than the effects of one will allow you to gain control and keep trust inside of the relationship. Punishing someone for something that they are truly sorry for doing, is like, punishing someone for regretting they did something to hurt you. And if we are not careful, it can cause something that someone was once sorry for, be something that they now don't regret!

Mistakes are the actions or judgments that are misguided or wrong and **can be** the very cause of sin. When a mistake is made intentionally, it changes from being a mistake into being a bad decision. **And k**nowingly doing something wrong **can** go from being ignorant to be**com**ing foolish.

Question: Why do someone intentionally make bad decisions?

Through the misguidance and deceptions of this world, what man considers good is wrong, and what is bad is considered good.

Through cultural influences, **the earth's population** is getting more and **more confused** about what is right and what is wrong. **Not knowing what is right and what is wrong will make us more conformed to this world and more likely to make mistakes.** By **becoming inclined to living** outside of God's judgment, it will give **a false** perception **that we don't need God and that** man **is** equal to **Him.** And for **some, even to** dare to think they are greater! By thinking consciously or subconsciously, thoughts that can put man anywhere close to being equal to **our Creator** will cause **a perception that because we are** imperfect, God has some imperfections too. **After all, it goes without saying, "If we are equal to God, that makes Him no better than us." Then by us not being perfect, through thoughts of reasoning, it will make us think that God isn't perfect either!**

Romans 1:21-25

21 Because that, when they knew God, they glorified him not as God, neither were thankful; but became vain in their imaginations, and their foolish heart was darkened.

22 Professing themselves to be wise, they became fools,

23 And changed the glory of the uncorruptible God into an image made like to corruptible man, and to birds, and fourfooted beasts, and creeping things.

24 Wherefore God also gave them up to uncleanness through the lusts of their own hearts, to dishonour their own bodies between themselves:

25 Who changed the truth of God into a lie, and worshipped and served the creature more than the Creator, who is blessed for ever. Amen. (Romans 1:21–25)

By definition, a bad decision is made regardless of the consequences to come. Consequences are a result of wrongdoing through an act or condition which gives purpose for punishment. Punishment, if used efficiently, is to make it where the consequences for specific actions are so unpleasant that it makes intentionally doing the wrong thing visibly not worth it. That's why God blinks at ignorance because ignorance is the condition of something done unknowingly. But if ignorance becomes a bad choice made intentionally, what was originally a mistake, will become, a choice that deserves the punishment obtained.

Acts 17:30
30 And the times of this ignorance God winked at; but now commandeth all men every where to repent. (Acts 17:30)

By definition, mistakes are made in ignorance, and through that ignorance, God gives His mercy. If we learn from our mistakes, it will make our errors no longer **be** thought of as mistakes but a much needed first step to do the right thing.

Often, it's easy to identify a person by the mistakes they make or the wrongs they do. **By doing t**his, **it** will allow a fluctuation of negative thoughts to be created, causing you to see **a person** differently than **you did** before the mistake was made. Many people suffer from categorizing others by their actions rather than their intent**, and by doing this, you are punishing a person for doing something they didn't want to do!**

Example: Having a loved one or a caring spouse who did something wrong that hurt you doesn't mean they did something to hurt you. If a person **is identified by their** actions, then "making a mistake," **by definition,** voids out what was done wrong and **should understandably place our attention on** what they were **actually** trying to do **that went wrong.**

Knowing and unknowingly, our days are full of mistakes. We sometimes base our perceptions on what a person does or doesn't do instead of the character that they possess. Not living up to one's expectations can create doubts, distrust, and wariness. That's why it's so important not to judge what anyone did, just by what they did, but we should view all things with fairness and kindness. If not careful, mistakes will change how you view your loved ones. It will start to change how you think and eventually will cause you to undermine not only their importance, but making mistakes can also even undermine your **very** own importance **and value of** your**self.**

By putting more focus on the why instead of the how, you will improve how you handle certain situations, allowing you to address them more accurately. By channeling your attention to the why, it will also enable you to resolve the mistake more efficiently, causing a positive impact on you as well as **in** your relationships with others.

Accepting that sometimes mistakes do happen will give you a **better perception and a** more empathetic **approach in life and within your many** relationships **with the people you care about.** By addressing the incidents **that happen** in your life correctly, it will also better equip you with dealing with **things that are done incorrectly or done by** mistake.

Take action now! (Turn to pages #243 through #265 for recommended fasts and exercises.)

13

The Power of Influence

Thoughts are the ideas and opinions created in our minds. It is our point of view and reality as we know it. Yes, thoughts are the most powerful trait humankind has, but over 90 percent of our thoughts used to define our **very** existence is controlled **through** the power of influences.

By definition, influences can restrain or increase **our** personal growth and development, and **it can** control **our** mood, and alter **our behavior.** By the use of persuasion, influences have the power to **change our character** and how **we** feel about every single thing **in the entire world**!

From the moment we are born, we **develop our cognitive skills through** the power of influence. **As b**abies, **we** are influenced to look **when we are called,** to laugh **when taking pictures**, and later **there is a** race **to be the first to get us to** say "mama" or "dada." While **we grow** into toddlers, we **are** influenced to walk, **to** use the potty, and to eat **our** vegetables. Throughout our lives, we can be influenced into choosing what to do, how to act, **what to eat**, what to watch, and what we listen to. We are later **in life** influenced on how to dress, whom to date, and how far to go when dating. In life, we are persuaded on which college to attend, wh**en** to get married, and when to start a family.

We encounter many influences in our lives, and we must be careful because the things we are influenced to do will be what determines what we are and how we live our lives.

Influences have always been with us, but the first record of it was when Lucifer convinced a third of the angels in heaven to rebel against God.

Revelation 12:4

4 And his tail drew the third part of the stars of heaven, and did cast them to the earth: and the dragon stood before the woman which was ready to be delivered, for to devour her child as soon as it was born. (Revelation 12:4)

Satan wants to hunt down and ultimately destroy human-kind. He is obsessed with tormenting us, and only because God loves us, he wishes to ultimately destroy us, one portion at a time. Through his deceit, he carefully changes the way we think and what we know, to be against the One who loves us the most. And he does it through his craftiness, and he also does it, with the power of influence.

Question: Have you ever noticed that sometimes it isn't until you've finished doing something wrong that you truly noticed how wrong that something you did actually is?

Example: When a person loses their virginity before mar-riage, the experience they feel is usually not at all as they had thought or hoped it would be. Instead of feeling deep pleasure and satisfaction, we typically have a feeling of dis-may and regret soon after it's over. It is usually through the influences of the world and the people in it, that causes us to think that the act of sexual immorality is okay. And despite the initial disappointment we felt, doing this same act often enough, can cause it to become normal and to be considered abnormal to resist. We become accustomed to sinning against our very own bodies, which causes us to become numb and guiltless to the convictions of our own wrongdoing.

To have influence over someone or something is to have a percentage of control, and that control has the power to change your thoughts into thinking something different. It will also create a difference in perception. Once the power of influence subsides, the power it has over our thoughts decreases, and we go back to thinking the way we did before these influences were inflicted upon us. And typically, we are left with a moment of regrets shortly afterward.

Example: People typically are more spiritually minded while they are incarcerated behind bars. With the lack of opportunity and without the negative power of influences, people normally revert back to thinking the natural way they are designed. When many of us are freed, we go back to how we were before we were locked up or imprisoned because of the recrudesced of opportunity and influence.

Quote: "I was under the influence."

Matthew 27:3-5
3 Then Judas, which had betrayed him, when he saw that he was condemned, repented himself, and brought again the thirty pieces of silver to the chief priests and elders,
4 Saying, I have sinned in that I have betrayed the innocent blood. And they said, What is that to us? see thou to that.
5 And he cast down the pieces of silver in the temple, and departed, and went and hanged himself. (Matthew 27:3-5)

Satan's control over Judas caused him to search for an opportunity to betray Jesus. Even though he walked with Jesus, witnessed the miracles, and felt His love, they were of no affect because of the power of influence. Satan had control over him, and it blinded his perception, and ultimately, his influences had control over the way that he felt. Once the betrayal was complete, Satan fled and left Judas to face his judgment alone. When Judas regained his thoughts, the realization of his actions was too overwhelming, and the effects of Satan's last influence was for him to take his own life.

Genesis 3:4-6

4 And the serpent said unto the woman, Ye shall not surely die:

5 For God doth know that in the day ye eat thereof, then your eyes shall be opened, and ye shall be as gods, knowing good and evil.

6 And when the woman saw that the tree was good for food, and that it was pleasant to the eyes, and a tree to be desired to make one wise, she took of the fruit thereof, and did eat, and gave also unto her husband with her; and he did eat. (Genesis 3:4–6)

Satan didn't stop with Eve in the Garden of Eden, but he pursued her husband next. Through the power of influence Satan had over Eve, he caused her to seek out her own husband, and through influence, Adam sinned also. If Satan can't get to you directly, he will often use others as a persuasion to get what he wants from you.

God had already cursed the serpent, and as mentioned before, it allowed Satan to freely eat **of** the **tree**. And after the forbidden fruit had been devoured, Eve went to Adam. And when he saw that she didn't die, Adam became deceived also by one of the strongest influences known to man—the persuasive power of sight!

🍃 **Example: Telling your child not to smoke while seeing you smoke all their life will encourage them to smoke more than it will discourage them not to smoke, even though you said not** to. Typically, it will create an opportunity to be led by Satan or by their own logical imaginations that you are being hypercritical. And often, shortly after that thought has been affirmed, they will later be persuaded to think that you are only trying to keep them from some kind of fun experience. And that thought will more than likely make a parent who loves their child and only wants to look out for their best interest be viewed as an enemy and a contributor to making their lives worse.

Quote: "Seeing is believing."

Sight is one of the most influential instruments known to man because sight gives light, and through that light, we recognize things that weren't recognized or seen before. Learning something new creates interest, and interest captures the thoughts in the mind of its thinker.

Question: Do you believe everything you see?

Advertisers run ads of smokers and partakers of particular food or beverages having the best times of their lives while using their products. Due to news ratings, reporters report stories and headline incidents and events that are more biased than ever before to capitalize off of the arguments created from characterizing with certain opposition and political issues.

Things are not always as they seem, and seeing certain things on television, on the internet, and even in life, can be deceitful enough to persuade you to think of something as only being fun and rewarding, when there are far greater consequences to come! It can influence people to make terrible decisions that they will often not know the full ramifications of their consequences until the act is done, or after it is too late!

Remember to realize; a bad choice is always a bad choice. Yet and still, we continue to be influenced to think differently or continue to be accustomed to thinking that some decisions that are proven to be bad for some people may be different for you. This way of thinking will continue to permit you to make a bad decision despite by definition, a bad decision cannot change and will always come with more regrets than rewards at some point in time.

God forbids us to **sin**, and just like Eve, we see many of these forbidden sins being cheerfully done by people with great pleasure. **When** Adam **sinned against God, he didn't die** that day, but by God's grace, he lived to be 930 years old before his full consequences were met. **An influence can cause you to believe in something or someone, and Satan mixes the truth of what we believe with false facts to execute one of the most substantial influences his deception has over us, the persuasion of doubt.**

Many times, throughout the Bible and throughout our lives, Satan uses **God's mercies given to us to turn our thoughts into a perception that causes us to take our Creator for granted instead of thanking Him for His forgiveness and for His grace.**

📚 **Example: You can become accustomed to doing something wrong by continuously getting away with it. Through time, you can grow accustomed to thinking of something as being normal and that there is nothing wrong with what you are doing. And even if you do think something is wrong, our decisions often don't change due to the fact that we think that we can always ask for forgiveness later in life.**

📚 **Question: How can you ask forgiveness for something you don't regret or feel sorry for doing? Or how can you plan to wish you didn't do something before you actually do it?**

The act of persuasion through sight can cause many acts of sins seen through life and in motion pictures to give the perception that wrongdoing can be done without ramifications or punishment. It gives an opportunity for us to be blinded by the perception of not knowing the consequences attached to our actions.

> *Quote: "One bad apple can spoil the whole bunch."*

Through social groups and affiliations, people have relied on one another to learn and grow. With the internet being so rapid and common amongst us today, it is easier than ever to influence a larger group of people than there ever was before. Once someone gives into another person's way of thinking, that person's way of thinking now has control over that someone. If that person's thoughts are negative, the other person will become as cynical as their influencer, and through the act of persuasion, they will become one and the same.

Influences have a level of control great enough to cause thoughts to occur and actions to take place that wouldn't usually ever have taken place before. And there are positive and negative influences all around us each and every day. That's why it's so important for us to know our thoughts, because what you are is how you think, and thoughts are what we know. Before long, how you are persuaded to think might turn you into someone you don't like and without realizing it, you can go through your whole life never knowing it!

One of the key things that make an influence good or bad is the thought and intent behind the persuasion. Positivity encourages growth in a facet that is helpful and pleasant, while negativity encourages wrong actions to occur through demoralizing and ridiculing individuals. Encouragement is a form of influence that motivates individuals to become the best themselves they can be. Motivation, in itself, is inspiring and uplifting. Throughout history, many encouraging and inspirational individuals set examples of how we can rise above significant challenges and set an example that symbolizes one of humanity's greatest abilities—the power to overcome and persevere.

Many great and wonderful people went against **oppression, ethnocentrism,** and **social injustice to fight** for what is right.

🍃 *Example*: Martin Luther King Jr. fought for civil rights and equality in a world where race dictated your importance and value in America.

Billy Graham was a Southern Baptist minister who committed his life to spread the message of Christ. He stood against racial segregation and bridged the gap between religious and secular cultures.

Malala Yousafzai, who grew up in a culture that was sexually divided, was inspired by her parents' work in humanitarianism. She began to shine a light on what life is like living in Pakistan under the influence of the Taliban regime. She is widely known for her work in education for women and for her resilience and bravery overall.

Desmond Tutu is a socialist known for his work as an anti-apartheid activist and fighting for democracy in Southern Africa for free and fair elections. He is the first person of dark skin to be appointed as dean of St. Mary's Cathedral in 1975, and he was the first to be appointed archbishop of Cape Town. His stand is for religion, justice, equality, liberty, and freedom for all.

> Psalm 139:14
> I will praise thee; for I am fearfully and wonderfully made: marvellous are thy works; and that my soul knoweth right well. (Psalm 139:14)

Negative thoughts caused by influences can make the most beautiful person ever to walk the face of this earth feel ugly. In some way, form, or fashion, we suffer through **similar** perceptions caused by negative influences **throughout** our lives. **The culture we live in defines the word *beautiful*, and if not careful, our culture will be used to define us as well. Some cultures ridicule certain human features, while other cultures are fascinated by these same features. Some regions look down on certain people based on their genealogy, while in different regions and areas, they would treat those same people like kings and queens for those exact same reasons.**

"Reality is determined through the eyes of the beholder."

Like snowflakes that never have the same pattern twice, each and every one of us has our own fingerprint. Our teeth are distinctly molded and even the retinas in our eyes are uniquely designed. For some intellectual people and scholars, beauty is identified as being unique, and by that definition, we are all beautiful in our own way!

God didn't go through all the trouble to make us different to make us doubt ourselves. He purposely made us different so that we could prove that even though we are different, it doesn't make any one person any better than anyone else. **And to be likened to Him, and followers of Christ, it is absolutely imperative that we treat everyone with the same manner of respect.**

Matthew 7:6
6 Give not that which is holy unto the dogs, neither cast ye your pearls before swine, lest they trample them under their feet, and turn again and rend you. (Matthew 7:6)

Our children are pressured to give up their innocence by the influence of their peers and friends. The lifestyles of characters played in movies and television no longer promote abstinence **but instead encourages** sexual infidelities throughout the whole world. **Insecurity comes from not knowing if you are living up to someone's standards, but if you become exactly what everyone wants you to become, it will cause you to lose some of yourself in the process.** The pressure from influences can be so intense it may leave you feeling like you have no choice, but know that the Holy Father gives us the power to choose. And no one, not even Satan himself, can overpower Jehovah and take **the** control *He has given* away.

Quote: *"I would rather for you to hate me for being me than to love me for pretending to be someone else."*

A person of less interest in something or interested in something else entirely will persuade others to share the same level of interest as they do. We naturally desire to be understood and mistakenly we think, in order to understand each other, we have to think just like each other. Once a person gives in to another's person way of thinking, they will become just like that person. If that person's thoughts are negative, through the act of persuasion, the other person will become as damaging as that person thinks.

Proverbs 22:24-25
24 Make no friendship with an angry man;
and with a furious man thou shalt not go:
25 Lest thou learn his ways, and get a
snare to thy soul. (Proverbs 22:24–25)

Through cultural practices, cultural standards are set by a result of the majority and by the people who are more influential than others. They set the standard of what things to value and even how to value ourselves. It has been proven time and time again that one person who grew up in a negative environment could have turned out entirely different if they had grown up in a more loving, stable environment.

Athletes, singers, musicians, and actors are given billions of dollars each year for endorsement deals because companies know they have the power to influence people to buy their products. Reality shows on television falsely portray how reality really looks, and that representation often sets the standards and moral values **for many** of their viewers. No matter which news channel you watch or what music you choose to listen to, we all are influenced in some way or another**; but through the power of choice, we can control who or what we allow to influence us.**

Matthew 5:13-16
13 Ye are the salt of the earth: but if the salt
have lost his savour, wherewith shall it be salted?

it is thenceforth good for nothing, but to be cast out, and to be trodden under foot of men.

14 Ye are the light of the world. A city that is set on an hill cannot be hid.

15 Neither do men light a candle, and put it under a bushel, but on a candlestick; and it giveth light unto all that are in the house.

16 Let your light so shine before men, that they may see your good works, and glorify your Father which is in heaven. (Matthew 5:13–16)

It's time for us to take back our power of choice by eliminating all influences in our lives that we don't want. We have the power to freely choose, and whether it is good or bad, a choice should only be made by the person who is making the choice.

Every day this world is taking away God's presence in our lives. We are so confused that we are ashamed to do good and proud to do wrong. Even the institution of marriage is taken away and made to be undesired through the influences of this world. Let the world know if you have an "*A*+ marriage," and if your marriage is not quite there yet, let everyone know that **an** "*A*+ marriage" is what you are **inspired** to **have**. Influence the world by letting everyone know that you're living an "*A*+ lifestyle" and that the right way is the best way to live!

By making this statement, God's people will reset the standards as we know it and lift up the teachings of Christ instead of living under the influences of man.

Quote: "*Everyone can have an influence on anyone.*"

Influence your children and your family to be the best persons they can be. Let everyone know as God's children, you are that light, and it's time for us to light up your world. Let everyone know that it is wrong to hate another person based on their nationality, for their beliefs, gender, or sexuality. Show them you are no longer subject to the negative influences of this world by taking back control over your life.

> 1 Peter 3:16
> **16** Having a good conscience; that, whereas they speak evil of you, as of evildoers, they may be ashamed that falsely accuse your good conversation in Christ. (1 Peter 3:16)

Gain back control over your life and let **everyone** know that through God, you will live an *"A+"* lifestyle! Serve Him with a purpose! Through the will of God, **rediscovering** the person you truly are, will allow you to **discover** the exact person you were destined to be.

Take action now! (Turn to pages #243 through #265 for recommended fasts and exercises).

14

Forgiveness

Forgiveness is the act of forgiving or the process of being forgiven. *Through this act,* any form of punishment or negative thoughts connected to what has been forgiven is exonerated from that exact moment forward. In conjunction with the gift of clemency and mercy, the act of forgiveness doesn't require worthiness in order to be accomplished. **However, what is required to forgive is a release of any and all thoughts associated with blaming or identifying the person to the actions that have been forgiven.**

Being unable to forgive is the same as being unable to move past the remembrance of the hurt and pain caused by someone, and its effects can last well beyond the life of the people involved. If you can't stop associating someone with the wrong that they've caused you, it will cause you to be unable to forgive. Or if you can't establish new thoughts to replace the negative thoughts that are connected to someone, it will make it nearly impossible to move the relationship forward in a more positive direction because you will always identify them by what they've done wrong. And, in doing so, you will be subject to reconstructing the same animosity and bitter feelings that you have already felt.

Proverbs 16:32

32 He that is slow to anger is better than the mighty; and he that ruleth his spirit than he that taketh a city. (Proverbs 16:32)

The mind-set of humbleness, being forgiving, and gentle natured will preserve the wrath of grudging pride. Conflicts and arguments that end with contention held for one another are **usually created by** things that are insignificant and **at the least of** importance. With the right temperament, the relationships you hold dear **to** your heart will grow stronger **through hard times by** surviving the contentions caused by the resentment we acquire each day.

> *Quote: "The one that needs the most forgiveness is usually the one that is most unforgiving of others."*

Forgiveness is the act of relinquishing any form of punishment caused by being offended, and it allows you to let go and be free of the moments that hold you bound. Resentment is the consequence of bitter indignation created by what is perceived as unfair treatment. And through the understanding of these actions, issuing out a punishment may feel necessary or appropriate regarding what has been done. But punishing someone for the wrong reason, or for something they've done that is actually right, can lead to afflicting a punishment on someone who didn't deserve to be punished. Also punishing someone out of habit or to cause them to become submissive to your desires can lead to you being the person who actually needs to be forgiven in the end.

Resentment is a feeling that captures the mind **of** its **creator** and consumes their thoughts **into a mind-set that ushers in its effects**. A mind-set is a pattern of thoughts, that not only controls your temperament and the way that you feel, but it also conforms your mood into what it may become. Resentment changes your mind-set to complement its meaning, and the way you feel and the mood you become accustomed to will be a direct product of its creation.

Punishment and consequences have two different meanings, and it is through their differences that it will be determined if someone has truly been forgiven, or not. Punishment is afflicted upon others in hopes of correcting their wrongdoings. It is implemented to generate a feeling of regret upon the person at fault. And consequences are simply the effects of an action that has already taken place.

Forgiveness displays an example of control, and it is through that control we have the power to control our actions. Through this power we have the authority to eliminate any form of punishment given, which will also allow us the opportunity to take control of our thoughts.

🍃 Example: Your friends or loved ones are people you desire, but if one of them has done something wrong, through the power of negative thoughts, it will draw you away mentally and often physically by its design. Even if what that person has done was done by mistake, having these negative thoughts will still have a negative effect even if the consequences are against your own willingness to forgive.

So, if you want to relieve yourself of feeling negative towards a particular person, you must take control of your thoughts. And with gaining control, erase all of the negative memories associated with that person that you want to or choose to forgive.

Consequences are the result of actions, and it has nothing to do with what has been forgiven. Consequences are often thought of as a form of punishment, but the reality of it is that they are only the results of an action or a condition of something that is or has previously taken place. This allows consequences to be good or bad according to the choices we make. And the consequences for our actions cannot be taken away through choice, which allows it to go far beyond the power to forgive.

🍃 *Example:* The consequences for making the right choice, no matter how hard it is, will make any situation better. And making the wrong choice, even by mistake, will be the cause of bad things happening even if these consequences are hidden from our recognition.

Through forgiveness, we are freed from our emotional restraints, and how we respond to a wrongdoing is no longer controlled through anger but by choice. If you find yourself wanting to forgive but can't, it is simply because you don't have enough authority to control your thoughts, thus causing you to have no power over controlling the way that you feel.

Unforgiveness is the unwillingness to forgive. Not letting go of the anger or hurt you feel for someone will ultimately cause hatred to occur. Once a negative thought is created, it will immediately cause a negative effect. These effects consist of anger, distress, and annoyance, generated by what is perceived to be wrong or unfair treatment.

Being unwilling to forgive will contain you in an undesirable moment in time without a way to escape. It will affect the decisions you make in the future and reduce your ability to grow. A big part of forgiveness is letting go and letting go is an act of not holding on to the past. It doesn't disregard the actions that someone has committed, but it does take away the negative effects that their actions have on you.

🍃 Example: I don't hate you for what you did, but I can't trust you as I did before, until you prove that you deserve to be trusted, like I trusted you before.

If a person has resentment toward someone, **it usually causes them** to be **frustrated,** irritated, outraged, or **even** disgusted by the **thoughts associated with thinking of that** person. **Resentment** often causes **a** person to become unremorseful, **unsympathetic,** and unapologetic towards the way they feel. This perception is powerful enough to cause a rift between brother and sister, father and son, mother and daughter, and even husband and wife. It breaks down the bonds between friends and family, and it causes a fence to be built between neighbors.

Colossians 3:12-13

12 Put on therefore, as the elect of God, holy and beloved, bowels of mercies, kindness, humbleness of mind, meekness, longsuffering;

13 Forbearing one another, and forgiving one another, if any man have a quarrel against any: even as Christ forgave you, so also do ye. (Colossians 3:12-13)

It can become very difficult to forgive someone when we don't understand **the reason as to** why something is. **Why gives reason, but that reason doesn't necessarily have to excuse or justify what someone did. In order to forgive, it** is far more important to understand why a person has done something rather than **what a person has done. *Why* guides you directly to thoughts, and if we refuse to change what we've thought, it will be impossible to change what we think.** And no matter the reason why someone did what they did, it still won't change the way we feel about what happened unless it changes the way we think about it.

Remembering **the way something makes you think is far more important than** what the something is that happens to you. Understanding the reason why we feel the way that we do will give us more control over our lives when bad things happen, and it will also allow us to identify how we feel and understand how our thoughts are affecting what we do. **To think, "I will never forgive" is like saying, "I will always remember the hurt and pain you caused me to go through for the rest of my life."** With forgiveness, it changes a negative into a positive **and** releases you to keep moving forward. Feelings are a product of our thoughts, and if the thought you remember of someone is negative, you may find it hard or even impossible to want to forgive.

Question: If you hold on to all the negative things that are done to you throughout your life, what room and time will there be left to think about and appreciate the good that is in the world around you?

If and when there are certain thoughts that we can't let go or we choose not to forget, it creates a partial forgiveness for who or what we are trying to forgive. Partial forgiveness qualifies as not letting go of every single bad thought but still remembering some of the hurt feelings that you feel. By doing so, it allows you to be somewhat cordial towards **a** person, but **it will never enable you to fully regain the relationship that was lost.**

> Quote: "Forgiveness creates a reason for positive thinking, which causes us to move forward, **and** forward progression, in return, causes a reason to forgive."

Everything that happens to you will either make you a better person, a worse person, or a little of both. When things that happen to us make our lives worse than it was before, and more importantly, when it makes us a worse person than we were before, it makes it hard or even impossible to forgive. Thoughts are everything and it is who we are. When something happens to make our thoughts turn negative, it not only changes the way we think, it also changes who we are.

Example: Someone committing a racial act towards you can cause you to reciprocate that same racial tension, not only to that person, but it can even cause you to have racial tension towards their entire race. By letting an event change who you are, you are allowing it to change the way you think. And you often will first have to remove the racial tension you've developed for that person in order to have the ability to forgive the person for their racial behavior.

If you are able to take any unfortunate event that happens to you and cause it to give you a reason to become a better person, you will have the power to take everything that was meant to harm you and change it into something that will cause you to grow stronger and better than you ever were before. This will not only cause you to be in control of your own life, but it will also cause you to be impenetrable to the effects of negativity, no matter how devastating they may be!

> Quote: *"Focusing on one dead flower can cause you to miss a field of lilies."*

The purpose of feeling ill will toward someone or something is for protection or to identify something as harmful. A mistake, by definition, is the commitment of an act that is out of a person's character. It is an unfair or wrongful act committed by a person unintentionally or accidentally with having some form of regret **afterward**. Without regret, a mistake becomes a choice, and any decision to repeat the choice to make a mistake will be defined as intentional.

Opposite of that, it will serve no purpose to feel any way other than forgiving towards someone who is truly sorry for the mistakes they have made. Punishing someone for something they already regret, usually doesn't cause them to be more regretful, but instead, it usually causes them to perceive that their regretfulness and repentance is unacceptable. This can lead to someone's regret becoming a resentment now felt for the person that they once sought for forgiveness.

> Quote: *"Forgiveness doesn't change the past, but it does change the future."*

Holding on to the negative thoughts of someone you love will follow you for the rest of your life unless you change your mind or let go of the old negative feelings you have towards that person. Everyone makes mistakes but reliving those mistakes and continuing **to** reflect on the bad experiences you've been through, or what others have gone through, will continually affect your perception and your life in the future. Being open to new experiences and creating new memories are what make this journey of life so rewarding. **This is not to say we should forget our history. But what it does say is,** being held back by the past will only leave you *stuck thinking the same* thoughts that are holding you down. **R**emembering the past with the mindset of a possibility to forgive will release you to grow into the future, not only wiser but also potentially better than you ever were before. Being held back by the past will only leave you **stuck thinking the same** thoughts that **are** holding you down. But remembering the past with the mindset of a possibility to forgive will release you to grow into the future, not only wiser but also potentially better than you ever were before.

Writing letters about how a person made you feel is a very strong, therapeutic way of getting out the resentment often kept in your subconscious mind. Later, if you decide to cut the pages up or deliver them to the person intended, the weight you've been holding on to will be taken away instantly. The act of burning the letter up in the fireplace is a symbolic gesture of letting go of your anger. Just by watching the sheets that hold the thoughts you've held on to for so long being engulfed in flames can help the healing process, even if that person has moved on or passed away.

Matthew 5:43-45

43 Ye have heard that it hath been said, Thou shalt love thy neighbour, and hate thine enemy.

44 But I say unto you, Love your enemies, bless them that curse you, do good to them that hate you, and pray for them which despitefully use you, and persecute you;

45 That ye may be the children of your Father which is in heaven: for he maketh his sun to rise on the evil and on the good, and sendeth rain on the just and on the unjust. (Matthew 5:43–45)

Forgiving others not only frees you; it shows an example of God's mercy He has given to us. Our Father asks us to love our enemies, and without the act of forgiveness, that would be virtually impossible to do. In the past few years, I've lived hating people I perceived to be evil because I've experienced and seen the worst in humans. I hated racist people for how they think. I've hated the rich for how they treated others. I hated the privileged for their arrogance and sense of entitlement. And I've hated the people who tried to hurt me because of the hate they've shown towards me. Somewhere in time, while writing this book, God spoke to me and took away the hate I hid in my heart. From that exact moment, I didn't hate the people I've always hated anymore! I no longer hated the racist or the privileged anymore. I did not hate the rich nor the ones who hated me.

When I possessed hatred, nothing changed **but me, and** I just became angry, full of vengeance, and more hateful. For that reason, God changed my thoughts, which changed my perception. So, I started to wish nothing bad ever happened to the persons I once hated; and that they will not endure vain suffering, but positive correction. I now have hopes that we can move past our differences, and one day learn to understand and respect one another. I now pray that they will see God, the same way I do, and that we both could live peacefully in this world and in the world to come together through His mercy and grace.

You see, hating someone for what they do is not the same as hating them for who they are. Who a person is and what a person is is slightly different, and if we fail to understand that difference, it will cause us to hate people for something they can't change.

Example: A deceitful person isn't deceitful because of how they look, but they are deceitful for what they do. I can dislike the dishonesty in a person without hating the person themselves. And I can love a person for who they are without loving them in a way that includes being fond or even accepting of what they do.

Having resentment towards someone for what they did doesn't mean you have to have resentment towards them for who they are. It is true, you are what you do, but resenting someone for who they are or for where they're from leaves very little opportunity to forgive because you will never see them for what they are now, according to what they do today. And this will cause you to only see them as a person that is a certain way simply because the thoughts of your perception have linked what they did to who they are.

It is impossible to change the past, and punishing someone for what they regret is just like putting resentment in a place where there was an opportunity to forgive.

If we can separate the actions someone did in the past from their present actions, it will protect our thoughts from becoming victim to other people's history, and instead, be an opportunity to let our thoughts form the history of the present choices we make.

Perception is not only how we see, but it also can control what we see, and sometimes because of what we see, it causes us to act in a way that is nothing like how we are supposed to be. But allowing individuals the opportunity to take control of their thoughts and change what they think will also allow us to take control over what we do and change what we are. In this scenario, what you are today may not necessarily be who you will be tomorrow nor what you will truly become *later in life!*

Example: If you are a hateful person right now, that doesn't mean that **it** is the type of person you will always be. Most people live one thought away from becoming a much better person than what they are at this very moment. Imagine if nothing bad ever happened to someone that caused them to hate. Imagine if no one was ever taught to hate another person or if a person never did anything else wrong to be hated for.

Question: Would that change the way that some people are today and *how we feel about them?*

Negativity or negative thinking not only produces negative results, but it can also take us from how we are supposed to be and change us to become something unimaginable. We are not designed to hate. Hatred gets in the way of God's glory. It causes a person to get upset because it takes away the power of choice. By nature, we want to be happy, but many people unknowingly live their lives every day possessing hatred in their hearts. They go day in and day out not knowing that it will prevent them from ever knowing how true joy feels. And not knowing what it feels like to be released from our negative thoughts will cause you not to know how it feels to truly forgive!

One of the most detrimental effects of pride is the unwillingness to forgive. If you are unable to forgive someone, give it to God. Listening to the right spiritual song or possessing the right frame of mind will allow the presence of God to overshadow you and consume any hatred you have toward any person for any reason.

God is an Omniscient, All-Knowing God. He is All-Powerful. That is exactly why by putting our problems we can't handle and our vengeance in His hands, it means putting it in the hands of someone who is more capable **and qualified** to handle our difficult situations than we are. Holding on to hatred and being unforgiving will eventually cause us to lose control, but trusting that by God's power He has everything under His control, will give you back the power and control you have over your own life!

> **Matthew 18:21-22**
> **21** Then came Peter to him, and said, Lord, how oft shall my brother sin against me, and I forgive him? till seven times?
> **22** Jesus saith unto him, I say not unto thee, Until seven times: but, Until seventy times seven. (Matthew 18:21–22)

In life, there are thousands of opportunities for you to forgive someone. In a relationship alone, an "A+" marriage requires the act of forgiveness almost each and every single day. This can seem overwhelming and impossible to achieve, but with the right mindset, it can take something impossible and change it into something that is truly possible. Remember, a mindset is a collection of thoughts, and the pattern of your *thoughts* will control your temperament, your mood, your ability, and your willingness to forgive.

Take action now! (Turn to pages #243 through #265 for recommended fasts and exercises.)

Memories of Thoughts

Thoughts are what we know, and memories are the containers that keep **the realization of what we think with us. We will** gather a vast collection of information **over the years**, and our memories are the centerpieces for **remembering** the information **we've learned.** There are people who have **frail** memor**ies**, and there are some **people** with extraordinary, photographic memories that **have the capabilities of** remember**ing almost** any and everything that happen**s** to them **throughout** their **lifetime.** Knowledge is **purely** knowing, and it is essential to know that **what you remember and in what way you remember it, will be what creates the** memories **of everything you know.**

Memories are only **previous thoughts created from** moments in the past that are not forgotten. They tell us stories of **the** people **of yesterday** and **of things that happened in years long ago.** They store **documents of past events created from** the perception **of historians, and they retell our history from a collection of facts and thoughts that we remember.** Just like computers that have accesses to information in their files, our past thoughts and feelings we've felt **throughout the years** are accessed through remembering thoughts that **we formed throughout** our **lifetime.**

📝 **Example:** Almost every guy who's ever played a sport can tell you stories of how they were the star athlete at some point in time in

139

their lives. If you listen carefully, you may notice that it's usually the same one or two stories told over and over again of how they made the difference in the game. Rather, it was making a **defensive stop** or scoring one of the winning points **to claim victory**, it was how they chose to remember their past. The one or two incidences **that** may or may not have happened the way they recalled, or **that** may **not** have even **happened at all like they remember it**, still **have the** power **through the use of memories** to make someone think of their entire and possibly short-lived athletic career to be regarded as a huge success!

That's how memories work, **and** they possess the **ability to preserve** that power throughout the test of time.

Quote: *"Memories are made of the moments that happened through the course of our lives."*

Moments are specific events taking place at a particular time that are important to us or have a significant effect on our lives. These moments give purpose to having memories, and the thoughts that are created from them will give meaning to the moments we share with others. Every time a moment is thought of, it enables us to relive a part of our past; and these experiences which we experience are capable of making moments that can be remembered beyond our lifetime.

One good moment or one bad moment can be the memory that tells what your life is like, what the people you know are like, and what the many things around you are like. Thoughts develop into moments, and those moments will classify almost everything that we know. And nearly everything that we know will be depicted by the moments that are stored in our memories.

🍃 **Example: Remembering one negative moment or remembering one positive moment can be the difference between having the memory of a good childhood or creating a reality for someone who's had a bad childhood.**

140

Positive and negative thoughts will give a perception to everything you remember, and from every lesson that you've learned, it will give recognition to everything that you know.

Anything you know prior to this moment; you know because you have a memory of it and the things you've forgotten are things you don't know anymore.

🌿 Example: Memories that are forgotten are like learning math all the way through school, and twenty years later, you find yourself struggling to help your child with their math homework.

Our entire history is only made up of moments, and the moments that make up our personal history are allocated only from the time we are given. Some of our most defining moments in time are typically only made of a few memories, and these remembered thoughts can hold the files to some of the most predominant moments throughout our lives. The moments we hold on to give a history of who we are and the effects that these moments have on us explain why we are the way that we are. What we remember will tell the tale of our lives, and rather it's a good memory or a bad memory, it will create the feelings that we feel about the thoughts of the past, regardless of if it's true or false!

🌿 Example: Having a best friend or someone close to you all your life that done something horrible to you only once, can nullify all the times they were there for you and everything that you both been through together up into that particular moment happened.

Memories can paint a picture that causes an effect as if something has just happened, and it can cause you to relive the past in your mind over and over again until you stop thinking about it or just forget. Each time a thought occurs in our mind, it intensifies the impact it has over us and strengthens the amount of influence it has over our lives. If it reaches a certain degree, these moments can create memories that will be impactful enough to even last years later, after an event has passed and is consciously forgotten.

🍃 *Question:* What was it like **for you** growing up?

There are many different moments a person will experience during their adolescent years, and some of these encounters will be good, and some of these experiences will be bad. However, it is only what you remember that will give an answer to how you respond to this question.

Each and every one of us can make memories, and every one of us has memories we will remember **more than others of** events that are significant to **us in our** lives. These memories are roads that lead to **not only** who we are **but also** to why we are the **people** we are today. *Outside of basic genetics and understandings; what we know is linked to our memories, and these memories are what define our lives today.*

🍃 Example: A neglected child can identify with rejection or hate before they can feel and understand what sacrifice means or to be loved. Likewise, an adult who grew up in a poverty-stricken environment might not understand the generosity or happiness found in giving. Typically hope is not there just simply because hope was never there at the beginning, and it will cause many people to be a victim of those circumstances instead of rising above expectations.

Your mind is captive to your thoughts, and that confinement causes you to only know what you know. The inability to think outside of what you know limits the knowledge you have to only be contained to knowing what you've experienced or thought of before. You cannot know anything outside of your own understanding. And this causes anything you learn, outside of memorization, to only be brought into your understanding and knowledge by connecting the things you acquire, to memories you already know.

🍂 *Question: Have you ever tried to explain to someone how a person looks that they've never seen before?*

If you said "yes," you may understand that the only way to do this is by referencing the person's appearance to a particular memory that the person you're trying to explain it to has.

🍂 *Example: "He looks just like your ex-boyfriend, but just a little bit shorter."*

Memories are the only thing **that** could be **used when we** consider answering any question that requires a **perception or** summarization to take place. **It is what storytellers use when giving accounts of the past, and it is what we use when giving an example of how something was.**

🍂 *Question:* What thoughts did you **remember when you gave an answer as to**, "How did you view your marriage?" in the first chapter of this book?

🍂 *Question:* If **the memories you were thinking of were entirely opposite of the memories you thought of at that moment,** do you think your **answer would have been any** different **than the** answer **that you gave at that moment?**

*A sign of having stored-up bad memories is referring to your spouse as a nag or someone who doesn't finish what they've started. Maybe you are being identified as irresponsible or accused of being selfish for something you did or didn't do in the past, or perhaps even uncaring for not showing interest in something. No matter what the reason is, if your thoughts cause you to live **in** the past and view people for what they used to do or used to be **as if nothing will ever change, it can drain out hope and replace it with resentment and bitterness.** It may even cause you to live right past your present by keeping you from basing your **perception** of things for what they are right now **and instead perceive things in the present according** to what they were in the past.*

Living in the absence of *forgiveness* **while** *remembering the time you had an argument or a time when your spouse made you* **upset can cause you to be stuck inside of a dreadful moment. Maybe it's a time when someone did you wrong or you felt misunderstood; no matter the reason, living in the absence of forgiveness will cause these negative memories to always be with you.** Basing a decision according to those memories can cause you to continue to remember someone or something **the same way** that damaged the way you think. ***And it can change the way you feel*** *to stay that way long after* **these** *memories have faded away.*

Example: Being mad at someone but can't remember the reason why you are mad. And the unfortunate part of it is, it doesn't decrease or stop the resentment you feel towards that person. It only hides the reason or thought behind your anger, which takes away almost any chance of addressing or correcting what was or was not done in that moment in time.

> Quote: *"It's not the future that is frightening, but* ***it is*** *the thoughts of the past coming back to life* ***that is the most terrifying."***

Memories are merely stored thoughts, and these thoughts can be seen as a blessing or a curse.

Bad things do happen, and when they do, sometimes it leaves you with **having** no control. Time is broken up into three main categories, which are, the past, the present, and the future. It is impossible to intermix these time frames physically, but **mentally** mixing them up **can be devastating or rewarding, depending on the thought**. Thoughts are your reality, and what you think will always equate to what you see. **A good memory can retain the way you feel about someone during a low time in the relationship, and a bad memory can be the cause of being unable to move pass the past.**

Question: **It is said that the past cannot be changed**, but what if **it could?**

🍃 *Question:* Would you go back in time and change what you did in the past to change the outcome it has on you?

If so, this means you've learned from your past, and **the situation that made you feel weak has now made** you stronger, and **the person that took advantage of you has now given you the opportunity to become** wiser than you once were before.

You only did what you knew to do at that moment, and **within** reason, that's all anyone, including yourself, could ever ask for. The purpose of the past is not designed to consume the present; **our present** is a totally different category in time. There are laws to time and space that prevents **us** from **actually re**living **moments** in the past and present at the same time. But learning from your past, and growing stronger in your future, can cause your present to serve a purpose for what it's meant to be!

Quote: "It's all in your head."

Remember, if thoughts are not helping you, they are hurting you; and if they are hurting you, let them go. You have the power to change your memories by changing what information you gather from moments in the past.

🍃 *Question:* What if your memories are negatively affecting you today?

When we reflect on the things from our past, we often refer to them as guidance to determine what could possibly happen in the future. Negative thoughts create negative actions, and the memories from these thoughts can create baggage. Baggage is long held thoughts or ideas with regard to things that are perceived as a burden, or hindrance, or obstruction. And these things are classified as being the cause for our difficulties. No matter if the classifications are correct or not, you have the option, through the power of choice, to put those bags down and leave them, or else, to carry them around for the rest of your life.

Psalm 121:1-2

1 I will lift up mine eyes unto the hills, from whence cometh my help.

2 My help cometh from the LORD, which made heaven and earth. (Psalm 121:1–2)

Moments are an important part of making life worth living, and to really take advantage of life and fully enjoy every moment takes appreciating a moment for what it is worth. Memories are **only meant** to **benefit you. A**nd that benefit is **meant to teach, inspire,** and comfort. When memories are looked back upon, they should encourage you to go forward, to give knowledge of what you've been through, and to know how you got through **your trials.** Memories are designed to remind you of where your help comes from and to inspire you to share this knowledge with someone else.

> *Quote: "The past is what makes us, but the future is what we will become."*

While someone may remember something one way, the memory of someone else can be totally different. This shows that through perception, you can control how you remember your past. In order to assess that control, you must come to the belief that this same control exists inside of you. Your past may lead you to remembering an event being so horrific or tragic that its devastation is still destroying your life today.

You could have gone through something so terrible, that it seems as if you will never live past it. If you have breath, you still have life! And where there is life, there is always hope. What it takes to live past those memories, is to place those moments behind you and place the constructive knowledge you've gain from those experiences in front of you. So that when you walk into your future, you will be walking into a better you, while leaving the worst in the past. And through the power of the mind, what we don't think of, we can't remember; and what we don't remember, are moments that do not exist anymore.

Quote: "What doesn't kill you will only make you stronger."

Persecution and toil may beat you down, but sometimes putting a seed in the ground is the only way to make you grow. Memories are the thoughts that tell the stories of our lives. Know that you have the power to control what and how you remember something or someone, and that includes how you remember your past as well. You are the author of your own story, and through forgiveness and understanding, you can erase or change those old memories that are negatively affecting your life today.

Quote: "Learning from your past will make you wiser in your future."

Thoughts are reality, and a person only notices what they think about. There is good and bad to every situation and there are two sides to every story. Remembering the good more than the bad can change your life and the way you remember it forever. Memories are what tell the stories of our lives, and knowing that how you remember things in your past will define how your life is in the present. And it will allow you to be the author of your very own tomorrow!

Take action now! (Turn to pages #243 through #265 for recommended fasts and exercises.)

Control

🍃 *Question:* How much of your life do you control?

🍃 *Question:* Do you control how you feel?

🍃 *Question:* Do you share the feelings you have with your loved ones?

🍃 *Question:* Do you understand how you feel and acknowledge what you think in a way that allows you to realize what you feel? **Or** do you **neglect** your thoughts **and hold them** inside as if your feelings **don't matter or** don't exist?

Maybe you don't know how to express how you truly feel, or perhaps **you don't do it** because of fear. Fear of what others might say or think. Perhaps it's fear of the unknown, or maybe it's fear of knowing how you truly feel. Either way, our thoughts are how we feel, and many of us live out our lives every day without knowing how we truly feel because we tend to not realize or understand exactly how we truly think.

How we express ourselves comes from how we think. **And the reason why you** hold back **your emotions and fail to build relationships according to how you truly feel** is that, somewhere in your mind, you are neglect**ing** some parts of what you truly think.

148

🍃 *Question:* Do you control how you act, or is your behavior a product of your environment, and is solely influenced by the people and situations that surround you?

🍃 *Question:* Do you control your thoughts, or are your thoughts mainly a **reflection of** your circumstances?

Your thoughts are your reality; it is your perception, and it is what alters the decisions that you make. It is what creates a quality of life, and it is a proven fact that your thoughts are truly what make up **what** you really are. The truth of the matter is, if you don't have control over your thoughts, it is virtually impossible for you to have control over your life. And not having control over your life is not having control over yourself, **what you think,** and what you do.

🍃 *Question:* So again, I ask you, how much of your life do you really control?

By definition, control is to have the power of authority, dominance, and command over something or someone; and that someone also includes ourselves. Control is the essence that gives us the power of choice, and it is the ability to have a dominant influence over someone instead of someone having a dominant influence over you!

🍃 *Example:* Thoughts are what changes the mind of someone who truly wants to go to a social event and have a good time into thinking they only want to go for a little while, or even into thinking they don't want to go at all simply because of having thoughts that consider what other people might think and say or who might be there.

Our thoughts are what makes the difference between that person going to that event to be the life of the party and that person only going to the party to show their face and leaving shortly after, just only to show people that they came.

🍃 *Question:* What if someone was able to change their thoughts from an *I don't want to go to the party* into **truly thinking** *I do want to go to the party* **and actually deciding to go**?

Quote: "Stop and think."

🍃 *Question:* What if someone was able to change an *I don't want to get up* **out of bed** into an *I am excited and* **can't wait** *to get up*?

🍃 *Question:* What if someone could change an *I don't want to exercise or take better care of myself* into an *I will start exercising and taking better care of myself* **right now**?

Studies show, on average, that the mind thinks of over six thousand thoughts every single day! Each thought is attached to a decision that we've made, an influence that has impacted us or an affect that has altered our character.

🍃 *Example:* Being affected by someone who is mistreating you, can cause you to grow cold and distant by simply thinking that, "No one appreciates how nice I am, so I might as well stop trying to be nice to people." It can change who they are to the point where they start mistreating others the same way they didn't want other people to treat them. And in doing so, it will make them be just like the people that they detest.

Quote: "Thinking different is being different."

A difference in thinking is what changes us, and it is the very essence that makes up the character that we possess. Going through many different experiences creates many different thoughts, and those thoughts are what make us grow and mature. By controlling the way you think, you will control what you do, and in doing **so,** it will ultimately control **what kind of person** you become.

🍃 *Question:* Do you like who you are, or are you unaware, or just being tolerant of the person that you've **become**?

🍃 *Example:* Hanging out with the wrong group of people just for protection or wanting to fit in, can cause you to later end up being just like the character of people you dislike.

🍃 *Question:* If thoughts are what you are controlled by, what is it, or who is it that is controlling your thoughts?

Thoughts are the ideas and decisions that we make, and these ideas and decisions are often controlled through influences. If we allow it to, influences will control the direction that we go and the way that we think. Most commonly, in today's world, many of our thoughts and decisions are influenced by entertainment, news reports, social media, and politicians. The danger is that everyone has an agenda, and some individual people's agenda can influence us to be biased or just plain wrong. And **the scary part is that, while it is happening,** we could have no idea as to what is **going on**! If you start to rely on the influences of others to make your decisions and determine your views, you will be living your life the way other people will have you to live. **And s**oon you can find yourself at a loss of control **because you've given control of your life to someone else**.

Quote: "I couldn't help myself."

People who are often known to lose control many times are thought of and referred to as being "weak-minded." By definition, a weak-minded person is one who shows a lack of determination, emotional strength, and focus **and is not** intellectually **strong**. They are easily influenced, easily distracted, and may find it hard to make decisions due to the fact **that** they frequently don't know what they want or what they need.

Due to our thoughts having control over our lives, a person of a weaker mind will have very-little-to-no control when it comes to how they think and what they do, thus causing **them** to have **no direction or goals in life.**

A weak-minded individual lacks the ability to control their thoughts. Thoughts are what takes you where you want to go, it gives you the ability to want to become who you want to be, and it determines what you would like to do. It does this every single day of our lives, and it does this automatically and without your permission!

Example: A person who knows that stealing is wrong can find themselves shoplifting because of hanging out with a crowd that makes stealing look cool and fun.

Many people who start doing drugs do drugs by being under the influence of something or someone outside of their own aspirations. No one usually decides on their own and being in their right mind to voluntarily become an addict, and no one usually wants to be under the bondage of having to take a particular substance just so they can live their life. But by the rejections and sorrows of this world, many of us find ourselves doing things we never would have done if we had clear control over our thoughts and over our lives.

Thoughts are not just limited to peer pressure or influence; they also inspire us to dream big or go further in life. And once you establish a purpose in your life, how you view yourself and value your life will be worth much more than the addiction to any drugs or alcohol can offer.

> Proverbs 29:18
>
> [18] Where there is no vision, the people perish: but he that keepeth the law, happy is he. (Proverbs 29:18)
>
> *Quote: "Resistance restrains the weak with doubt, but the fortitude of the strong will overcome the deprivation of uncertainties."*

A person of a stronger mind is the opposite of one of a weaker strength. A strong-minded person is a person who maintains the majority of control over their lives by having control over the majority of their thoughts. A person of a stronger mind isn't easily convinced or persuaded. They are more confident in their thinking and less likely to reverse their steps or change how they think and feel. Having a strong thought about something can be useful to the extent where it causes someone not to lack focus, not often be subject to influence, and rarely lack assertion and determination. In contrast, a person with a stronger mind can also be stubborn, unyielding, and uncompromising.

Quote: "You can't teach an old dog new tricks."

As adults, we are less likely to change our minds due to habitually thinking and doing things the same way for a long time. For this reason, we are often more acclimated to our own thought **patterns** and are more comfortable **staying in our** way of thinking. It takes away the ability to think differently, which will result in having **less** control over **the** fewer choices that we make. And because we are not open to many options, it will cause there not to be many options to choose from either.

Matthew 18:2-4
2 And Jesus called a little child unto him, and set him in the midst of them,

3 And said, Verily I say unto you, Except ye be converted, and become as little children, ye shall not enter into the kingdom of heaven.

4 Whosoever therefore shall humble himself as this little child, the same is greatest in the kingdom of heaven. (Matthew 18:2–4)

Humble people are more submissive than a person with stubborn pride. Humbleness is the quality of being deferential, unpresuming, and is the act of showing attentiveness. Pride keeps us from being humble, and without humbleness, it causes an unwillingness to serve. A closed-minded person is commonly known to refuse new ideas and also known to reject new teachings. The danger in that is a lack of growth that stems from a lack of knowledge, and being stuck in your own way of thinking can cause a person who is unsaved to stay that way.

Having control is the ability to choose the best option rather than the first option; it is the ability to change your mind when you are presented with something new or something better than before. And it is having the strength to say "yes" when you have to and to say "no" when you need to.

Romans 12:2
> 2 And be not conformed to this world: but be ye transformed by the renewing of your mind, that ye may prove what is that good, and acceptable, and perfect, will of God. (Romans 12:2)

Thoughts are everything! They are how we feel, who we are, and what we believe. Someone who's in a good mood can be taken out of how they feel just by one bad thought. But by replacing your negative bad thoughts with good positive thoughts will give you the control you need to change your mood back to how it once was. Through the power of choice, we can take the negativities of a strong-minded person and the uncertainties of a weak-minded person and transform it into the type of mindset that glorifies God with an unwavering, steadfast, and unshakable faith; a faith that cannot be compromised.

Matthew 14:28-31
> [28] And Peter answered him and said, Lord, if it be thou, bid me come unto thee on the water.
> [29] And he said, Come. And when Peter was come down out of the ship, he walked on the water, to go to Jesus.

³⁰ But when he saw the wind boisterous, he was afraid; and beginning to sink, he cried, saying, Lord, save me.

³¹ And immediately Jesus stretched forth his hand, and caught him, and said unto him, O thou of little faith, wherefore didst thou doubt? (Matthew 14:28-31)

Question: Have you ever wondered why tight rope walkers are taught to never look down?

Tight rope walkers should never look down because it takes their thoughts **away from** their target goal and **re**places it **with** fear. Fear increases the **prob**ability of failure. And once doubt enters your mind, it takes control of your thoughts and places new thoughts in your mind, contrary to what you are trying to accomplish.

> **Quote: "To lose control** means to be out of control, and to be out of control is to have no **control at all."**

"I lost control" is a phrase many people often use, but so very often many of us **don't real**ize the truth in that statement. **Mentally,** at that **moment,** that is precisely what has taken place. To lose control over something technically means you've **relinquished the ability to** have a say-so or to have any power over something or someone, which also **very often** includes not having control over **yourself as well.**

It is typically at this point that the mind is no longer able to process information at a sensible rate, **and it can cause** someone not to think, **which will also cause us to** suffer due to a lack of thoughts. It can cause someone's actions to become reactions. And in return, it creates a behavior similar to the instincts of a more primitive species that may include say**ing and doing certain** things without proper judgment. Once a loss of control occurs, **quite often,** the actions that are taken are outrageous or overly exaggerated, which is frequently followed up by experiencing some form of regret afterward.

🍃 **Question: When was the last time someone made you upset?**

When someone makes you upset, it is just that: they made you upset. You didn't choose to be upset on your own or even wanted to get upset. But through the mere thoughts of the action or thoughts of others, you were forced to be upset. **Remember, upset people have upsetting thoughts. And** having control over our thoughts and over our lives is what makes having a choice possible. And the only way that choice can be taken away is **through** a loss of control.

Quote: "I was under the influence."

Our influences have a direct effect on our character and behavior. It also can affect the development of something or someone through the use of its authority and control. Being under the influence simply means **you are** not being who you **truly** are and at that particular time generally you're lacking adequate control over your life as well. But once the influence has worn off, it can leave you stuck in a situation worse than what it was before you left it. If this **continues** to happen, it can cause the image you now portray to be **unrecognizable** to others and even become unrecognizable to yourself **as well.**

🍃 Example: The agony of a tragic event took me on a downward spiral. And I lost my home, my dignity, and my family because of it. And now when I look in the mirror, I only see a shadow of my former self.

Perceiving your problems to be only obstacles in your way, rather than an **unchangeable circumstance**, will allow you to stay hopeful and positive about **overcoming your problems.**

Focusing on the circumstances that you cannot control rather than putting your attention to what is in your control will take away the option to make a conscious decision that will better your situation. And many times, it will also cause you to make an excuse **to give up** rather than creating a reason to overcome what you are facing.

📖 **Example: Someone who suffered a drastic change in life or is being tortured by a negative thought can often attempt to drink away their suffering. It can lead to the thought of thinking** that "this is how life is going to be from now on." And that will lead to the act of giving up instead of doing whatever it takes to make the situation better. For every problem, you can always find a solution, even if the solution is seeking **the help of a professional.**

> *Quote: "Focus on the possibilities and not on the obstacles."*

📖 *Question:* Do you find it hard to read or focus on one particular thing while the television plays in the background?

Having control over our minds is what makes having control over our lives possible, and sometimes distractions can stand in the way. There are some things we will personally find harder than others to **stay focused on, and there are some situations we will find ourselves in that we will feel like it's impossible to maintain our composure through.** Just because something may be hard, doesn't make it impossible to accomplish; it just might mean that it **is going to** take a little more **effort and practice** to achieve.

Studies show that it is very close to impossible for someone to have 100 percent **of** control over their thoughts, but **yet in still**, your thoughts can still be adequately managed **through discipline and exercise.** The brain is a muscle, and it needs proper exercise to grow stronger. Meditation is a form of exercise that can be use**d** to help strengthen those muscles.

Meditation entails attentiveness and concentration to repetitively think. Putting focus on **one** thing for a set period of time requires patience, and through its performance, it blocks out all distractions, disturbances, and interruptions we encounter day to day. And if **it's done correctly, it will strengthen the mind's ability** to stay more focused. It will also enhance the mind's ability to maneuver through the challenges of today with a great deal of authority.

Trying to meditate for the first time may come off hard at first, but the more you do it, the easier it will be, and the easier it becomes will demonstrate the greater control you have over your thoughts. Without a struggle, there is no growth, and without growth, the mind can become stagnant and weak. But with patience and practice, in time, **the mind will** grow stronger and ultimately powerful enough to **obtain** control **over the way we choose to think. There is always more focus w**ith fewer thoughts, and **with** being **more** focused on the things that matter the most, **it** will create a determination in you that cannot be easily doused.

We all possess different levels of **control** based on the situations and circumstances we find ourselves in. Some situations can go beyond our power of control, creating the thoughts you choose not to produce that will ultimately develop feelings you choose not to feel and actions you do not want to take. It will make any situation an uncontrollable circumstance, and you may find yourself not controlling a situation but a situation possessing control over you.

Romans 7:14-15

14 For we know that the law is spiritual: but I am carnal, sold under sin.

15 For that which I do I allow not: for what I would, that do I not; but what I hate, that do I. (Romans 7:14–15)

🍃 *Question:* **Have you tried to not think of something and found it impossible to do?**

The difference between being in control and being uncontrollable is having the power to do what you decide. Know that even in an uncontrollable situation, there is a **lways a possibility of control by controlling how the situation causes you to think. And if not,** you can **still maintain control by** making the choice to completely **remove** yourself from any situation that you may find uncontrollable.

> *Quote: "Take control over your life, or else **your** life will take control over you."*

In the business world, many owners and CEOs of Fortune 500 companies believe that when it comes to making business decisions for the company, stockholders' votes should always remain under 50 percent while keeping the founders' percentage slightly over 50 percent of the vote. It is a customary practice because owners put a high value on their companies. To have less than 50 percent of the vote means that **in extreme circumstances,** they **may not have a majority of** control over the business they've built.

Question: How do you value your life?

Question: And if you find that life is priceless, why do so many people trade it for such extraneous things?

The meaning of consumption is the act of using up a resource, and **in many instances, that resource is time. By some** definitions **of consumption,** it is **used** to **describe the effects of** a disease that causes the body to waste away and can even lead to death. **And also, by definition, consumption** is the act of consuming, which overshadows the ability to think or do as desired. Being consumed absorbs all **attention and** leaves no room **to consider or think about something else.** Life is full of moments, good and bad, big and small, and important and insignificant. One particular moment will never measure up to who we are, and who we are at one particular moment will never measure up to what your life is truly worth!

Know that by knowing life is more important than what it is usually recognized for and saying and believing that you are more important than what consumes you, will give you a new perception and put the authority God has given **to** you back in your control!

Quote: "You made me mad."

Matthew 21:12-13

12 And Jesus went into the temple of God, and cast out all them that sold and bought in the temple, and overthrew the tables of the money-changers, and the seats of them that sold doves,

13 And said unto them, It is written, My house shall be called the house of prayer; but ye have made it a den of thieves. (Matthew 21:12–13)

Question: When someone makes you mad, do you lose control, or is your anger managed through discipline and serves a purpose?

Anger is appropriate for certain occasions and instances as a display of emotions to show how you feel in a moment of discontentment. For other situations, it is also properly used to add emphasis or to make a stronger point. Anytime someone makes you mad out of your own will; it is due to being just that, they made you mad.

People don't normally wake up and freely decide to be mad. As humans, our nature and desires are to be happy and not be mad or upset. Once you're taken out of your natural element, the next step usually involves going into a more subjective deportment or behavior, which forces you to act or react in a certain way that is not desirable, such as becoming defensive or even offensive in a heated moment.

It is very important to understand that relinquishing the ability to process thoughts or the act of **not being able to** control your thoughts **because of** the actions of others takes away any control you have over your emotions, leaving you partially or totally vulnerable to the influences **and** the decisions **based on what** other people have made.

🖋 *Question:* How would taking someone's life and being faced with the consequences to come, make your life any easier or better than what it is right now?

To take someone's life is not part of our natural DNA. By nature, we are designed to procreate, not degenerate. That's why, unfortunately, many soldiers come back from war suffering from PTSD. To put your life on the line for the sake of others is one of the most honorable and noblest sacrifices anyone has the capability to ever commit, but to kill someone that is not due to self-defense or the welfare of others but due to selfishness or even hatred is the most disgraceful and weak-minded acts a person could ever do. It proves that you have absolutely no control over your own emotions and that, at that moment, you've lost any power a stronger-minded person would have had to get past that moment of desperation.

Other than for protection, to take the life of another human being is one of the most disgraceful and worse acts anyone could ever commit. We all live by the decisions that we make, and we all will have to answer for our decisions sooner or later. **Through the power of choice, w**e are given the ability to choose, to choose what we want out of life, and the choice to choose who we want to be at this very moment.

Deuteronomy 30:15-19

15 See, I have set before thee this day life and good, and death and evil;

16 In that I command thee this day to love the LORD thy God, to walk in his ways, and to keep his commandments and his statutes and his judgments, that thou mayest live and multiply: and the LORD thy God shall bless thee in the land whither thou goest to possess it.

17 But if thine heart turn away, so that thou wilt not hear, but shalt be drawn away, and worship other gods, and serve them;

18 I denounce unto you this day, that ye shall surely perish, and that ye shall not prolong your days upon the land, whither thou passest over Jordan to go to possess it.

19 I call heaven and earth to record this day against you, that I have set before you life and death, blessing and cursing: therefore choose life, that both thou and thy seed may live. (Deuteronomy 30:15–19)

We are given the power **to choose**, and that power is only offered through the supremacy and power of God. That's why no one can ever take that power, which is the power **of choice** away.

Often a choice is inadvertently made through **our** actions, **and often those actions are influenced by** a course of events taking place or due to certain circumstances we are in **that has an impact on our behavior**.

Example: Growing up poor or being in debt can cause someone to give up on hope or lose self-worth. And that new perception of thought can cause them to choose to do things that would otherwise be out of the question. In order for them to gain control of their life, they will have to find a more positive way of thinking. And those positive thoughts will motivate positive action that will ultimately take them out of their circumstances and place them in a more constructive reality.

There are good things and bad things that are going to happen to us throughout our lives, deserving and undeserving, and these things will have a big effect, small effect, **or anywhere in between in every one of** our lives. To move past the struggle**s in life,** sometimes **we** have to go through **tough times with a humble spirit. Every experience we go through will have an effect on us, but the way**

you think through those moments will absolutely determine how the things that you go through will have a direct affect on you.

📖 *Question:* It is said we should rejoice for the good things that happen to us, but is it possible also to rejoice for the bad?

> Romans 5:1-4
> **1** Therefore being justified by faith, we have peace with God through our Lord Jesus Christ:
> **2** By whom also we have access by faith into this grace wherein we stand, and rejoice in hope of the glory of God.
> **3** And not only so, but we glory in tribulations also: knowing that tribulation worketh patience;
> **4** And patience, experience; and experience, hope. (Romans 5:1–4:)

> Quote: *"It is not always what happens to us that **mostly** matters, **but** it is how it affects us that matters the most."*

When we suffer through tribulation, it often creates a feeling of misery, distress, and hopelessness. What we feel is often created through thoughts, and by being subjected to these thoughts, through the power of choice, we have the ability to change how we feel by changing what we think.

📖 *Question:* It is quite common to create a feeling of hopelessness through difficult times, but what if instead of creating a feeling of hopelessness, it created a feeling of hopefulness?

As babes, we are born neither bold or shy; but as we go through life, we are faced with many challenges. The way we think in these challenges will form the characteristics that define us individually throughout our life. And through the effects of a cause, we can find reasoning.

🍃 *Example:* Before an occasion ever existed, we were neither positively self-assured or confident nor negatively despondent or discouraged. But now through circumstance, we have cause, through even **in the most** difficult times, to create in us characteristics that includes patience, hope, and also appreciation and prayer. **By controlling your thoughts, you can change the narrative from a reason for disparity into a reason to rejoice. And if something happens and creates a reason to bring us down, through the power of control, we can take that same thing that happened and make it a reason to lift us up and make us better than we were before!**

Taking away the negative effects that negative thoughts have on us and replacing it with positive thoughts, will gives us positive results, and ultimately, we will have a better outcome. Just imagine if we took that power and applied it to every bad situation that ever happened to us. In every situation we suffered through, every resentment we**'ve** felt, and every regret we**'ve** pondered **over and over** again, **o**ur stumbling blocks will disintegrate like dust in the palm of our hands. Through the power to control your thoughts, you can go back in the past and change your future! Through the will of God, we have the power to change any tragic situation into a reason to rejoice by controlling the affects it has on us.

🍃 *Example:* A loved one's untimely death is one of the worst things anyone could ever experience. It can cause years of suffering, and it can even have you questioning God! But allowing it to give you a more significant appreciation for life not only honors the dearly departed but also honors God. By taking back the control that this tragic event once possessed, you are taking away the negative energy it possesses, and instead, you are redirecting that same energy in a positive direction to motivate you and to make you stronger. Even though you can never change what has already happened, it doesn't mean you cannot change the effects it is going to have on you today!

It is unfortunate that we cannot control the decisions others have made, especially when their choices directly affect us. But through the beauty of choice, what others decide doesn't change who we are; it only changes who they are. We are only changed through the thoughts and choices that we make, and no one else's. And those decisions and choices are determined by what we think.

Example: **The** horrific tragedy of rape is one of the worse experiences a person can ever endure. It can be one of the most challenging experiences to go through while **still** trying to maintain control over your life.

That's why it is **very** important to know that this horrible act is not done through **consent, and without permission, it doesn't qualify to fall under the law of** the power of choice. One person's decision doesn't have control over you or your ability to choose. Take comfort in knowing, by virtue, the purpose of this act cannot be fully fulfilled by force. Love is so powerful that not even God can force someone to love Him, and for that reason, not even the act of lovemaking can be forced by man. A person who exposes someone to conditions that are not offered by choice can never get the real experience or satisfaction felt *when someone* freely *offers their virtue* to another person, instead of them having to take it.

Outside of free will, a choice cannot be truly made, and the experience you have will **merely be** an imitation of how God designed it to be.

> *Quote: "You **cannot** have peace of mind unless you
> are in your **right state of mind.**"*

The **effects** of substance **abuse will cause** you not to **serve the purpose God h**as intended for you. It can even cause you to **feel** that you have **no purpose at all**. Once we find ourselves drowning in negative thoughts, it may lead us into deciding to do whatever it **takes to relieve us** of the feeling it produces, even if it's only for a moment. By drugs and alcohol being relied upon for you to keep going or get through everyday life, it may be the very **thing that destroys** your life or causes you to lose it entirely.

🍂 *Question: Exactly what thoughts go through someone's mind right before they decide to engage in substance abuse?*

While under the influence of drugs or alcohol, you have no control and this can cause you to do things you would never have allowed if you were in your right mind.

Being in your right mind is the same as thinking in the correct content of your character, and thinking outside of the influence of drugs and alcohol can cause you to make the best decision according to what you know. Being under the influence means not being yourself, and if not being what you truly are isn't good enough, maybe it's time you gain back control and change what you are by changing how you think!

Remember, you are what you do, but you do what you think, and all it takes to change how you think is to change one thought at a time. That's why it's so important to take your thoughts seriously. Not knowing what your thoughts are and not understanding the effects they have on you is just like being in a fight blindfolded or in a war you don't even know you're in.

Identifying an enemy, whether it is a person, situation, or thought, is the best step in defeating your antagonist. Gear up, because we are fighting a battle at this very moment, and many of us still don't know the fight has already started!

Ephesians 6:10-18

10 Finally, my brethren, be strong in the Lord, and in the power of his might.

11 Put on the whole armour of God, that ye may be able to stand against the wiles of the devil.

12 For we wrestle not against flesh and blood, but against principalities, against powers, against the rulers of the darkness of this world, against spiritual wickedness in high places.

13 Wherefore take unto you the whole armour of God, that ye may be able to withstand in the evil day, and having done all, to stand.

14 Stand therefore, having your loins girt about with truth, and having on the breastplate of righteousness;

15 And your feet shod with the preparation of the gospel of peace;

16 Above all, taking the shield of faith, wherewith ye shall be able to quench all the fiery darts of the wicked.

17 And take the helmet of salvation, and the sword of the Spirit, which is the word of God:

18 Praying always with all prayer and supplication in the Spirit, and watching thereunto with all perseverance and supplication for all saints. (Ephesians 6:10–18;)

The only way to truly break free from any torment is to break free from the thoughts that hold you there. Thoughts are reality, and all it may take to change your reality and take control of your life is to change the way you think and take control of your thoughts!

Finally, pray! Pray to God without ceasing for strength, and not only that, pray for wisdom, knowledge, and understanding in all things. Pray that He will protect your mind and guide your thoughts, creating in you a new life and a start to a new beginning.

Finally, pray for your marriage as well as yourself. Pray that you and your spouse may be blessed and grow together. Pray for happiness, and in doing so, pray for His strength to lead you **and** guide you to take back control over your life!

Take action now! (Turn to pages #243 through #265 for recommended fasts and exercises.)

Neglected Thoughts

Neglect is the failure to remember, a failure to care for, or a failure to think of. It is the opposite of realization, and through the act of neglecting, any form of consideration or taking notice is overshadowed by its disregard. Neglect can be referred to as things that are mistreated, uncultivated, or things that are left unattended. Negligence by design can cause abandonment, isolation, and even create a feeling of rejection. The acknowledgment of everyone and everything that we know comes from our thoughts. Therefore, any form of disregard that causes us not to recognize or forget about anyone or anything we actually know, is essentially a form of neglected thoughts.

Neglect is to ignore, to pay less to no attention to, and it is to not take notice of. It is through the power of our thoughts that our perception of everything is created, and it is through that perception that anything or anyone who is thought of is perceived. Everyone and everything that is not considered, can eventually become of little to no concern, and it is through neglect that a particular person or thing will have very little to no impact on our lives.

The hard truth of it is, whether it is consciously or subconsciously done, one of the main ways the mind distinguishes what is essential to us at a particular moment is defined according to how we are thinking when we are in that moment. And depending on what those thoughts are and the time we spend thinking on a particular thought will be the determining factor of how much those particular thoughts will control what we think.

🍃 Question: What is the first thing that comes to mind when you think of your favorite thing to do?

🍃 *Question:* Would your answer be any different if you had more time to think about it and go over the things you love to do?

If you said "yes," this shows the effects of neglected thoughts. And if you said "no," it means you realize what you like and dislike better than most people.

🍃 *Question:* What do you think would happen if you spent less time doing the things you like to do, or you stopped thinking about the things you enjoy doing?

Typically, our thoughts will determine what we enjoy, but if we are neglecting to think of our own enjoyment, it will cause our lives to be less enjoyable. And these neglected thoughts can have this exact same effect on anyone we know. At this very moment, we can be neglecting something or someone who is very important in our lives. And at the same time, by us not knowing that our lack of thoughts is making the people we know and the things that are around us less significant in our lives, it will cause them to be less desired to spend time with as well. Neglect is so powerful; it can cause distance in the relationship between a parent and child, a friend or relative, or a husband and wife. Even God Himself can become a distant thought in our lives due to the effects of neglect.

🍃 *Question:* Have you ever felt like God's presence in your life went away?

Through choice, we often neglect or fail to acknowledge the presence of our Heavenly Father. It **is through our actions that** we act as **if** He's not here with us. Neglect is to disregard, and if our Heavenly Father is always here with us, by taking no notice of His presence, by our neglect, we will be disregarding the direction He is trying to lead us, and **it will cause us to be** solely living by our own merits. And due to our ignorance, it can cause our actions to serve no real purpose, **which will also cause** our lives to have no real meaning. By neglecting our Heavenly Father, it can cause the feeling we use to feel of God's presence to be often less felt; **and after time passes, the thought of wanting to feel His presence again can become a distant memory of our past**.

> **Zechariah 7:13-14**
> **13** Therefore it is come to pass, that as he cried, and they would not hear; so they cried, and I would not hear, saith the LORD of hosts:
> **14** But I scattered them with a whirlwind among all the nations whom they knew not. Thus the land was desolate after them, that no man passed through nor returned: for they laid the pleasant land desolate. (Zechariah 7:13–14)

Realization increases knowledge, but neglect takes away the opportunity to gain understanding. And even the things we know, if they are neglected, will be the things that are ignored and are forgotten. We know only what we know, and failing to recognize the important things in your life will leave you not realizing what is truly important.

🍂 *Question:* What would you do if someone ignored you?

What I've learned in my relationship with God is that our connection fluctuates based on the thoughts I invest in Him. Neglecting to recognize God or **failing** to think about **Him** and **all He is doing for me** has always caused me to feel distant, even when I'm going to Church or working in ministry.

Unfortunately, doing something for someone doesn't always mean that **we** were thinking of **that** person **at the time we** were doing **things** for **them.** This can cause miscommunication inside of a relationship because one person can think they are doing something nice while the other person can think that what the other person was doing was done out of habit, without any merit or any real thought for **consciously choosing to do** something nice. Thoughts are everything, and if a person has done something without thought, it means it was done without them thinking about what was done or why they did it! And it applies to any relationship we have with anything and anyone, no matter how important they are to us.

🍂 *Example:* Going to church **every week can be in vain if we are only going out of habit and not going to learn or better our relationship with God. Also coming home every day to your spouse or loved one doesn't mean you are there for them, especially if thinking of** them is the furthest thing from your mind.

🍂 *Question:* **If you neglect to think about the same thoughts that caused you to fall in love with your spouse, would that make the time you once shared together that created those feelings that caused the love that was once there not to exist anymore?**

🍂 *Question:* **If we still reflected on the things that inspired us the same way we thought of them in the past, will that allow those things of the past to still inspire us the same way today?**

Neglect is a failure to remember, a failure to consider, and a failure to think of. Any form of concern or consideration at that particular time is disregarded and henceforth will go unnoticed. You are what you do, and you do what you think; but if what you did is not considered anymore, it may cause what you have always done to be forgotten or not thought of anymore through the process of neglect.

🍃 *Example:* **A man who wanted to lose weight went to a trainer who told him if he ate healthier, smaller, more frequent portions of food throughout the day and often exercise, the weight will eventually come off. So the man did as the trainer had instructed him to do and lost over fifty pounds in a short period of time! Once he dropped to his ideal weight and time passed by, the man stopped eating healthier food options and stopped exercising, which caused him to gain all the weight he lost back. So the man went back to the trainer to inquire about how to re-loose the weight that he once lost. The trainer told him to eat healthier smaller portions of food more frequently throughout the day and exercise often. The man told the trainer, "I did what you said at first, and the weight did come off, but that wouldn't work for me anymore because I gained back all the weight I originally lost." The trainer said to him, "It is not that the method doesn't work any longer. The reason why you gained back all the weight you once lost is that you've neglected to continue to do what it took for you to lose the weight that you had lost in the beginning. If you want to lose the weight again, do what I had instructed you to do the first time we talked and never neglect or completely stop doing my instructions if you want the weight to stay off."**

What works, works, and just because you've gotten a little older or heard the same advice more times than you can count doesn't stop what has been working from working anymore; it may just mean that you need to continue to do it or maybe do it more often.

🍃 *Question:* What is important to you?

Life is full of choices, and these choices stem from things we need to do, things we have to do, and things we want to do. Through neglect, we tend to procrastinate on the things we need to do, making them hard to accomplish as time passes by. The things we have to do are self-explanatory, but it can cause us to feel overwhelmed and may leave very-little-to-no time for the things we need to do or even **the things we** want to do.

🍂 *Example:* In the relationships we have with other **people**, there are things we need to do to sustain a good relationship, and there are some things we **have** to do in order **to keep** the relationship **alive. The feeling of misery comes from having to do the things we don't want to do, and by doing so, it can make any relationship become unbearable. Sometimes we make choices to neglect and not take care of the things we don't want to do. Through procrastination, neglecting to do the things we have to do will cause us to fail to take control of doing the things we need to do, which can even prevent us from doing the things we want to do.** If we could use the power of thoughts to control our minds to **converting** the things we need to do **and the things we have to do into being** the things we want to do, it will create a **much more rewarding** relationship **with anyone,** and **it can** possibly **even** be your key to obtaining **a much better lifestyle and even creating an "*A+*" marriage.** In this instance, there will be no need or reason for neglect because it creates a circumstance where you want to do the things you **need** to do. **And in doing so, it cancels out any cause for misery or reason for being in agony for doing the things that we have to do.**

🍂 *Question:* **Do you have someone you love that you've stopped thinking about as often as you used to in the past?**

🍂 *Question:* **If your answer is "yes," how does this lack of thinking affect the relationship you have with that person today?**

People who go unnoticed are those who go unthought of, and the people we don't think about will eventually cause us to move through life without them being a present figure in our lives. If we fail to produce the proper attention it takes to maintain a good relationship with our loved ones and our spouse, it will cause problems to occur inside our relationships.

NEGLECTED THOUGHTS

Quote: "A good gardener knows how to grow a garden, but a great gardener knows how to tend to one."

Example: Thoughts are like plants, and your marriage is the garden. If it's not cared for, other vegetation will begin to grow and consume the plants in your garden. If your garden is not protected, the fowls of the air will swoop down and take the thoughts right **from** out of your garden. If you neglect your garden, insects will fester and devour the life from it, and the vast vegetation of thoughts you once had will disintegrate and soon be forgotten.

Neglected thoughts can be anything from not being aware of our spouse's or loved ones' contributions to not realizing the mistakes we make. We are what we do, and we do what we think. Neglecting specific thoughts **that** may affect your decisions and the choices that you make in life will always make the difference in the way we live.

Neglecting specific thoughts that strengthen you and cause you **to** grow, can be detrimental in your development and the relationships you have with others. **Neglecting to do what's right can cause what you do to be what's wrong, but also neglecting to do what's wrong can cause you to do what's right!**

Neglecting resenting thoughts can cause you to forgive, and neglecting to hold animosity towards someone else can cause you to learn to love other people. Neglect, in its worse form, causes us to ignore the presence of God, and failing to notice Jehovah in thought or through the lack of prayer can prevent our Heavenly Father from being a part of our lives. Through hard times, we learn to **be grateful,** and through **our** struggles, it makes us **more** sympathetic **towards others.** But if we neglect to develop the thoughts that cause us to be appreciative **of what we have** and **to** sympathize with others, it will cause the trouble **and pain** we go through **to** be **all** in vain.

174

Quote: "Without appreciation, it is impossible to be thankful; and without showing thanks, it is impossible to feel appreciated!"

In life, we sometimes forget, and because of neglect, we tend to not recognize the moments that made us who we are today. Remembering those critical moments in life that define us will remind us of how we truly feel and **who we truly are. It will bring back to remembrance, and the realization of** what is truly important to us, **and it also will give a clearer conception of what your true purpose is in life.** Reflecting on the **things that are** important **to us**, outside of all the other influences in our life, will bring back the thoughts we fail to remember.

Our thoughts are everything and what is frightening is, the thoughts that are neglected can be the very thoughts that bring meaning to your life. Take time out to get to know and appreciate the things and people that really matter the most. This will continually build a healthy and happy relationship with all your loved ones **and** especially with your spouse. It is the best approach to prevent neglected thoughts from reoccurring, and it is the best step in cultivating your marriage **and your life** into the beautiful garden it was meant to be!

Take action now! (Turn to pages #243 through #265 for recommended fasts and exercises.)

18

In the Mood to Feel

There are millions of different moods and feelings people *will experience* in their life, *and there are* often *many different moods and feelings we will typically go through in a day*. A person may start the day off feeling sad, and something changes to cause that person to feel happy later on, *that* same day. That something **that happened** caused a change of thought, **and those thoughts** ultimately changed the mood that person was in. Thoughts are a high contributor to what causes the mood that we're in, **and the mood that we're in is often only a mere accumulation of the feelings that are felt.**

How we feel is often a product produced by a reflection of our perception, that is **created from our** thoughts. To feel is to be aware of, to touch, or to experience. A mood is a temporary state of mind, and emotions are expressions used to demonstrate how **we** truly **feel and** think.

A feeling can describe how someone thinks as well as how someone feels, or **in many cases**, it could be used as one and the same.

Example: Asking you how you feel about something in particular, is **usually** the same as asking you what you think.

Outside of how your body makes you physically feel, your thoughts **are what determines** what you are feeling. Thoughts will also determine your opinion**s towards anything, your** feelings towards **everything**, and how you feel towards any person in particular **or persons as a group**.

📖 *Example:* If you've **ever been** excited **about something or someone**, the excitement you **felt** comes from specific thoughts that made you feel excited. If these thoughts **had** never **been created**, the feeling you felt would have never existed.

No matter if it's through **your imagination** or through **occurrences that** actually **did exist,** your thoughts will have a direct effect on **every one of** the emotions you go through **in your life**.

An emotion can be created through **pretending** or produced truthfully by the way you actually feel. **This means that** the mood that **you're in, pertaining** to almost any situation, can be controlled through **the development** of thoughts! Moods are impossible to produce without the power of thoughts, **and it is** highly common for the moods that we are in to be created through the **way that we think**.

📖 *Question:* Have you ever tried to make yourself cry?

If you said "yes," it is highly assumed that it was attempted by using depressing or sad thoughts that made you emotional. A depressed person cannot be depressed without creating depressing thoughts just like a happy person wouldn't be the way that they are without thinking the way that they do.

Quote: **"I had to laugh to keep from crying."**

That phrase comes from choosing to view a tragic or disheartening situation in a humorous way versus letting the natural thoughts settle in and causing oneself to feel depressed. Sometimes you can only feel the way that you think, and if you refused to feel down and depressed for an extended period of time, it means you will have to start thinking the way that you want to feel.

People don't normally choose to be sad, but the thoughts of something disheartening can force your heart to feel sorrow. Contrary to that, through neglected thoughts, it will be highly unusual **for a person** to be sorrowful and/or sympathetic toward anything **without having compassionate thoughts.**

🍂 *Question:* **What were you thinking the last time you were depressed, excited, happy, angry, frustrated, or even became emotional or irrational?**

Endogenous opioids are receptors in the brain that causes emotions to occur. These receptors can be activated by **the production of** endorphins **or the use of** morphine, which is served as pain killers. The nicotine in cigarette smoke can also affect these receptors, causing a person to relax, **but they are extremely addictive and can cause other health and life-threatening problems to occur. Through the use of these receptors, you can also control how you feel** just by controlling **how you think.**

🍂 *Question:* Did you know **that** the power of thoughts **can activate the** endogenous opioids **inside your mind?**

🍂 **Exercise: #8**

Try to make yourself feel **excited.**

🍂 *Question:* What thought **or thoughts** went through your mind to produce this effect?

Try to make yourself feel **joyful.**

🍂 *Question:* What thought **or thoughts** went through your mind to produce this effect?

Try to make yourself **laugh.**

🍃 *Question:* What thought **or thoughts** went through your mind to produce this effect?

Finally try to make yourself feel **thankful**.

🍃 *Question:* What thought **or thoughts** went through your mind to produce this effect?

🍃 *Question:* Did these series of thoughts make you happy or unhappy?

Try to make yourself feel **depressed**.

🍃 *Question:* What thought **or thoughts** went through your mind to produce this effect?

Try to make yourself feel **aggravated**.

🍃 *Question:* What thought **or thoughts** went through your mind to produce this effect?

Try to make yourself feel **mad**.

🍃 *Question:* What thought **or thoughts** went through your mind to produce this effect?

Finally, try to make yourself **cry**.

🍃 *Question:* What thought **or thoughts** went through your mind to produce this effect?

🍃 *Question:* Did these series of thoughts make you happy or unhappy?

🍃 Example: If you thought of a theme park or surfing waves on the ocean, you would have had to think of it as fun to do those things to make you feel happy. You could have thought of just lying on the beach or walking down the shore to produce the feeling of happiness. But either way, at that moment, your perception of happiness was to have fun or just relax.

🍂 *Question:* **From all of these, which emotion was the easiest to produce?**

🍂 *Question:* **As you go through life, which emotions do you feel the most?**

🍂 *Final Question:* **From this same list, which emotion would you like to experience more of? And put them in order from greatest to least.**

A vast majority of us will say we would rather be happy, but at the same time, we are less likely to take time out to create happy thoughts; nor are we commonly doing the things that would generate and produce pleasurable thoughts.

🍂 *Example:* **Wanting to be happy while spending your time all day criticizing and complaining about things to someone in person or on social media will only make you feel the way you think.**

Quote: "**You can only reap what you sow.**"

Some **feelings** may be easier **to relate to than others** due to the fact that through characterization, we tend to **recreate** certain **emotions easier than others. And this can** cause us to be more like what we think and less like how we want to be. It is because "we are how we think," and ultimately at that moment, we tend to create the **type of** thoughts **that will lead to the path of least resistance.** Thoughts follow us each and every day, controlling the moods and emotions that we **feel.**

In most cases, due to the pattern of thoughts you become most aquatinted with, it will be the type of personality **and behavior** you are most likely to display. That's why, **the only way to change our behavior is to change how we think. Remember, you are what you do, and to change what you are to something better starts with making the correct choices.**

🍃 *Question:* If there was a rule at your job, that you could only work with the people you got along with, how many people would **that be?**

If you said "everyone," it is more than likely that you are the type of person who **is forgiving and** never holds grudges **for very long. And it is typical for these types of people to never** have bad thoughts about anyone.

If you said, "almost no one," it is **more than** likely that you **are the type of person who has** a negative thought associated with almost every single person that you work with on your job and, quite possibly, everywhere else you go also.

You may be the type of person who watches the news just to find something wrong in this world. This may be a little harsh, but even if a percentage of that is true, **these** negative thoughts will follow you, affecting your mood, which creates a pattern of behavior that doesn't bring out the best in people, and that includes yourself. Maybe this is okay with you, because bringing out the worse in people, only gives confirmation about the **negative** way you think **about people** already.

With the many jobs and tasks we have to do every single day, with the many people we come in contact with and have to relate to on an everyday basis, **it** causes us to experience many thoughts and emotions throughout the day. And being so involved with **everyone** and **every**thing around us can cause us to often lose ourselves in **other people**. Meditation will help take away any distracting thoughts and oppositions out of our minds and place our thoughts back into a place where we can freely determine who we truly are **and how we truly want to feel.**

Thoughts have a significant influence on the way we feel, and so often our human emotions and the mood we're in are caused out of habit. This will have a significant effect on our normal behavior, and the mindset of the way we think. All moods serve a purpose, and the mood you choose to be in will affect everyone around you. Some moods will influence a person to be close to you, while other moods can drive someone who is close to you away. Just from the effects of having negative thoughts. You are what you do, and to change who you are for the better, starts with making better decisions.

Quote: "No one better speak to me today."

The use of narcotics weakens the ability and desire to activate neurons in the brain, causing us to rely on the effects of nicotine and other sedatives to function properly.

Example: Being grouchy in the morning because you didn't get your morning coffee is often caused by the effects of having less functioning neurons in your brain.

Question: If this example is similar to you, how did you relax, be joyful or feel at peace before you started to drank coffee, smoke cigarettes, or any other thing you have to do now in order to just be cordial?

The way you feel will affect how you think, and **both the way you feel and the way you think** will affect the choices that you make. Remember, you have the power to control your mood or the way you feel by utilizing the power you have to control your thoughts.

Example: Once at a water park, a fourteen-year-old Indian boy was with his family at the top of the line getting ready to slide down the tallest slide in the whole park. All of a sudden, there was a big uproar! With his entire family, who just got off the slide, anxiously waiting at the bottom, the attendant asked, "For the last time, are you going to slide down?"

The boy shook his head and said, "no" as he turned slowly around and started back down the stairs. People were screaming out words of encouragement and others were laughing and making fun of the young boy as he held his head down in shame.

As he passed me, I reached out my hand to get his attention. When he looked up, I asked, "Why didn't you go down the slide?" He answered, "I am afraid of heights." I asked, "Do you want to go down the slide?" He said, "Of course I do, but I am **too** afraid." He went on to tell me how his mother even promised to buy him a funnel cake with ice cream on **top** if he would slide down. I **then** asked him, "What are you afraid of"? He told me he was afraid of falling.

I told him that I was afraid of heights too, and there was nothing wrong, because everyone is afraid of falling. And then I asked him if he wanted my help in getting over his fear of heights. He lifted his head and said, "Sure." I told him, "To start, it sounds to me that you are not afraid of heights, but just like everyone up here, you are only afraid of falling." I told him of the thoughts I have when I look down from being up high, to gain his trust, and then I asked him a question that may change his life forever. I asked, "If you never had a single thought of dying, or better yet, if the thought of falling never crossed your mind, would you still be afraid of going down the slide?" He looked to be confused for a moment and said, "I guess not." He paused and asked, "If I didn't think about it, why would I be scared?" I told him, "Exactly!" I **went on to say to** him, "Go back up there and do whatever it takes to take your mind off **of** falling." I told him, "Now take control over your thoughts, and **when you** look down, **think about anything except getting hurt**. The slide isn't that far down, and just **put your thoughts on imagining**, when you're finished, how **good** that funnel cake is going to taste after you prove to everyone you can do it."

As he began to climb back up, he paused and turned to give me one more look as if for assurance, and he disappeared as he **went through the line and** got closer to the top. Seconds later, I heard a big cheer and clapping coming from the top of the stairs. I looked down with excitement to see if he had done it. And then I saw the boy climb from the bottom of the slide to give his mother a hug. His little brother was jumping up and down with enjoyment **and** his big sister standing afar off, clapping beside their father, as he stood tall with a proud look on his face.

Later that day, a massive craving for a funnel cake with ice cream on top came over me. I guess, all the talk about funnel cakes was enough to persuade me to get one as well. As I walked over to sit down, I was shocked to see the same kid from the slide running up to give me a hug! He said, "Thank you," and went on to tell me how he got a chance to slide down all the rides he was once too scared to go down before. As he walked back toward his family, I was left with a feeling of pride and joy knowing that I made a difference in the life of someone I probably would have never spoken to in an ordinary circumstance.

If you are feeling scared, excited, weary, happy, or depressed, know that your thoughts are in the center of it all. Whether it's being greeted as you enter a restaurant that makes you feel welcomed or hiring a motivational coach to call you each day and tell you, you can do it. It all comes from thoughts.

Philippians 4:8

8 Finally, brethren, whatsoever things are true, whatsoever things are honest, whatsoever things are just, whatsoever things are pure, whatsoever things are lovely, whatsoever things are of good report; if there be any virtue, and if there be any praise, think on these things. (Philippians 4:8)

In this world, life is full of twists and turns; and it is full of challenges, disappointments, and triumphs. Think about the things that will make you the best person you can be, when you are faced with challenges, and think on only the things that you can control, when times get hard. We are not designed to go through this life by ourselves, because if we were, we wouldn't need God. So if and when you are feeling overwhelmed, take a step back, pray, and readjust, to do the best you can possibly do with any situation you are in, and give everything else to our Heavenly Father!

Matthew 11:28-30

28 Come unto me, all ye that labour and are heavy laden, and I will give you rest.

29 Take my yoke upon you, and learn of me; for I am meek and lowly in heart: and ye shall find rest unto your souls.

30 For my yoke is easy, and my burden is light. (Matthew 11:28–30)

The beauty of life gives many reasons to show emotions. There are things we will be thrilled and elated to think about, and there are some things that will be scary and discouraging to us. At your worse, when things don't look promising, put your thoughts and trust in our Heavenly Father, having faith **and a joyous emotion** in knowing that He **is** with you, and He's got you covered!

Take action now! (Turn to pages #243 through #265 for recommended fasts and exercises.)

19

A Lighter Side of Humor

The act of being humorous causes laughter and amusement, but humor is not only the act of being funny. Humor also comes from the condition and temperament of your character. Fortunately, you do not have to possess the ability to make someone laugh to have a humorous perception of life. All you have to do to possess humor is to be in the right mood and have the right state of mind.

Laughter caused by humor has a physiological effect on the mind. Humor releases endorphins inside the brain, which is scientifically proven to have an analgesic effect, and is useful in fighting pain and stress in the body and mind. **That is why it is widely common for dentists to use** Nitrous oxide, commonly known as laughing gas, to distract their patients from feeling discomfort and pain. **It is also why you can be in the center of the worse moments of your life, and the effects of someone causing you to laugh will instantly have a positive impact.**

> **Proverbs 17:22**
> 22 A merry heart doeth good like a medicine: but a broken spirit drieth the bones. (Proverbs 17:22)

Most people admit that they take life too seriously. Taking something too serious can cause anxiety, depression, insomnia, and even high blood pressure. Studies show that humor and laughter reduce stress hormones, lower blood pressure, and increase circulation in the bloodstream, which makes us more resistant to getting infections.

Laughter is a state of mind; a state of mind that knows that bad things do happen, but what doesn't kill you will be a funny story to tell once it's over. Looking back at something humorously that happened in the past, not only will bring enjoyment to a rough situation, it will also give reason for the mind to produce happier memories.

Laughter causes you to feel secure when the rest of the world feels insecure. Through laughter, it can bring joy to a less-joyous situation, and to a world that is full of sadness, it can bring a brief moment of pure cheerfulness.

Quote: "You look so much better when you smile."

It is not for sure that smiling actually makes a person more attractive, but it does make a person seem more approachable. Laughter also has a positive influence on anyone that is in its presence. **So the next time you smile, know that even though we may question whether it actually makes someone look better or not, it will definitely influence positive thoughts; and positive thinking will make anyone feel a whole lot better.**

Quote: "When you smile, I smile."

Question: Did you know it takes fewer muscles to smile than it does to frown and that this can reduce aging?

Quote: "Humor is mankind's greatest blessing."
(Mark Twain)

Marriages are usually happier when at least one spouse has a sense of humor. Laughter helps build a closer relationship and causes a stronger bond between loved ones. Laughing together creates a joy that lets the other person know that they're understood. At least, for that moment, you are like-minded and happy together. And happy moments together **creates happy memories of being together, and it is all because of having happy thoughts**.

Quote: "I have to laugh to keep from crying."

Humor offsets the pain and agony we go through and gives a lighter perception to every situation in life. Life is more enjoyable when you can celebrate your success and also find some humor in your failures. It gives you the ability to learn a lesson from any circumstances and move past it, instead of being stuck reliving a bad experience over and over again.

Proverbs 15:13

13 A merry heart maketh a cheerful countenance: but by sorrow of the heart the spirit is broken. (Proverbs 15:13)

Question: Have you ever encountered Christian believers that always appear to be mad or depressed?

The world is full of troubles, and a look of sadness or anger creates a perception through negative thoughts. You can worship God one day a week or every day alike, but you will never preserve true joy unless you start giving your problems to Him.

Matthew 11:28-30

²⁸ Come unto me, all ye that labour and are heavy laden, and I will give you rest.

²⁹ Take my yoke upon you, and learn of me; for I am meek and lowly in heart: and ye shall find rest unto your souls.

³⁰ For my yoke is easy, and my burden is light. (Matthew 11:28-30)

Our Father wants us to give our problems to Him. Trusting in our Creator is trusting in who He is, and if we trust in the power of

God, we will trust that He has the strength to take care of us when we are weak. By doing so, we are honoring Him, and through this act of obedience, our attitude will show a gratifying countenance that will relay to everyone that you don't have to carry the burdens of this world alone, but instead, you have someone to give your problems to!

Quote: "Don't worry, be happy."

Just like there are always two sides to a story, there is always a bad and a good way to look at things. A sense of humor not only increases joy in people's lives, but it also trains the mind to look for the lighter side of every situation. **And by recognizing the humor in some of our worse experiences, at the end of the day, we can look back and say, "at least it made me laugh!"**

Quote: "A person without a sense of humor is like a wagon without springs. It's jolted by every pebble on the road". (Henry Ward Beecher)

Our **brain** naturally tries to defend us from worrying by rethinking the reason why we are worrying over and over again, which sometimes makes things worse until a solution to the problem is found. If we have a negative reaction to an uncertain or untimely event, it can cause us to experience some form of anxiety. Anxiety doesn't come from our situations, but it comes from the reactions we have to **a situation.** Laughter allows you to go through unforeseen situations with minimum damage, because it reduces the negative thoughts that negative results are created from.

Quote: "A day without laughter is a day without joy."

Growing up, my family never had a lot of money. When we would go out for dinner, we automatically knew to look at the $1 menu or the cheapest section on the list. Sometimes we would make jokes about not being able to afford anything more than the basics when eating out. Adding cheese was a privilege and buying a drink was unheard of, but we had appreciation in knowing, that if we complain too much, we can always go back home and cook! Growing up in a humorous state of mind allowed us to joke and laugh at our difficulties, creating a joyous childhood even though we didn't have much. We appreciated what we had rather than feeling stressed about being deprived of the things we could not afford. And as long as we had each other and laughter, there wasn't really too much left we could complain about!

> Quote: *"Life only gets too serious when it keeps you from smiling."*

There are some things in this world that deserve to be taken seriously, and there are some things that are not. When you are faced with problems, taking the **path of the** lighter side of things will not only sustain you but will also give you a new perspective on negative thoughts when bad things do happen. This will cause your character to not be stuck in the "how come" or the "why not," but it will allow you to continue to mature and grow as you were naturally designed to. And once you've developed a sense of humor, you will be able to appreciate all that life has to offer, the good, the bad, and the humorous!

Take action now! (Turn to pages #243 through #265 for recommended fasts and exercises.)

Reflections of Thoughts

A reflection is an act of throwing back the surface of light, air, or sound without absorbing it. **It is the celebration of ideas, and it is the consideration of thoughts. Reflections reveal the course of our actions, and they give reason to the conduct of our behavior.** Software engineers frequently use reflections to create programs that would modify and examine the behavior of their applications. And just like **software programs, we also alter and change our behavior by reflecting on the thoughts and the choices we make.** Reflections **create an** outcome **to every**thing we know. Our** experiences will **depict** what we see, and **what** we **see** will reveal an external image **from the reflections of** what we think. The outcome of your reflections **will determine the way you feel. And** what you *become* after applying the knowledge you gain *from* reading this book will ultimately be a reflection of the effects that the *Interest of Love* will have on you.

> *Quote:* "A reflection is merely the act of throwing back the surface of light."

🍃 *Question:* When you look in the mirror, what do you see?

If you've ever gone through a house of mirrors, you've seen how, when light reflects **off mirrors, the** mirrors can bend and skew **that** light to portray an illustration **of a reflection** different from **the image standing right in front of it**. Through our perception and **through** the influences around us, we tend to see things differently from what they are. **And no matter the cause of what you see, the reflection you have of yourself can be altered according to your perception of thoughts.**

🍂 *Example:* **If all your life you've been treated awful or as if you were nothing, it is common that you will grow up thinking of yourself the same way. Unless you go beyond how you've been treated and perceive an image greater than how you've been raised to believe, you will keep that perception of yourself with you, until you discover the person who you truly are.**

This **example illustrates the power of persuasion. The thoughts** we have about one another, including ourselves, can be bent and manipulated through the **power of thoughts to cast an image of what we see to be the image of what we think.**

> **Psalms 139:14**
> **I will praise thee; for I am fearfully and wonderfully made: marvelous are thy works; and that my soul knoweth right well. (Psalms 139:14)**

Reflecting is also the process of **contemplating our** thoughts, **and that process causes us to** think deeply and carefully **without interruption.** When **we are in the act of** reflecting on something, it is as if time stops, and all **of our** thoughts are **centered** on that one **single** thing. One incident can produce a cluster of many feelings, good and bad, but depending upon which thoughts **you understand to be true,** will **be what** determines the outcome **of what you see.**

> *Quote:* "Reflections give meaning to things we don't understand. Through it, we gain clarity; and by its outcome, we **gain** certainty."

🍃 Exercise: #9 Think of an orange. Now think of an orange.

🍃 *Question:* **Did you think of the same thing for both oranges, or did you think of something different for each orange?**

If you imagined two different oranges, it is logical to think you thought of two different oranges because you believed the Exercise was asking you to think of two different oranges. And it is also logically believed that the first orange that you thought of would be the example of an orange that is most common to you.

🍃 *Question:* **Did you notice the only thing changed was adding the word "now" to begin the second sentence.**

🍃 *Question:* **How did asking you to, "now think of an orange," make you feel about the first orange?**

Now take out a moment to ask yourself if you think this exercise was asking for two different types of oranges, or if you think it was asking for the same orange twice. And once you're confident in your answer, try to explain how you came up with your response.

Reflecting is the act of considering and to consider means to take into consideration more than one possibility to come up with the best possible solution. When asked a question that you don't automatically know the answer, it causes you to think. Thinking is an act of reflecting, and it causes us to concentrate our thoughts on something for a certain period of time to find the most accurate and logical answer.

When you thought about the oranges, you had to go through a moment of reflection to gain clarity of what you thought. And it usually takes us going through a process of separating what we think from how we feel. It is through this procedure that you will gain knowledge and understanding. Without it, nothing is known that is not already understood, and if nothing is understood, we are often left with using other people's thoughts or other resources to find answers while giving up to get an understanding from ourselves. It is mainly through reflections that we obtain a degree of knowledge, and it is through your understanding that your thoughts will become certain.

🍂 *Question:* When asked to think of the oranges, did you envision the orange you understood the question to be asking for?

If your answer is "yes," explain in detail what that the image looked like.

🍂 *Final Question:* While you were giving a detailed description of the orange you imagined, did you realize that the exercise never asked you to picture an orange, but it appeared automatically from the thoughts you were thinking?

Often what we think is linked to what we see. It is how the brain routinely determines what it understands to be accurate. That's why, through reflecting, it is common to picture images of our thoughts to have clarity and gain proof of what we think. Envisioning is sometimes used to show how you honestly think, but it can also be used to control your thoughts.

🍂 *Question:* If you could go on vacation anywhere, where would it be?

🍂 *Question:* Now, in detail, explain what thoughts came to mind?

🍂 *Question:* Did you notice how your thoughts didn't show anything wrong with the place you would like to visit?

🍂 *Example:* If you thought of a place that's tropical, chances are you didn't picture it being too hot, even though it often is; and if you thought of a place that's cold, chances are you didn't think of freezing because the image would go against the decision that you made.

Life is full of possibilities, therefore, only things that can be imagined are the things that can be thought of as possible. Failing to imagine will cost you to lose hope, and failing to reflect on certain things, will cause you not to see. But as long as you can keep dreaming, you will always know where you want to go. And as long as you can see, what you see, no matter how big or how small it is, the possibilities will always be there.

Our thoughts reflect what we think, but unfortunately, at times, what we see will also impose a reflection on what we believe. That's how when someone sees a person who looks differently than they do, it can lead that someone to treat that person differently even if they have almost identical personalities. It is also how certain people can see some things one way while other people can see the exact same things in a totally different way. You can only see what you think, and anything outside of our perception of thoughts will often go unseen or unnoticed.

Example: Projectors function by reflecting light off a mirror, and when the reflection goes through an LCD lens, an image is created. Perceptions work the same way. It is the process of **our thoughts, reflecting a picture of what we** think. And also, **what we think, can** form **a view** as to **what** we see. **That process is how we gain access to how we see** the world, and **it is how** the world sees us.

Reflecting is an essential part of knowing who we are, and taking time out to know what we think is still the best way of knowing what is happening in our lives. It is also a significant part of knowing what to do in certain situations and how to view certain circumstances we find ourselves in. Yet and still, due to the demands and responsibilities of being an adult, it leaves less time to think and reflect. And without reflecting on our life, life would be just accepted as it is and with very little to no concern or recognition on how to make life better.

A change in life always requires a change in thinking. Whether you are just getting married, just getting separated, losing someone in your life, or finding salvation, everything that changes requires a change in thoughts. If you fail to think of how to adapt, you could find yourself living with the same mindset or thoughts that are not suitable for who you are or what your life requires at this particular moment. And it can even cause you not to know what you need while you're in the midst of your circumstances.

> **Romans 12:2**
> 2 And be not conformed to this world: but be ye transformed by the renewing of your mind, that ye may prove what is that good, and acceptable, and perfect, will of God. (Romans 12:2)

Reflecting is how we renew our minds, and it is the process of how we clarify what we think. Our thoughts are the realization of what we know, and it is what transforms our way of thinking. Thoughts give meaning to everything that we know, and it is what creates a purpose for our lives. Without establishing why God created humanity, it will be impossible to know why we exist. And not knowing your real purpose in life can cause your whole existence to exist without any real rhyme or any real reason for living.

In some ways, perceptions are to reflections as reality is to actuality. It doesn't take a deliberation to form a perception, and it doesn't require us having to contemplate to define our reality. Reflections are distinct in forming a more objective opinion than a more subjective belief. It requires taking more into consideration of the evidence involved, and through thinking of the effects of a cause, it reveals a more detailed description of the circumstances of an outcome. When we reflect, all of our thoughts are gathered to try and figure out what something actually is. And through reflecting, we go through a process of gathering all of the thoughts formed, to strategize, and come up with a determining factor in consideration of our thoughts.

Quote: "I just had a change of thought."

Your goal may be to make a million dollars, get married to the person of your dreams, and start working on a family all before **you reach the age of forty**! Maybe life brought you a few mishaps, and perhaps you've had a few surprises along the way that caused you to think of yourself as a failure. And maybe the negative thoughts that were created through these mishaps left a lasting impression on **the opinions that you have** of yourself.

A reflection is the redirection of light, and maybe all you need to do is to **apply the teachings you've learned so far through this book to** redirect your **thoughts and your desires to** change **the image** of how you see **yourself and how you live your life**. Remember, life will not always go as planned, but all you can do is your best, and that best may include taking all of the negative things that happened to you along the way and manipulate it to reflect the best image of yourself!

Example: **Situations you face can cause your life to stop, but fighting through those setbacks will show everyone that you are a fighter and that you will not let anything or anyone else, including negative thoughts, stand in your way!**

> Matthew 5:14-16
>
> **14 Ye are the light of the world. A city that is set on an hill cannot be hid.**
>
> **15 Neither do men light a candle, and put it under a bushel, but on a candlestick; and it giveth light unto all that are in the house.**
>
> **16 Let your light so shine before men, that they may see your good works, and glorify your Father which is in heaven.** (Matthew 5:14–16)

You are what you do, simply because what you do shows a reflection for everyone else to see. Reflections are the outcome of what our mind generates. It is what gives reason behind the determination, and it is the purpose behind the inspiration. When light rays reflect off an object, it enters through the lens of the eye and into the cornea. The light that enters **through** the eye has to bend to focus its **radiance** on the retina. **In return, t**he retina ultimately communicates **the rays of light** to the brain. **Now what you think will automatically become what you see. If we choose to give our lives to God, we must let His light shine through us to reflect a different image than what we were before. And it is only in His likeness that we can reflect a light powerful enough to light up the darkness in our lives.**

Example: **The moon doesn't produce light, but the sunrays of light reflect off of the moon to brighten up the night sky. And if it wasn't for that beacon of light, it would be impossible to see how the moon actually looks like.**

When I became truly saved, I started to act differently than I did before. When I truly began to understand God **and His purpose for creating me**, I began to think differently. When I thought differently, I started to **be** different. My perception **of life** became different, and I be**gan to truly live** differently **than I had before. In the midst of living for God, I gained true purpose; and it** wasn't that I was forced **to,** but I chose to, **through the power of choice that I was purposefully given.** And w**hen I learned the effects of wrong and right, it** made more sense to me **to do what was right.** To be a Christian is to be Christ-like, and being Christ-like, **reflects the image of God even onto sinners like us.**

> *Quote: "How you treat others is a reflection of yourself."*

I've both wondered how certain people in this day and time can have the same racist mentality of oppressors that lived decades before they were born. I've also wondered how someone of a different heritage and race would sacrifice their own lives to give equality and opportunity to the less fortunate. I've wondered how a child can have the knowledge, integrity, and respect for others established in them at such a young age.

I've also wondered how certain children can be raised to have very little respect for authority or can disregard their own lives. I've wondered how someone who is created can live with so much disrespect for the God that created them, and I've also wondered what causes people who go through so much not to change or learn from their actions. You are what you do, and you do what you think. Our thoughts are the one and only thing that separates us. It is our thoughts, and the ideas that we encourage other people to have, that reflects the influence we have on them.

> **Proverbs 22:6**
> **Train up a child in the way he should go:**
> **and when he is old, he will not depart from it.**
> **(Proverbs 22:6)**

Even though each and every one of us has the power of choice, we all are still subject to many different types of influences **and choices that are made** in this world. **Many of these influences directly affect the way that we are raised, and many of the choices that our parents make good and bad, are the results that help shape our lives. That is how** generational curses **work, and that is also how the blessings pass down to our children can help their generation to grow.** There are times when all it takes to **break up a curse is to train up** a child to **think better than the generation before them. And what it takes to bless a generation is to leave them with something more than what the generation had before them.**

Thoughts **are generated from many different sources, and they are what make up what we will become. What we inspire our children to be is what is perceived to be what is expected from them. And what we fail to teach our youth will very likely be the thing that they wouldn't know growing up. Our children are subject to the examples we make, and the examples we make can have a strong enough influence to encourage them to become just like you, or it** can be powerful enough to cause them to grow up being nothing like you. **Either way, what examples we choose to set** can give our children an advantage in life, or it can be something they will have to overcome in order to take advantage of the life they were given.

> *Quote*: *"A person's behavior is a reflection of the music they listen to."*

Growing up, when I wanted to **be** bad, I couldn't listen to music that was joyful, **and w**hen I wanted to make a statement, I had to listen to music that made a **similar** statement. **W**hen I use to spread hatred, songs that promoted that same **hatred** was the type of music I **found myself** listening to. **And any type of sin that I struggled with, it seemed to ironically be encouraged through the type of music that I was hearing**. To listen to something or someone requires taking notice of what they say, and to listen, without any form of rejection or denial, is to hear the words being spoken with reflection or consideration.

Music is spiritual, but the words inside of a song relate to your thoughts. You cannot talk without thinking, and by think-ing of what you are hearing and saying, even though you may not realize it or regard it as being true, it still possesses a level of persuasion of the perception that is constantly evolving inside of your mind.

Music was around before the creation of man, and it's been an influence to help shape **the** culture **of humanity since time began. By its design, music has been** sung **through spiritual hymns** during oppression **that lifted our spirits. Antiwar** songs **have been sung to give a message** against fighting in the times of war. There have been songs **to inspire us to move on in the time of despair. But there are also songs that promote sin, violence, promiscuity,** and **discrimination towards others.**

🍃 *Question*: **With so many genres of music that exists today and with it sending so many messages to its listeners,** *i*s it our cul-ture that encourages the types of music we listen to, or is our culture a reflection of the **type of** music **that** we hear?

Imagery through music videos can be used to reflect a picture through electronic devices to perceive an illustration that is deceitful enough to fool anyone into thinking the bad they see is good, and the wrong they see is the right thing to do. Just by redirecting our thoughts through sight can portray something different than what things actually are, and by creating a false perception of things, it can create an image of something that is nothing like what you see.

I can recall times when I've heard songs being played for the first time on the radio or videos shown on television and was shocked at what I saw. I remember songs being banned, and I remember many people saying it was a violation of our freedom of speech. But I can also remember feeling upset and even disgusted at the messages of certain songs. Now that I am older, I can look back into my innocence and see how through music and videos, shortly after I listened to these songs I didn't like, it was soon after, I found myself reciting and dancing to the same songs I found to be repulsive when I heard them for the first time. Only simply because they had a nice beat.

Question: What types of songs are you listening to and letting your children listen to right now? And how are these songs influencing the way you think and the way our children behave in this world today?

To make it clear, any song that downgrades and violates someone, it is a song that is created for sinful purposes. And any song that is not comforting, and inspiring; or a song that is not teaching us to become a better people; are all songs with messages that go against the will of God!

Music is spiritual, and it can be used to put thoughts into the minds of its listeners. And just like the songs you recite and listen to, so will you think and soon you will resemble.

Satan was the first to sin, and he is the influencer of our sin. He was once considered the most talented musician in heaven, and it is widely believed that through his music, he uses its power to fulfill his agenda still today.

Quote: *"You set the example."*

Question: Have you ever wondered why you can **sometimes** tell where a person lives by how they speak or by how they act?

We are a reflection of our environment, and our reflection**s are** what describes **the** society **we live within**. How people look at our generation, our **race, and** even our family's **name** will be a reflection of **the things that we** do. **We are judged by what we do, and what we do is a reflection of the way that we think. Reflections are the effects in the cause and effect method, and in that effect, it will affect our marriages, our growth and development, and our attitude towards anything or anyone we know. If you are loving, you are looked at as a loving person, or if you are violent, it can easily cause you to be viewed as destructive and harmful to yourself as well as others. To change what you reflect, you must change what you do, and to change what you do, it must be done through the reflections of your thoughts.**

If you are reading this book, you are now a reflection of it, and the power it has over your life will be the image that is displayed. When you go out in the world, you will reflect its teachings by what you do. And by what you disregard, it will reflect the message that everyone has a choice, even if the choice is to choose not to change.

To think negatively will always cause a person to doubt. An optimist always sees hope; there is a *but* with every pessimist and a silver lining **whenever** we think positive. Rather, you decide to make changes in your life **through the knowledge God has provided through these teachings, or you decide to throw what you've learned all away.** What you do and where you go from here with regard to **God's word** will all be an image of what you decide to reflect!

Take action now! (Turn to pages #243 through #265 for recommended fasts and exercises.)

21

Sense of Thoughts

Our senses use the physiological capacity of organisms to provide data to create thoughts, and through these thoughts, a perception is formed. We as humans have five basic senses **which are:** taste, sight, smell, hearing, and touch. Each of the**se** five senses is associated with using specific sensing organs to send information to the brain. Through this communication, it helps us develop thoughts; and also, through thoughts, **by the use of our senses,** we can **better** understand and perceive the world around us.

Question: Have you ever noticed that strawberry candy doesn't really taste like strawberries?

Companies use dyes, images, and some even use smells to make us think that a particular product really tastes like what they advertise. Man cannot create **something from nothing,** so we as humans gather material that already exists to form something new. Creation in its purest form is to bring into existence **something that is entirely not there, and that form of creation can** only be achieved by God, Himself.

Question: How do real strawberries smell?

🍃 *Question:* Do artificial strawberry flavored products smell anything like real strawberries?

Through our inability to create, at times, it causes us not to be able to relate or understand our Heavenly Father for who He actually is. And it also leads us to question His divine power. We often begin to ask questions like, "If God created everything, who created God?" By not fully understanding the supremacy, authority, and power of God, we create hypotheses such as the big bang theory to explain what we can't understand.

🍃 *Question:* If all that exist were created through energy, space, and time, who was it that created energy, space, and time?

The only way to manufacture a real strawberry taste is to use real strawberries; other than that, everything else is only an imitation of the real thing! The trick to thinking you're eating what is advertised is to cause our senses to activate and send signals to the brain to create qualities of the product that manufacturers are trying to sell. Once enough senses agree, a complete thought is formed. And since our thoughts **make up** our reality, we will soon find ourselves **believing we're** eating **real** strawberry candy, while in actuality, it doesn't really taste anything like strawberries.

By putting the right images on packages, using the right colors, and even applying the right smells to any product, companies can have you thinking that you are eating almost anything they desire. So, the next time you buy a box of candy with a variety of flavors inside, close your eyes and taste a piece to see if you can guess the taste of what flavor the product is advertising.

🍃 *Question:* What thoughts do you gather from your senses?

Ecclesiastes 2:24
24 There is nothing better for a man, than that he should eat and drink, and that he should make his soul enjoy good in his labor. This

also I saw, that it was from the hand of God.
(Ecclesiastes 2:24)

- Taste stimulates the brain's cerebral cortex, which is a significant part of what forms your consciousness. Through the sensual taste of chocolate, its creamy, rich texture can produce a feeling of infatuation to its taster. Through our senses, we are to enjoy the fruit of our labor. Appreciating what you eat, drink, and what you do, can be the key to a happy life.
- The smell of barbecue can give you the perception of delicious food, and the taste of grilled food can remind you of a particular holiday or family event. Olfactory receptors are cells in the nose that are linked to the limbic system of the brain. The same system of which, that governs our emotions, our behavior, and our long-term memories.

  Many businesses and companies use smells to influence consumers to purchase anything from a shirt to buying a home. The scent of citrus gives off a sense of freshness, while the smell of vanilla makes a home feel cozy. The lively aroma of green tea restores harmony while the scents of pine and cedar can put you in the mind of holiday festivities.

  Smells can wake you up or soothe you to sleep. The smell of natural oils can heal you and lower your stress levels. The aroma from oils also has the power to influence your mood and heighten the intimacy levels between a husband and wife.
- Through the sense of touch, feeling the sunshine **on a sunny day** can cause you to think of summer or being on vacation; while the chill of the cold air can cause you to think of the **many fond times you've had at** Christmas. Touch is a major part of communication, and **it is** how humans connect with one another. Oxytocin is a feel-good hormone that is stimulated through the use of touch. Babies are comforted through the embrace of their care-

giver, while adults bond through a warm embrace, or simply by holding hands.

- Music has the power to instantly change the temperament of your mind-set to be just like it's designed. Music is spiritual, which makes hearing one of the most influential **senses** God has ever created. Hearing a particular song has a way of taking you back to a place and time where the song was relevant. It can make you go from being outrageous to loving everyone, all in the message and rhythm of a song. Replaying your wedding song can have you reliving one of the happiest moments in your marriage. Even listening to a powerful spiritual song can be one of the key things that leads you back to God.

1 Samuel 16:23

23 And it came to pass, when the evil spirit from God was upon Saul, that David took an harp, and played with his hand: so Saul was refreshed, and was well, and the evil spirit departed from him. (1 Samuel 16:23)

Music plays a major part in influencing you mentally and spiritually. During times when life gets hard, or you feel beat down, playing your favorite songs will lift your spirit without hesitation.

- Through sight, movies can place you into the center of the action. And without getting a scratch or a bruise, you will experience the journey the producer takes you on, while you're safely inside of your home. Before sweet wines like Moscato became popular, many wine drinkers today did not like the wine itself but were fond of the perception of drinking it. Through taste, caviar, despite its flavor, is served at high-end events because it gives off the sense of elegance.

A vast majority of cigarette smokers don't like the smell of cigarette smoke and are wary of the effects of smoking.

🍂 *Question:* So why do so many people smoke?

Cigarette companies hire advertisers to target young people to smoke by posting up sexual images, and scenes of a beautiful, more mature life to encourage people to smoke. Usually, once we start **to** smok**e cigarettes, the** addictions of nicotine causes **us** to think **we** need cigarettes **to function correctly**. Addiction is the act of being dependent on something, and people who are addicted to cigarettes or any other substance, often rely on them to produce dopamine.

🍂 Example: Dopamine is a substance produced naturally by our body that causes the feeling of happiness and motivation. But when **the brain sends signals to the body to release dopamine caused by narcotics and alcohol, it affects the brain's natural ability to produce dopamine all on its own. This causes drug users to rely** on the use of these foreign substances **to feel good** instead **of producing dopamine naturally from using our senses.**

Being under the influence can cause sensory organs to send signals to the nerve cells to release dopamine in the limbic system of the brain, and they can also prevent the body from naturally releasing dopamine, which can cause depression. Soon we can become dependent on these narcotics and fail to realize that dopamine can naturally be generated through thoughts. Just taking a gentle stroll outdoors, noticing the beauty of **the world, and** taking out time to enjoy nature can naturally produce these neurotransmitters in order to feel pleasure.

By recognizing the opportunities we have and the blessings of just being able to wake up in the morning and get out of bed is enough to make you feel optimistic and excited about life. But when the **body starts to rely on the help of certain sedatives, just to function, it can be hard to naturally appreciate anything anymore**, and that is often when addiction occurs. Thoughts are a reality, and we only realize what we think about. **T**hrough the use of drugs, the many things around us that we can get pleasure from would be worthless to us if something **prevents us from naturally taking** time out **to** enjoy what we have.

Quote: "Seeing is believing."

Question: How many times were you convinced you could fly or that you have some sort of special ability after watching a super-hero film?

Through the power of perception, the retina is used to communicate images directly to the brain. That's what makes sight so compelling when it comes to the influence it has over our thoughts.

Through sight, movies can encourage you to work out like a boxer training for a fight. It can have you thinking you can move objects if you thought hard enough or sing like your favorite character from a musical. Even though our intellect tells us some of these things are not possible, some small part of us still believes it, because "seeing is believing" and perception is sight.

The **images** in a romantic movie can communicate to the brain the reality of a couple that loves each other even through the thickest of times. In relation to this, **it can** influence **us** to try harder in loving our spouse as seen on the movie screen.

Through using our five primary senses, we can enhance our lives by surrounding ourselves with positive thoughts. Thoughts of encouragement, reflecting on why you first fell in love, or just a remembrance of fond events and happy experiences in the past, are healthy habits to have in creating a positive, loving reality.

There are thousands of thoughts caused by our senses each day. Through watching movies that inspire us, to listening to the music that strengthens us, we have the power **to** control **our thoughts** through our senses. With control over the mind, we are encompassed with the ability to create a positive and healthy environment that we can taste, see, smell, hear, and touch every day, for as long as we live!

Take action now! (Turn to pages #243 through #265 for recommended fasts and exercises.)

22

Past Tense

The term *past tense* refers to **the element of thoughts** relating to the past. **It is** a condition of someone or of something that no longer exists, and it pertains to an event that has already happened. It **can** also **be** acknowledged as a state in progress, a continuance of an act being habitually done, or something customarily reoccurring. **But** it is **most often** used **for** signify**ing or referring** to something that is now a part of **history.**

> **2 Corinthians 5:17**
> **17** Therefore if any man be in Christ, he is a
> new creature: old things are passed away; behold,
> all things are become new. (2 Corinthians 5:17)

As Christians, we believe baptism to be a symbol of rebirth and a new beginning. Putting away the things you used to do is a sign of growth, and no longer doing habitual acts that have been done in the past is an indication of maturity. If you do things the same way you always do and think the same way you've always thought, no matter if it's good or bad, it will make you precisely be the same person you've always been. **This can mean that you are not easily receptive to influence; but this can also give you the mindset of someone whose thoughts and memories are out of date and not equipped to function properly in this new and constantly changing world.**

🍃 *Question:* If we stay in the past, how can we exist in the present, or live for tomorrow?

Know who you are right now and don't look back regretting the past. Regrets are worthless without change, and being that we cannot change what we did in our past, **it** gives **a** good reason for the things we used to do **to not** be allowed to affect our happiness in the **present or in the** future. No matter what has been done in the past, there is always a chance for forgiveness. And by being given an opportunity for forgiveness to occur, we should always **be willing to ask for forgiveness or be receptive to forgive others.** But to live with regrets without change is worthless, and it will hinder the future growth you can develop **at this precise time and in the** moments to come.

If you've ever experienced going to a shrink, you know, the first thing they will ask, is for you to tell them something about yourself. And soon after that, they ask for you to tell them something about your past. The past is what defines you, and **it** is a history of occurrences that leads up to why you are the person you are today. **It shows why we think the way we do, and it gives the history to your life leading up to now.**

🍃 *Example:* Studies have shown that a person growing up in a family that never embraces one another or shows any form of **affection or** emotions **is** prone to draw away from displays of **endearment.** And it is also commonly known for that person to have some signs of emotional issues as well.

> Quote: *"Give a man a fish, and you feed him for a day. Teach him how to fish, and you feed him for a lifetime."* (Chinese philosopher Lao Tzu)

The past can make you a better person if you learn from it or a worse person if you repeat it. Based on the type of situations you are faced with, and according to the type of thoughts you take away from those situations will determine the effects that your past will have on you. Using the past as an excuse for the present or for a reason not to try may be the cause of history repeating itself **time and time again.**

Isaiah 43:18-19

18 Remember ye not the former things, neither consider the things of old.

19 Behold, I will do a new thing; now it shall spring forth; shall ye not know it? I will even make a way in the wilderness, and rivers in the desert. (Isaiah 43:18–19)

What defines you is your past, but your past is continually changing every day. You are **what you do, which causes you to be** identified by **the things that** you do. But remember, today will be your past tomorrow! So if you want to change your past, you can begin as early as **changing it right now!**

Exercise: #10

Question: Imagine if I've been your lawn man for the past two years, and you ran into me while you were out with your friends. And after we've spoken, your friends ask, "Who was that guy you just spoke to?"

Question: How would you identify me?

Imagine if another year had gone by, and since then, I've no longer done maintenance to your lawn. One day your child unfortunately gets sick, and you take them to the ER for help. After all the tests have been administered, I walk in wearing a white lab coat and start to describe the distressful conditions your child has been experiencing. I later write you a prescription to get for your child, and then I address you informally and ask, "how have you been doing."

🍂 *Question:* When I **walked into the room**, what would be your reaction? And explain in detail why your reaction would be the way that you've answered.

One day, while you are out with the same friends as once before and it just so happens that you bump into me again. We speak for a brief minute and address any updates with your child, and I leave mentioning if you have any questions, to give me a call. **Your friends say**, "That guy looks familiar," **and again asks, "Who was that guy you were just speaking to?"**

🍂 *Question:* What would be your answer?

🍂 *Question:* Did you describe me the same way as before or was the description **you gave any** different from the one you told your friends the first time they asked who I was? And **if something changed, try to explain why.**

You are what you do, and if you want to change who you are, you must first change what you do!

🍂 ***Example:* I was known as your lawn man once because I used to cut your lawn. Now that I've treated your child's illness, I am considered or viewed as a physician. You are what you do, and by that reasoning, if you change what you do, it means what you are will change also!**

A liar is a liar because he lies, and a thief is a thief because he steals. But what if you never lie anymore? What if you never stole again from this day forth?

🍂 *Question:* Will that change the way people see you, or more importantly, would it change the way you see yourself?

1 Corinthians 13:11

11 When I was a child, I spake as a child,
I understood as a child, I thought as a child: but
when I became a man, I put away childish things.
(1 Corinthians 13:11)

What if you said, "I will no longer be biased" or "I will no longer live in hate?" What if you said, "I'm not going to quit **or give up** trying **anymore**" **or that** "I will finish what I start for now on?" What if you vowed to start making better decisions in life instead of making up an excuse or causing things to get worse? What if you said, "I'm going to change the way I think, the way I feel, right now, starting today?"

Question: Will that make a difference in who you will be on tomorrow?

> **Quote: "Sometimes all it takes to stop viewing or living your life in the past is to start looking forward to life in the future."**
>
> **What if you said, "I am going to trust in God for now on" or "I am going to leave the past behind me?" What if you made your mind up to stop making excuses and to only start making progress? What if you said, "I will no longer live regretfully in the past" and that "For now on, I am going to live my life and place my thoughts on the here and now?" What will happen if you began to have hope again and said, "I am a new person, and from now on, I'm going to be better than I ever was before?"**

Question: Will that make a difference in the way that you feel right now, in this very moment, and what kind of person you will be tomorrow?

Our past defines who we are right now, but what we fail to realize is what we do today will be the past that defines who we will become in the future. The decisions and choices you make will continue to represent you each and every day of your life. But don't be concerned, because change is in your control. If you take control of your thoughts, you will take control over **your actions and** the choices **that** you make. Having control over the choices you make today will immediately put you in control over your past tomorrow and your future to come. Starting right now!

Take action now! (Turn to pages #243 through #265 for recommended fasts and exercises.)

23

The Power of Thoughts

Thoughts are the opinions **we have; they are the** decisions we make, and **they are what form** the ideas and dreams in**side of** our minds. **Our t**houghts are **what dictates** our **presence** in this world, and it is the tunnel that every communication and every interaction **we experience** has to go through. It is the very thing that **makes** us as human **being**s **human, and through its creation, it is what separates us** from every other living organism on the **entire face of the planet**.

> **Jeremiah 17:7–8**
> [7] "But blessed is the one who trusts in the
> Lord, whose confidence is in him.
> [8] They will be like a tree planted by the water
> that sends out its roots by the stream. It does not
> fear when heat comes; its leaves are always green.
> It has no worries in a year of drought and never
> fails to bear fruit." **Jeremiah 17:7–8 (NIV)**

Thoughts can take you from loving to hating in a matter of minutes. Thoughts can **cause you to like something** or **dislike something** according to how you think. It has the power to determine **what** way we **think** about everything, **and it has the ability to establish how we feel about everyone, including** ourselves.

A thought can be the difference between **believing** in God and **trusting in His authority completely, to** entirely not believing in Him at all. It is what gives encouragement and inspiration, and it is what takes it **all** away. *Negative thoughts are what cause* us to be discouraged, and **when we are in doubt, it is what causes us to be afraid of the unknown.** They can create a feeling of peace within ourselves that enables us to live in harmony or paint a picture that displays an image that causes chaos and distress inside our lives.

Question: **What thoughts do you think goes through someone's head to encourage them to shoot innocent children at a school?**

In recent times, we as a nation have witnessed more mass shootings and terroristic acts than ever before. Investigators go through hundreds of files and thousands of personal e-mails in **search of one** link, one **clue, or** any **sign as** to **why these things keep happening. They know if they can find something that links a person's thoughts to their actions, it can give reason to why and possibly prevent** these horrific tragedies from happening again.

Question: **What can make someone think that they're more valuable than someone else?**

Before the civil rights movement, countless African Americans were beaten, and some brutally murdered, for the simple fact that they were not white. There **has been** segregation inside our school systems, judicial systems, and even **in** the job **market that goes back for decades. And there are some of these same systems and thoughts that exist with us, still today.**

Question: What can cause a person to hate someone **or want to take a person's life** simply based on **what** they look **like on the outside?**

Thoughts have the power to encourage us to love one another. They are what give us the ability to determine right from wrong, and they can **even** give **us** the courage to sacrifice our very own life for the sake of others.

🍃 *Example:* Our military, police force, firemen, evangelists, journalists, freedom fighters (from all origins and lands, black and white), martyrs, activists of every nationality, missionaries, pastors, community *leaders*, and the list goes on and on...

Thoughts have the power to determine the will of all humanity, and they have the power to will the decisions of every single man **and** woman on earth.

🍃 *Example:* Our judges, lawyers, government officials, prosecutors, lawmakers, the judicature society, educators, members of Congress, local city mayors, law enforcement, even the president of the United States, and individuals such as every one of us.

A single thought has the power to *bring into existence anything that can exist, and it has the will to produce* life or to *take life away!*

An attempt to commit suicide is the greatest mistake any person can ever make. Yet there are thousands of cases happening around the world and in cities and towns just like yours of individuals desiring **and choosing** to take their own lives. **Al**though there are cases where attempts fail, yet one attempt that is successful is way too high. **In regards to** suicide, once it's done, it's done, and there is no coming back!

This means there's no chance of waking up tomorrow and moving past yesterday. No chance of ever making the right decision **or correcting the wrong mistakes we've made**, no chance of making things better, no chance of knowing how it feels to live life carefree again or how it feels to feel a **gentle** breeze blow in the cool of the day. No chance of knowing how it feels to be touched *again*, to understand what it means to be loved again, or to have the pleasure of seeing your loved ones grow up and develop into the persons you always knew they could be. Never a chance to listen to the waves as they crash onto the shore or witness a single snowflake fall from the sky and touch the surface. It means never knowing what tomorrow may bring. And it means not knowing that you were possibly just one thought away from entirely turning your life around and totally changing the way you see yourself at this very moment!

Just one thought, "I don't want to live anymore," "I want it all to end," or "I'm better off dead," can take away your life and nullify the plans and purpose God has for you.

Question: What point would it make to take your life when choosing to take your life **means** taking away **the one real and true thing you actually have?**

Everything that is on this planet is made of dirt, created by the Spoken Word of God, and transformed to the use of man. The life and the spirit that we have is the only thing that was given directly from Jehovah the Father, and it's the only part of us that is directly a part of Him.

> *Quote:* "It's often perceived that the things around us are what give us meaning, but in actuality, it is us that give everything around us a purpose."

Perception is reality, and to make things better requires some sort **of change** to take place. **That change starts with the power of thoughts, and those thoughts begin with you.** You have the power to change because you have the power to **choose. Making a different choice takes creating a difference of opinion, and having a difference in opinion is created through a difference in** thoughts. Through **thoughts, a** choice **is made, and that choice is the only thing that truly matters!**

> *Quote: "Making a change can be as simple as changing one thought or as hard as **being reluctant to change the way you think**."*

Billion upon billions of dollars are poured out, and hundreds upon millions of hours are spent each year teaching and training people **on** how **the mind works**. People go to school for **years** in hopes of becoming a psychologist, neuroscientist, or doctor; and some people study for years to get degrees in philosophy, biology, and sociology. There are some people who study in mental and physical health to understand **how and** why people **think the way that** they do. And it seems that no matter how hard or how much we try, we will not know all there is to know. At the end, every last penny spent, every last hour sacrificed, every last effort exhausted, are all to have the ability to do one thing, and that **one thing** is to have the ability to **understand or** change one single thought.

Divorce, **similar to** suicide, takes away **any** opportunity for making things better. Some couples don't go all the way through with **it,** but instead, they suffer in silence while **living** physically and mentally separated from their spouse.

Divorce is not giving up, it's letting go, **and** I personally think **that** divorce **isn't an unpardonable sin some religious entities make it out to be**. Marriage is not made to suffer through all the days of your life. **It is a partnership, a love story, a compromise, a friendship, an achievement, and a commitment.**

Although divorce **has its purpose, having a good reason to get a divorce doesn't stop the devastation it** causes. And its destruction will affect everyone in its path. Its effects will not only touch the lives of the individuals involved, it **also will** touch the lives of their **children,** friends, family, and **the communities where we live**. That's why it's so important to make the best effort to not only stay married to our spouse but also to remain happily married together. **All it takes to make a bad choice in life is only to entertain one negative thought!**

Matthew 25:40
40 And the King shall answer and say unto them, Verily I say unto you, Inasmuch as ye have done it unto one of the least of these my brethren, ye have done it unto me. (Matthew 25:40)

Misery is so familiar to us that we can hear stories about others suffering and neglect **to ever** stop what we are doing to think about the needs of the individuals **who are affected** or how we could help. Life is full of many challenges, but often what it takes to overcome some of these challenges **in life** is **to possess the correct pattern of thoughts**!

One change of thought can lead you from taking your own life **to living your life with no regrets**. One change of thought can **possibly stop** you **and your spouse** from being **separated to staying not only married, but staying happily married together**. To refrain from negative thoughts that discourage you, all it takes is one change of thought. To turn from giving up on your dreams, to living life to the fullest, may only take one single thought. **A variation of thinking can even be the difference between being saved and unsaved. One change of thought can take you from hating yourself to loving who you are. And sometimes,** all it takes is one simple change of thought, to change our minds into **creating** a whole new perception of life!

1 Corinthians 10:13

13 There hath no temptation taken you but such as is common to man: but God is faithful, who will not suffer you to be tempted above that ye are able; but will with the temptation also make a way to escape, that ye may be able to bear it. (1 Corinthians 10:13)

Thoughts have the power to create a conversation with the most powerful Being that will ever exist. The same One who brought Israel out of Egypt, the same One that created the heavens and the earth, who by speaking one word caused the water to flood the land, who by taking one breath separated the Red Sea and gave safe passage to His people. The Great I Am, and the same One who gave His Son to die for all our sins. A thought has the power to allow us to have the most intimate conversation we will ever have in our lifetime with this same Omnipotent God, without saying one single word!

Philippians 4:6

⁶ Be careful for nothing; but in every thing by prayer and supplication with thanksgiving let your requests be made known unto God. (**Philippians 4:6**)

With one thought, **it can lead** you **to** becom**ing happier** and **healthier** than you've ever been before. Positive thoughts can lead you to become more successful in life. One thought can change a "no" into a "yes," it can change an, "I don't care," into an, "I do care," and from quitting a task, into finishing the job. Being faced with a decision to take your own life, a single thought can be the difference between life and death. By one thought, you can go from signing divorce papers to taking the first step, the right step, you need to make your relationship work. And not only work, but **creating** a good **relationship with others and an** "A+" marriage **with your spouse**!

Thoughts are what divide nations apart, and it is what Jesus meant when He said, "Satan wishes to sift you as wheat." But a thought also gives you the power to become anything you want to be in life. It is what separates us from becoming the person we are, to becoming the person we ought to be!

Take action now! (Turn to pages #243 through #265 for recommended fasts and exercises.)

Introduction

In our youth, we spend most of our time fantasizing and daydreaming about the things hoped for. As children, we know what we want to do **and where we want to go in life. It is at this age when we even know what we want to be** when we grow up. **It typically consists of** being an astronaut, **doctor,** veterinarian, **police officer,** firefighter, and some sort of athlete, singer, **or actor.** We spend time using our imaginations on **what it would be like as adults as we play house. We also play in the mud as we pretend to make the most delicious foods and desserts. And we sing along with our favorite artists as we listen to our favorite songs.**

In our youth, we imagine what it would be like to have the superpowers of our favorite superheroes. It is also the time when we host the most wonderful and elaborate tea parties while being accompanied with the most inquisitive and sophisticated guests. As children, we also never hold on to any grudges or negative thoughts, but instead, we keep moving past these moments, not seeing the world for what it is, but only imagining the world for what it could be.

Growing **slightly older and not wanting to be treated like a baby anymore, we insist on being called a big boy or a big girl, and we are determined to be treated like so as well. We still enjoy watching our favorite television shows and playing dress-up in lavish makeup and modeling extravagant clothes. We continue to** enjoy playing video games and **creating action scenes** with our favorite toys. **A**nd on the weekend, we also enjoy going outside to play **our favorite games** with our **neighbors and** friends. It is typically at this age when all we want to do is just have fun without any real worries or any major concerns, and we are perfectly content with just being who we are **and not like the rest of the world.**

These particular moments in time are commonly seen as **one of** the happiest years of our lives. And without yet fully experiencing the devastation of living with any doubts or regrets, it leaves us spending less time looking back on our past and more time looking **forward** to the future.

Yet and still, **as we get older, things** start to get more competitive as we begin to get more involved in sports and athletics.

A short time later, it becomes less about having fun and more about winning and losing. Despite it all, it is at this age where we don't take much notice or serious thought about the aspects of each day. It causes the years to go by so quickly that it makes it hard to remember anything more than just a few bits and pieces of what life was like, at this time in our lives, when we were young and carefree.

Now entering into our preteen years, a majority of our lives now are being spent on going to school, balancing athletics, and competing in competitions. Our social lives consist of **being on the phone, posting on social media,** and hanging out with **our** friends. **When** we're not **busy**, we just simply **like** spending time at home listening to music, watching something on television, **and being on our cell phones.** As we become more independent, we become less connected to our family, and it is at this age where our values begin to develop. **Outside of home, we begin to enter into social groups, which only involve being around the people in our circle. And that's fine with us because these are the only people who seem to get us, and everyone else is either too lame or way too self-centered to be around for a long period of time.**

It is also at this age is when our bodies start to change, and now we become increasingly more self-conscious, and begin to **develop insecure feelings about ourselves. We don't realize everyone around us has the same lack of confidence as we do, and it causes our insecurities to make us feel even more insecure. And now** that **we are experiencing a physical and mental growth** mixed **in** with our emotional development, **it can cause** it to be one of the **hardest** times in **our lives, because this is the first time we feel like we're going through something alone. And feeling like we're by ourselves can be devastating when all we want to do at this age is be liked and fit in.**

Entering midway into our teenage years, we still don't fully understand how to handle our emotions, so we find a connection with the music we listen to because it seems like it is what can best explain how we are feeling at this time **in our lives.** So the music we listen to becomes a part of what defines us, and it is also something **we identify ourselves with** as well. **It is at this age when fashion is how we express ourselves, and now our primary goal is to climb up the social ladder by keeping up with the latest trends and impressing the right people. Also, life becomes one of the most confusing times at this age, because we tend to see ourselves now for how other people see us. We also typically begin to think more about what other people value and think, and less about ourselves and what is important to us.**

Next, entering **into** our **later** teenage **years, we become even more independent, which causes us to be separated even further away from our family.** And in some instances, it also can cause us to be separated from **the** values **we were taught growing up as a child. Now, with being only left to relying solely on our own thoughts and feelings, we are only influenced by who we let influence us. And still without fully understanding how we honestly think and in what way we truly feel, we are subject to say things we don't really mean and do things we don't fully understand the effects of yet. Social media starts to be where we find most of our information, and what is important to us starts to be based on how many likes we get or followers we have.**

Life is far from perfect, but we enjoy it because it's at this age where we are the closest to becoming fully grown without having the full responsibilities as an adult. **Yet, it is at this age when we start to take more control over who our friends are, and we become more independent thinkers of who we are and what kind of person we would like to be. We also become more accustomed to the social statuses that we are in, but it can also lead us to question ourselves and to wonder if we will ever be happy.**

On the weekends, we still like hanging out with our friends, attending sporting events, or simply **talking and texting on the phone.** We make **some** mistakes, and we learn through **most of those** mistakes, **but we will not find out until later in life, how some of the lessons we will learn will be some of the lessons that**

will teach us some **of the most** important lessons **we will ever learn in life. At this particular moment in time, is when we begin to make crucial decisions on where life is going to take us.**

For some **of us,** this transformation will create **anticipation for the upcoming** opportuni**ties we will have.** And for others, it may develop **a feeling of skepticism** and start us to question **if we will ever accomplish what we want to achieve in life.** On top of that, many of us start to realize that life isn't as easy **at this age** as we thought it **would be** when we were kids. **For some of us, life looks promising, and for everyone else, it leaves us with a sense of uncertainty. And now, with doubt starting to rise even higher, we begin to question what life really has to offer. Despite of everything else, we still have some very memorable moments. And with the thought of liberation and adulthood just around the corner, it brings an excitement to life even though reality is just around the corner.**

Unfortunately, a vast majority of us will never become that singer or athlete we always thought we would be. **It takes a tremendous amount of money and schooling to become that doctor or veterinarian we always said we would become.** Being a police officer or firefighter is very challenging and demanding work, and the opportunity to be an astronaut feels like it is as far away from us as we are from the stars. **Some of us will achieve our dreams but will shortly come to realize that our dream jobs were not as exciting and glamorous as what we fantasized about.** Now we're left compromising with our **childhood** fantasies and the realities of life, and it leaves many of us stuck right in the middle of a world where we don't know which way to go.

Later in life, some of us will be finishing up with our enlistment in the military. Some of us, **having graduated** from college and **began our careers, will soon look forward to getting married. There are some of us who will have already started families, and there are others of us who will have not done either. Either way,** these decisions and accomplishments will start a fresh beginning to a new life or a new beginning to a life now with a family **or as a single parent. Now completely being on our own,** our future become**s** clearer to us**, and good or bad, we can see almost exactly where life is going to take us next.**

*"You are what you do, **and you do what you think**."* And now, when we **meet** other **people**, we are identified by nothing outside of what we do **at work or what we do at home. And to be perfectly honest, that is the majority of what we typically think about throughout each day as well. In your career**, you are this person; when you **are at home,** you are that person; **and** when you're out with friends, you are another person. **W**hen you visit your mom **and** dad, you are that little boy or **little** girl they always **see** you as, **and because thoughts are a reality, when you are all alone, you don't really know who you are or where you want life to take you next. With doing everything else, you have very little time to think about yourself, and it leaves you with a lot of unanswered questions and unseen concerns about your life.**

Thoughts are everything, and now everyone knows you by what they perceive you to be. In this world, you are forced to become the person that you have to be, and **in your life,** your responsibilities require you to be the person that you **need to be.**

🍃 *Question:* If you are absolutely honest with yourself, and if you were asked to **explain** who you **really** are, at this very moment, **without describing what you do at home** or **what you do** at work, what would you say?

24

Think of Me

🍃 *Question:* Do you know who you are? And if so, who?

When asked questions such as these, there are very few of us who can explain who we are in detail, and there is no one who can possibly answer questions like these without thinking about it first! To think is the pathway to the knowledge of our understanding and to know can only be derived through our thoughts. A thought is an idea or opinion we have about something or someone, and an opinion is what we think from our perception of thoughts. To effectively think requires us to reflect on all ideas and feelings, and it takes having an open mind to consider every idea and all opinions. We live in a society, and in a world today, were very few of us know who we truly are, and there are fewer of us who have any idea or concern as to why we are created. It takes noticing who you are to realize who you are, and if you are too consumed with doing other things or with life itself, it could cause you to never have time to think about yourself and for yourself. And it even may cause you to go through this life without knowing what life really means and what it has to do with you.

Matthew 10:39
39 He that findeth his life shall lose it:
and he that loseth his life for my sake shall
find it. (Matthew 10:39)

Your life contains a history of thoughts and choices made throughout your lifetime, and your decisions causes you to have a prominent effect on everyone you have ever had contact with. To think, "I'm not important" is an invalid thought, and to think, "I have no real reason for living" undermines the reason why this whole world and everyone in it was created. We are all connected in some way, and what you do with your life will either better humanity or cause it to falter due to your neglect.

Genesis 1:26-27
26 And God said, Let us make man in our
image, after our likeness: and let them have
dominion over the fish of the sea, and over the
fowl of the air, and over the cattle, and over all
the earth, and over every creeping thing that
creepeth upon the earth.
27 So God created man in his own image,
in the image of God created he him; male and
female created he them. (Genesis 1:26-27)

We all have reason, which means we all have a reason for living. It is true, we all have purpose, but to know that you are not only a part of the life you have but you are also a part of life itself, is the beginning of understanding your purpose for living.

Quote: "There are many facets to making me
who I am today. To know is to think, which
means getting to know me more requires me
starting to think about me more."

🍂 *Question:* Are you happy with where you're at in your life right now?

🍂 *Question:* Are you happy with how you are and who you are with no regrets?

🍂 Last Question: Do you know how you got to be where you are today or how you got to become like you are right now? And if so, how?

A person who doesn't know what they do is a person who doesn't know what they are doing. If thoughts are knowledge, not thinking of how you are and of what you do will cause you to not know where you are in life or how you got there.

🍂 *Example:* Many people suffer from depression and don't know they're depressed. If you haven't laughed or felt some sense of gratitude recently or for example, approximately the past ten days, chances are you're suffering from some type of depression. Certain health specialists say that different forms of depression can last up to fourteen days or more. It is so common among adults, that you can be depressed, and no one would ever notice that anything was wrong.

An excellent practice to obtain happiness is to count your blessings. By waking up in the morning and saying what you are thankful for will make you more appreciative of what you have, because it will cause you to think of what you have. With the use of positive thoughts, writing down your goals, no matter what they are, and recording the steps you're taking to reach your goals, will create a higher awareness of your accomplishments, and what other steps it will take to get to where you're trying to go.

Everything you go through has an effect on you because it has an impact on the way that you think. Every time you change the way you think, you change the type of person you are, and the more consistent the thoughts are that changed you, the better chance of that change becoming a permanent part of your personality. And it often happens without us even knowing it!

We are what we do, and we do what we think. When I don't know how I feel or can't understand why I don't feel a certain way about certain things anymore; when my thoughts are all over the place, and I find it hard to control what I feel and how I feel; or when I'm confused and don't know which steps to take next; that's when I set aside from everything else and pay close attention to what thoughts I've been thinking in my head.

There is a reason for everything, and there is a reason to why you are the way that you are. The decisions we make are caused by the way that we think, and the way that we feel is only accumulated through a notion of ideas and thoughts inside of our minds.

Example: As humans, we can get addicted to gambling because of the feeling it gives us to win. And if we lose, we can also get consumed with gambling by thinking to ourselves, "I can't stop until I get back what was unrightfully taken from me." These effects are common among most people, and it leaves us helpless from escaping the thought of gambling. This experience is also how a system built on taking, can do just that. If we can change our thoughts into fully understanding the feelings that gambling produces are the feelings that make what it's designed to do work, and the feelings that we feel is what causes us to fall victim to gambling. Then you would know the only way to truly win is to gather what you have left and walk away from it altogether. If you say losing doesn't bother you, it is not that losing doesn't bother you anymore, it's that you've trained your mind to live with the feeling of losing. And likewise, by not thinking of what you've lost causes you to become accustomed to it.

To not think of what you do is the same as not knowing or understanding what you do. Thoughts are how we feel, and as long as we feel we can win, no matter what the odds are or what is

at risk, the way we feel is powerful enough to make us powerless to the way that we think.

Example: The odds of winning the lottery are usually somewhere between 1 in 300 million. Yet, many people waste away the money that they need to live and pay bills each and every day in hopes of becoming rich. The unfortunate actuality is, people who feel they will win, usually will never realize they didn't really have a real chance at winning, until they lose. And if we are being honest, if you think you will win, or that it's your lucky day, or that you have some kind of sign from God to play a certain number, why would we gamble away so much money trying to play the odds, instead of only playing that one number that we feel like was our destiny to win?

Exercise: #11

You are how you feel, and you feel how you think. A happy person has happy thoughts, a sad person has sad thoughts, and a person who is always angry or mad must continue to have thoughts that continuously make them angry or mad, or else they will have no choice but to feel a different way! A person who is loving will have loving thoughts, a sincere person will think sincerely, and an emotional person will commonly think in a way that causes their feelings to show. So when answering these questions, remember that the type of person you are always comes from the kind of thoughts that you think.

Question: What type of person are you?

Question: Do you act and think like the type of person you truthfully are or did you allow the things and people in your life change the genuine nature of your character?

🍃 *Question:* If so, what things happened, and what thoughts occurred from those things that caused you to be how you are right now?

🍃 *Question:* Do you know why these things have this specific impact on you?

🍃 *Question:* Do you know the things that you like and the things that you don't like? And if so, name some of these things that have impacted you the most?

🍃 *Question:* Is it possible that some or all of these things are affecting the way you are, the way that you feel, and the way that you are thinking at this very moment?

🍃 *Question:* Being who you truly are and referencing how you truly feel, what are some of the things you want to do and what are some of the characteristics and attributes you truly want to have?

These are the things that make you, you and not knowing what I like and don't like, and the reason it is that way is only because somewhere in life I stopped thinking of me. And that can cause me not to understand why I am the way I am and think the way that I do.

🍃 *Question:* What is your favorite **food or favorite drink? And why?**

🍃 *Question:* What is your favorite **genre of film and music? And why?**

🍃 *Question:* What is your favorite **movie and song?**

🍃 *Question:* How does it make you feel or think of when you listen to your favorite song or watch your favorite movie?

🍂 *Question:* What is your favorite color? And **what feelings do you feel, or thoughts do you think when you see it?**

🍂 *Question:* **If you can go anywhere in the world or do anything you want to do, what would it be?**

🍂 *Question:* **Have you noticed any patterns yet? And if not, go back over your answers to find out if you can connect any dots!**

The answers you give are the things that make up who you are, and if you are ignoring it or are never setting time aside to learn these things, it is the same as not knowing why you are special.

🍂 **Final** *Question:* **A**re you the kind of person you want to be at this moment? And if not, **and if you had the choice, what would you change?**

You know what you know, and the only thing you know is what you take the time out to think of. The **answer to these** questions **are the same answers that** tell the story of who you are **and why. It makes up the evidence of what causes you to have a certain personality, and it is** why you like **the things that you like and not like** the things you do **not like. Knowing who you are takes thinking of who you are. And to think of myself** is a part of understanding **who and what I am.**

🍂 *Question:* **If you don't know who or what you are right now, how will you know what steps you need to take to become the person you want to become later on in life?**

Your thoughts will always be your reality, and it will always be what you recognize and what you know to be true. Many of us live out our lives day by day, never **taking the time out to consider or** think about ourselves.

In life, years pass by so quickly that it often leaves us wondering, "Where did the time go?". **But by being in the moment as it happens and recognizing our thoughts alone the way, will help us gain better control over the enjoyment of those moments and what we take away from the important events in our lives.**

Never neglect to notice the good **things about you and what you do** because the good **you do** is what you're good at, and it **will help you maintain confidence and belief in yourself.**

Also, never neglect **to recognize** the bad **things,** because knowing the bad is knowing what **you're not good at and what** you need to improve on. **Don't** get discouraged **by making** mistakes because **by definition,** mistakes are never made intentionally**, but are only done accidently. Mistakes acquire improvement and creates an opportunity to learn from the things done in the past. With n**oticing the good without noticing the bad, and also noticing the bad without noticing the good in **what you are and in what** you **do** will always paint an unfinished picture, and you will never completely see yourself for who you truly are.

Everything we recognize is processed through thoughts, and everything we understand comes from the perception of what we think. Psychiatrists get paid lots of money to explain our thoughts and why we feel the way that we do. Even though they're worth every penny of what they get paid for, if you could link the way that you think to the way you feel, you will find yourself with more control over your life and more understanding of who you are than ever before.

Example: **If I'm afraid of taking chances or trying something new, it would most likely be caused by me being afraid of failing or scared of something not coming out as I had hoped for. But if I thought more on succeeding or things turning out great, through the power of thoughts, I would think that chances are that things would come out just how I imagine them to be. It would also give me less time to think about failing or on things turning out badly, and because of that, it will** cause me to be more eager to take chances or to try something new in the future.

> *Quote:* "Your thoughts are what you are, and if you don't know why you think the way that you do, it means you don't know why you are the way that you are."

Most people spend the majority of their lives doing for other people. You have to be this person for this group of people, and then you have to turn around and be a different person for another group. You have to be just like your friends so that you all will have something in common. And at the end of the day, you can release and unwind and start all back over again tomorrow.

You are what you think, and if you are constantly trying to be like everyone else, being yourself will never be good enough. If not careful, you will find yourself living inside a hollow shell looking through the eyes of others in search of your own happiness.

Many of us **also** spend a majority of our adult lives worrying about our job or worrying about our careers **or worrying about other people**. We come home either thinking about what we need to do, **where we need to go, and who we need to call.** We **go from one thing to the next** for some of the best years of our lives, **but it's okay because being productive is how things get done.** But if we never take a break or break protocol **from making** sure everyone around us, including the pet, is taken care of, we will find ourselves taking care of everyone around us and not taking care of ourselves in return.

Luke 10:38-42

38 Now it came to pass, as they went, that he entered into a certain village: and a certain woman named Martha received him into her house.

³⁹ And she had a sister called Mary, which also sat at Jesus' feet, and heard his word.

⁴⁰ But Martha was cumbered about much serving, and came to him, and said, Lord, dost thou not care that my sister hath left me to serve alone? bid her therefore that she help me.

⁴¹ And Jesus answered and said unto her, Martha, Martha, thou art careful and troubled about many things:

⁴² But one thing is needful: and Mary hath chosen that good part, which shall not be taken away from her. (**Luke 10:38-42**)

Quote: "If you give everyone all that you have, it will leave you with having nothing left to give."

It is true that the people who are around you are the people who are the closest to you and are typically the people who count on you the most. But neglect is the absence of the presence. And before long, you might discover that the best part of your day is when you look on social media to see what everyone else is doing in their lives. That's why it is essential to know that while everyone who circles you needs you the most, it is you who is standing right in the middle of it all and desire your attention as well, and if not more.

Mark 8:36

36 For what shall it profit a man, if he shall gain the whole world, and lose his own soul? (Mark 8:36)

Putting yourself first doesn't automatically make you selfish or self-centered. Putting yourself first can also mean not jeopardizing your morals and your values for the sake of others. It also means not letting anything get in the way of your salvation and peace of mind.

Life is tricky, and we are born in sin. This means sin is all around us, and it is in our nature to sin. Sometimes what it may take to put you first and to make your salvation your primary goal is to put things that you and everyone else want second and the things that we need first. Right is right, and wrong is wrong, which means, when making choices in life, especially when it comes to your wellbeing, making the right choice will absolutely always be the best choice to make!

> Quote: "*What lies behind you **doesn't measure up to** what lies in front of you, **and what lies in front of you,** pales in comparison to what lies inside of you.*"

"What" and "who" you are, are two totally different things! "What" describes in action or what we have developed into or what we have become. "Who" describes ownership, purpose and is only derived through creation. We all have a purpose placed inside of us and that purpose gives each and everyone of us a reason to keep living!

> Quote: "It is not how long you live that is important; it is the way you live that counts the most."

Maybe you want to start traveling or go out dancing. Perhaps you want to get on a boat and go fishing, plant a garden as a way to relax and unwind or get saved. Either way, it is important to know that time is needed and wanted the most when we don't have it; and yet, it is appreciated and valued the least, when we do have it.

> **Quote: "*Thinking you can do something, puts you halfway there.*" (Theodore Roosevelt)**

It's up to you to start making a **decent** attempt **on starting** that business you've always wanted **to start or develop a relationship with the person you've** always wanted to have. The best time to mend a rift between loved ones is now. And the only way to do anything you want to do is by first thinking of doing it! And the next step needed to begin making your desires become a reality is by making the choice to take actions!

> **Proverbs 25:28**
> He that hath no rule over his own spirit is like a city that is broken down, and without walls. (Proverbs 25:28)

> **Quote:** *"Getting married and having children doesn't mean giving up on your life. It means having a new life with your spouse and with your children together as a family."*

Allow your children to get to know who you are, and do things with them that you always wanted to do. By raising our children, we are supposed to teach them right from wrong, good from bad; and give them a better chance at creating a life worth living. And if we are not doing that, "we are just feeding them" and letting them figure out everything else on their own!

We give up so much for our children and try so hard to give them the things and opportunities we didn't have, so much in fact, that often we leave out the most important thing, and that is giving them you. *Know that understanding who you truly are, and sharing the best you with your family, is the best gift you could ever give them next to God.* The most important thing we can give our children is God, and the most important thing we can do for them is to spend time with them.

> **John 1:1-9**
> ¹ In the beginning was the Word, and the Word was with God, and the Word was God.
> ² The same was in the beginning with God.
> ³ All things were made by him; and without him was not any thing made that was made.

⁴ In him was life; and the life was the light of men.

⁵ And the light shineth in darkness; and the darkness comprehended it not.

⁶ There was a man sent from God, whose name was John.

⁷ The same came for a witness, to bear witness of the Light, that all men through him might believe.

⁸ He was not that Light, but was sent to bear witness of that Light.

⁹ That was the true Light, which lighteth every man that cometh into the world. (**John 1:1-9**)

Quote: **"Life is the most precious thing on the planet, and that life would not exist without light. It is light that makes all things prosper, it is light that gives us the ability to live, and it is light that gives life unto all the world."**

The mind is like a computer with all the hardware and components of the most expensive and complex computers on the planet. And just like every other computer, the mind has to occasionally reboot itself for your software to run correctly. The mind has to log off sometimes to shut down all the other **applications,** programs, and thoughts that have been continuously running inside of our minds. And **to efficiently continue to move effectively in the present, takes leaving the things that are not effective from the past, in the past**. Listening to music that soothes you or music that takes you back to a more peaceful, happy time in your life, **even** for **only** a minute, can make all the problems of today go **away**.

Looking up at the stars on a clear calm night can help put things back into perspective, and you will see that the universe is greater than just what is in front of **us**.

You can build hope through watching your favorite movie or find **joy in discovering** your next favorite **place to visit**.

The smell of vanilla can calm you, while the warmth **and** tranquilities of a soothing bath can wash away the sorrows of this world. Even stepping out and enjoying the pleasure of a good meal can refresh your mind and give you the energy you need to continue the tasks at hand. The touch of a massage can heal you, even **if** it's not coming from a professional massage therapist or masseuse.

By just breaking away, if only for a moment, it can clear your mind, and **can** give you a whole new look on life. The world teaches us that our children come before anything else, but **the bible teaches us to put God first, our marriages, which include the people in it, second, and our children next. You are more important than what you do. And if we put our jobs and everything we do for everyone else first, it will often cause these things to be more important also. In addition, it can generate a flustered and troubled lifestyle and an unhappy marriage as well.**

God's greatest desire is to have a relationship with you, and even when we're too busy to think of Him, He is patient with us. Not knowing what it feels like to have a relationship with your Creator is the same as not knowing why you were created, and not knowing why you were created is the same as not producing the thoughts that it takes to understand why you exist.

Once upon a time when we were kids, we thought as kids, we knew what we wanted in life and what we wanted to do. As life moved on, it got more complicated, and as we matured, we started to lose the simple understandings we had when we weren't too conformed into this world. The power of our mind is controlled by our thoughts. Thoughts are what we are. It is why we like what we like and dislike what we dislike. Our thoughts control our actions, our perception, and our lives. You can only know what you know and what you think always starts with one singular thought.

Through the power of choice, we choose who to forgive, and we choose who to trust. Realization comes from what we know, and what we see comes from our point of view. Through our real-

ity, we can make new memories to replace old memories. And through the power of the mind, we can change what we remember mostly about anything and everything we know. A negative thought causes negative or complacent actions, and a positive thought always motivates and produces positive results. To say, "It's too late" is only a negative thought, or to say, "It can't be done" is merely a negative state of mind. There are positive and negative things that happen to all of us in our lives, but with an open mind, we can control how anything will affect us, and by that, we will gain control over how we choose to live.

Quote: "The most important person you will ever know is you!"

Knowing that every relationship is important, **but the people inside of the relationships we have are what matters the most,** will allow you to build **healthier and happier relationships** with everyone around you.

The most important lesson I could ever learn is that I am important. And the best way to find out life's true meaning is to know my actual purpose in life. That's why it's so essential for me to occasionally stop in the midst of everything else I am doing, and take time out, to "think of me."

Thoughts equal interest, and interest equals love. *You will not think* about something or someone you are not interested in, just *like you cannot* be interested in someone or something you never think about!

I hope you found joy and enlightenment from this book. Continue to read over the **teachings in these chapters** and study **God's message** as much as you need, to **get the understanding that you want to have.** Let's change the way we think **together** by changing our thoughts. And **together, let's change the world we live in, and our life in it, to an "A+" life, and our marriages to an "A+" marriage, one thought at a time!**

God bless!

Fasts and Exercises

Cleansing

Cleansing is a process or period of time designated to rinse away or clean out any impurities. It is designed to purify and wash away any toxins in the body, spirit, and mind. Your body is a temple, your spirit is its host, and the mind is what controls it. By cleansing out your body, you will rid your mind from the toxicities in its proximity. And by cleansing the mind from these infirmities, you will also cleanse the spirit from the iniquities of this world.

Ephesians 6:12

12 For we wrestle not against flesh and blood, but against principalities, against powers, against the rulers of the darkness of this world, against spiritual wickedness in high places.

Quote: "A fight isn't a fight unless we put up some resistance."

We are in spiritual warfare, and evil spirits are constantly attempting to control how we act, what we do, and what we think. By not having control over our thoughts, we are giving the evilness of this world the power to have control over our lives. And unless we cleanse our minds and bodies of the infestation that torments us, it will cause agony and suffering throughout our entire existence.

2 Corinthians 7:1

1 Having therefore these promises, dearly beloved, let us cleanse ourselves from all filthiness of the flesh and spirit, perfecting holiness in the fear of God.

Jesus was perfect and never sinned, and yet He died as a sinner for us, that we can be saved. By accepting His sacrifice, we are covered by His blood, and through His power, we are saved. And by God's mercy, we can cleanse our minds and bodies so we can return to developing into the person we were originally meant to be.

Cleansing Fast:

Duration: 10 Days (Beginner)
30 Days (Advance)

Time: 5 Minutes (Beginner)
10 Minutes (Advance)

Instructions: Take time out of our lives each day to pray to God, in the name of Jesus, to rebuke any wickedness or troubles that we face. Ask for His strength when you are too weak to deal with the sins and the evilness of this world. And pray that our Heavenly Father will cleanse your mind so you can clearly utilize your power of choice freely to make the decisions you choose to make.

Prayer is very similar to having a conversation with God, but it is also reverenced as a form of worship. Through prayer, you can give Jehovah praise for what He's done and who He is in your life. And also, through prayer, it can be a time set aside to surrender yourself to Him.

In times of despair, we must call on someone who is greater than us for help. Through the power of God, our bodies can be cleansed of all the infirmities and evilness that exist in the world today. I ask that you keep the faith and be fervent in your prayers to allow Yahweh to move through you and work with you as you take this journey through life.

Objective: Cleanse our minds, bodies, and soul of the impurities of all forms of negative energy affecting our lives. Create a more purposeful life, guided by our Heavenly Father, in the way that He designed for it to be. God doesn't force us to make certain choices, but He gives us free will, not only to ask for His help but also to allow Him to be part of our lives. Evilness and good cannot occupy the same space. And through this fast, we will remove sin so that the grace and Spirit of God can move in us.

In this fast, you may include adding any obstructions from certain foods, narcotics, and alcohol to increase the effects this spiritual fast has on you. Keep in mind, this is an advanced level, which will make it harder to accomplish. It will take more discipline and a stronger mind to complete. But the greater the sacrifice and the effort to achieve, the greater the reward and the satisfaction will be obtained once this fast is completed.

Purpose: To overcome any evil influences, negative thoughts, and struggles that we face in our lives. To provide a time to seek God for His protection and His counsel in our lives. It is also a moment created to give praise and thanks to God for what He has already done, and it is a moment to honor and recognize Him through prayer. By creating an opportunity to seek His counsel, it also allows us to find the answers to the problems we face. With so much going on around us, even the best of us sometimes fail to remember that our purpose for living is the same purpose for why we are created. This fast serves as a reminder that only through God's purpose, will we ever have true value in life.

Stipulations: An outline of your fast is needed to give details of your course of action if something happens or doesn't happen.

🍃 Example: If I break my fast, I would either start over or add a certain amount of time.

State any preconditions or requests.

🍃 Example: Controlling my thoughts is hard, so I will only be required to do my best to complete this fast. Or this is a busy time for me, so I want to oppose lenience of missing one or two days of completing my fast.

State if there are going to be any other fasts that are going to be combined with the fast you've chosen. And if so, specify when any other fasts will be added to the original fast you've selected.

🍃 Example: I will include the Positivity Fast when I'm half-way through with the Negativity Fast I've selected.

Compiling two complimentary fasts together will significantly increase your results. And combining two complimentary fasts together will also improve your performance during the original fast.

🍃 Example: Adding the Meditation Fast to any of the other fasts will reveal your thoughts to help you complete the original fast of your choice more efficiently.

Recommendation: It is highly recommended that you think over these terms and conditions in prayer before accepting a fast. It is also recommended that you communicate to Yahweh the reason why you chose to fast.

🍃 Example: Spiritual growth, favor, insight, healing, etc.

It is important to know that fasting is a sacred act, and it must be sincerely done with the utmost respect. Fasting is not designed for vain reasons, and it is not meant for obtaining any form of selfish gain. It is for physical and spiritual growth and serves to offer up a pure sacrifice to God. It has the power to restore your spirit, and through the sacrifices you make, it has been known to even move the heart of our Heavenly Father through this act of faith.

Ecclesiastes 5:4-5

4 When thou vowest a vow unto God, defer not to pay it; for he hath no pleasure in fools: pay that which thou hast vowed.

5 Better is it that thou shouldest not vow, than that thou shouldest vow and not pay.

It is highly recommended to ask God for His guidance in deciding if you are mentally and spiritually ready to offer this sacrifice. Also, pray to God for His acceptance and His blessing as you go on this journey.

My prayer is that God will give you the strength, motivation, and focus to get through the fast you've selected.

God bless!

Communication

Communication is the act of exchanging information between individuals. To communicate verbally only takes one person to speak, but requires all persons involved to listen. A lack of communication often consists of a failure to talk or listen to someone clearly. And failing to have an effective conversation with someone can not only prevent you from having a productive relationship with the person you wish to know, but it can also even prevent you from forming a relationship with God.

> **Matthew 7:21-23**
> **21** Not every one that saith unto me, Lord, Lord, shall enter into the kingdom of heaven; but he that doeth the will of my Father which is in heaven.
> **22** Many will say to me in that day, Lord, Lord, have we not prophesied in thy name? and in thy name have cast out devils? and in thy name done many wonderful works?
> **23** And then will I profess unto them, I never knew you: depart from me, ye that work iniquity.

A significant line of communication is developed through the act of transferring information clearly and truthfully, and it must be heard with open-mindedness to completely receive all of the information given. If one part doesn't exist, it cannot be classified as an effective line of communication, and communicating ineffectively can be the one difference between being saved and unsaved.

> *Quote:* "Having a conversation is the act of transferring the knowledge of existence to someone else. And acknowledging someone else's existence is the most significant sign of communicating effectively."

Having a conversation is the act of exchanging information, and exchanging information is the process of getting to know someone. It is an experience shared amongst two or more individuals, and it is the pathway to establishing a unity that builds a relationship with God.

Communication Fast:

Duration: 10 Days (Beginner)
30 Days (Advance)

Time: 5 Minutes (Beginner)
10 Minutes (Advance)

Instructions: Take time out each day to have a conversation with God. The time designated to have a conversation can be during any part of the day you choose. And the designated time can even be changed at your discretion, as long as the time allotted is continuous with little to no interruptions. Since God knows everything, this can be a time spent with our Heavenly Father, to be vulnerable and open to communicate without having to hold back the way you genuinely feel. The more open and truthful you become, the greater the reward will be. And the more time shared with our Father, the more it will build a stronger line of communication and a stronger relationship with Him.

There should be measures set in place to prevent any distractions. Things such as cell phones and electronics should be cut off or turned on silence as a token of respect. Traffic should be barred from coming in and out of your space in order to secure the intimacy level established through your connection with Jehovah. And taking notes and jotting down your thoughts throughout the day will help you remember the things you want to talk about with your Father.

Objective: To build and strengthen our relationship with God. Creating an opportunity to seek God's counsel and direction in our lives not only gives our Creator respect, but it also gives Him the honor to be held in high esteem in this regard. In time, our goal is to build a closer relationship with our Creator and to consider and seek His guidance more, concerning the choices we make.

Purpose: Break down the walls that keep us from effectively communicating our thoughts and feelings to our Creator. Life gets so busy at times that we forget to take out time to think of what is most important in our lives. "Our thoughts are our reality," and not thinking of what is important to us is like making it seem as if what really matters in our lives doesn't really matter that much. This can also cause God's presence in our lives to not have any real influence in our lives at all. Thoughts are everything, and just setting a time out of your day to spend with your Heavenly Father will encourage you to acknowledge Him more and pursue His divine will in your life.

Stipulations: An outline of your fast is needed to give details of your course of action if something happens or doesn't happen.

🍃 Example: If I break my fast, I would either start over or add a certain amount of time.

State any preconditions or requests.

🍃 Example: Controlling my thoughts is hard, so I will only be required to do my best to complete this fast. Or this is a busy time for me, so I want to oppose lenience of missing one or two days of completing my fast.

State if there are going to be any other fasts that are going to be combined with the fast you've chosen. And if so, specify when any other fasts will be added to the original fast you've selected.

🍃 Example: I will include the Positivity Fast when I'm half-way through with the Negativity Fast I've selected.

Compiling two complimentary fasts together will significantly increase your results. And combining two complimentary fasts together will also improve your performance during the original fast.

🍃 Example: Adding the Meditation Fast to any of the other fasts will reveal your thoughts to help you complete the original fast of your choice more efficiently.

Recommendation: It is highly recommended that you think over these terms and conditions in prayer before accepting a fast. It is also recommended that you communicate to Yahweh the reason why you chose to fast.

🍃 Example: Spiritual growth, favor, insight, healing, etc.

It is important to know that fasting is a sacred act, and it must be sincerely done with the utmost respect. Fasting is not designed for vain reasons, and it is not meant for obtaining any form of selfish gain. It is for physical and spiritual growth and serves to offer up a pure sacrifice to God. It has the power to restore your spirit, and through the sacrifices you make, it has been known to even move the heart of our Heavenly Father through this act of faith.

> *Ecclesiastes 5:4-5*
> **4** When thou vowest a vow unto God, defer not to pay it; for he hath no pleasure in fools: pay that which thou hast vowed.
> **5** Better is it that thou shouldest not vow, than that thou shouldest vow and not pay.

It is highly recommended to ask God for His guidance in deciding if you are mentally and spiritually ready to offer this sacrifice. Also, pray to God for His acceptance and His blessing as you go on this journey.

My prayer is that God will give you the strength, motivation, and focus to get through the fast you've selected.

God bless!

Meditation

Meditation means to think, contemplate, devise, and ponder. It is practiced by directing the mind to be channeled on one singular thought, free from distractions. Similar to weightlifting, the mind is strengthened through meditative practices, and these practices are often exercised among many successful pioneers, business leaders, and spiritual leaders of the world today.

Psalm 19:14

14 Let the words of my mouth, and the meditation of my heart, be acceptable in thy sight, O Lord, my strength, and my redeemer.

There are so many objectives, demands, and influences occurring in our lives today that creates a disruption in our mental state of mind. Through meditative practices, you will be able to mentally be clear of those distractions in order to achieve an emotionally calm state of mind.

Quote: "Meditation empties the mind of its many thoughts so that the mind can have room to fill itself with mindful thinking."

Research shows that meditation has neurological, cardiovascular, and psychological health benefits. It may be used to reduce stress, anxiety, depression, and pain. Meditation will also increase and strengthen your utilization of peace, awareness, and self-concept.

Meditation Fast:

Duration: 10 Days (Beginner)
30 Days (Advance)

Time: 5 Minutes (Beginner)
10 Minutes (Advance)

Instruction: Focus your mind on one single thought or image of your choice and hold it there until every other thought is silenced. It may be hard at first to separate your mind from the numerous thoughts coming in and out of it. That's why it is essential to develop patience before you begin to meditate.

Expecting too much before you begin meditating can cause frustration and anxiety to develop. And if you cannot relax, it can cause it to be that much harder to focus. Meditative positions are not specified in this exercise. Still, it is important to know that comfort is essential when relaxation is required, and being too comfortable can cause you to fall asleep. If you are having trouble focusing, a good start will be to focus only on breathing, to isolate your thoughts. Your breathing levels should stay consistent, and your posture should alter no more than slightly as you meditate.

Your success depends on your state of mind, levels of stress, energy, and determination. The rewards can be great, and even though the results may take some time, the more you practice meditating, the greater the return will be!

Objective: To explore the mind through silence and discover our true thoughts on a deeper level. Or you can simply stay focused on nothing, causing your mind to enter into a relaxed environment and begin to regenerate in its silence. Becoming more aware of your thoughts and of the effects they have on you will allow you the opportunity to gain knowledge of how you became the person you are today.

Exploring your thoughts will allow you to change the way you think by simply changing the thoughts that are hidden in your subconscious mind. Being mindful of the way you think and your internal thoughts will also reveal the feelings you hold inside. And knowing how you feel inside will open you up to a better understanding of who you truly are.

Purpose: To train the mind to become more focused, aware, and resistant to unwanted thoughts. Meditation will reveal how busy the mind can get with the numerous thoughts, visions, sounds, images, and memories continuously flowing through it every day. Meditation can also serve as an excellent method to relieve anxiety, depression, and stress by locating any negative thoughts being stored privately in your head and relinquishing them away from your mind completely.

Stipulations: An outline of your fast is needed to give details of your course of action if something happens or doesn't happen.

🍂 Example: If I break my fast, I would either start over or add a certain amount of time.

State any preconditions or requests.

🍂 Example: Controlling my thoughts is hard, so I will only be required to do my best to complete this fast. Or, this is a busy time for me, so I want to oppose lenience of missing one or two days of completing my fast.

State if there are going to be any other fasts that are going to be combined with the fast you've chosen. And if so, specify when any other fasts will be added to the original fast you've selected.

🍂 Example: I will include the Positivity Fast when I'm half-way through with the Negativity Fast I've selected.

Compiling two complimentary fasts together will significantly increase your results. And combining two complimentary fasts together will also improve your performance during the original fast.

🍂 Example: Adding the Meditation Fast to any of the other fasts will reveal your thoughts to help you complete the original fast of your choice more efficiently.

Recommendation: It is highly recommended that you think over these terms and conditions in prayer before accepting a fast. It is also recommended that you communicate to Yahweh the reason why you chose to fast.

Example: Spiritual growth, favor, insight, healing, etc.

It is important to know that fasting is a sacred act, and it must be sincerely done with the utmost respect. Fasting is not designed for vain reasons, and it is not meant for obtaining any form of selfish gain. It is for physical and spiritual growth and serves to offer up a pure sacrifice to God. It has the power to restore your spirit, and through the sacrifices you make, it has been known to even move the heart of our Heavenly Father through this act of faith.

> *Ecclesiastes 5:4-5*
> **4** When thou vowest a vow unto God, defer not to pay it; for he hath no pleasure in fools: pay that which thou hast vowed.
> **5** Better is it that thou shouldest not vow, than that thou shouldest vow and not pay.

It is highly recommended to ask God for His guidance in deciding if you are mentally and spiritually ready to offer this sacrifice. Also, pray to God for His acceptance and His blessing as you go on this journey.

My prayer is that God will give you the strength, motivation, and focus to get through the fast you've selected.

God bless!

Negativity

Negative thoughts are thoughts that are damaging, harmful, dismissive, unsupportive, and uncertain. They will always shine a light on the worst of every situation, and they will reveal the mistakes people make without resolution. It opposes positivity, enthusiasm, and optimism. You are what you think, and your thoughts make up the reality that you live in. Negative thoughts are designed to be argumentative, discouraging, and bestow destruction to not only the thinker but to anyone and anything negative thoughts are subject to.

> **Mark 7:20-23**
> **20** And he said, That which cometh out of the man, that defileth the man.
> **21** For from within, out of the heart of men, proceed evil thoughts, adulteries, fornications, murders,
> **22** Thefts, covetousness, wickedness, deceit, lasciviousness, an evil eye, blasphemy, pride, foolishness:
> **23** All these evil things come from within, and defile the man.

Reality is what you know, and what you know absolutely comes from what you think of. Memories are nothing more than past thoughts, and if these thoughts are negative, they can easily sway you into thinking something or someone is worse than what they actually are. If they are not controlled, negative thoughts will consume you, and in doing so, it will create a negative state of mind. And everything and everyone around you will be subject to its effects.

> *Quote:* "You reap what you sow, and if negativity is what you sow, its effects will not only affect what is thought of, it will also have a negative impact on you as well."

256

Negative thoughts can change the perception of how you look at someone or something, and consistently having these negative thoughts can ultimately change the way you feel about everything. Peace cannot coexist within a negative state of mind, and developing negative thoughts will cause disruption and chaos in the lives of whom it exists. If negativity continues to take place in your life, it can not only cause you to think negatively; it can also cause you and your entire life to be negative as a whole.

Negative Fast:

Duration: 10 Days (Beginner)
30 Days (Advance)

Instructions: Hinder and reject any and all forms of negative thinking throughout the duration of the fast. It can be hard to control the way we think, and without having experienced it yet, it can seem nearly impossible to take control of our thoughts as well. It takes a tremendous amount of practice and self-awareness to address how you feel, and it takes a much greater effort and determination to try to change the way you think. That's why it requires a tremendous amount of patience to complete this fast because you not only have to control what you think, you have to gain control over how you think also.

The Negativity Fast is not subject to take on the same instructions and requirements as the Positivity Fast. As humans, we are inherently negative thinkers, and by dividing the two fasts apart, it will allow you to focus only on one fast while taking away the added pressure of having to address multiple thoughts all at once.

Objective: Eliminate the effects of negative thoughts. For the duration of the fast, you will not entertain nor engage in any negative interactions or have any negative feelings about anyone or anything. It is practically impossible to totally stop every single negative thought from happening, but what you do after a negative thought is created is what will establish the difference between having a negative thought and being a negative thinker.

One negative thought doesn't make you a negative person, and having multiple negative thoughts doesn't make you a negative thinker. Entertaining these thoughts and letting them change the way that you feel is what makes you a negative person. But by rejecting to listen or engage in the negative thoughts you think, or by changing how you think altogether, is what will keep a negative thought from being a negative way of thinking.

Example: Saying fixed statements like, "this always," "I will never," or referring to things like they will never change are all classic instances of negative thinking. By changing these statements into thoughts that ushers in a possibility of change can take away any blame and, instead, look at a negative incident only as something that just needs to be addressed.

For beginners, you may choose specific things or certain people to refrain from thinking negatively towards. It will reduce the pressure of eliminating all negative thoughts, while still allowing you the opportunity to compare the normal way you think to the way you think outside of thinking negatively.

Purpose: To reveal the effects of having a negative state of mind. By experiencing the difference of what your life was like with negative thoughts and what life is like without the influences of negative thinking may encourage you to reduce the number of negative thoughts you have. Ultimately, by creating a clear concept of life and creating an accurate perception of the world around you and the people in it, you will see that it will leave you with no time to live a productive and peaceful life and also entertain negative thoughts.

Thoughts are everything, and ultimately you will see how your thoughts play a vital role in how you feel about a specific person or in everything in general. And one day, you will realize that your thoughts have always been the most decisive factor in how you've felt about everything and everyone throughout your entire life!

Stipulations: An outline of your fast is needed to give details of your course of action if something happens or doesn't happen.

🍃 Example: If I break my fast, I would either start over or add a certain amount of time.

State any preconditions or requests.

🍃 Example: Controlling my thoughts is hard, so I will only be required to do my best to complete this fast. Or this is a busy time for me, so I want to oppose lenience of missing one or two days of completing my fast.

State if there are going to be any other fasts that are going to be combined with the fast you've chosen. And if so, specify when any other fasts will be added to the original fast you've selected.

🍃 Example: I will include the Positivity Fast when I'm half-way through with the Negativity Fast I've selected.

Compiling two complimentary fasts together will significantly increase your results. And combining two complimentary fasts together will also improve your performance during the original fast.

🍃 Example: Adding the Meditation Fast to any of the other fasts will reveal your thoughts to help you complete the original fast of your choice more efficiently.

Recommendation: It is highly recommended that you think over these terms and conditions in prayer before accepting a fast. It is also recommended that you communicate to Yahweh the reason why you chose to fast.

🍃 Example: Spiritual growth, favor, insight, healing, etc.

It is important to know that fasting is a sacred act, and it must be sincerely done with the utmost respect. Fasting is not designed for vain reasons, and it is not meant for obtaining any form of selfish gain. It is for physical and spiritual growth and serves to offer up a pure sacrifice to God. It has the power to restore your spirit, and through the sacrifices you make, it has been known to even move the heart of our Heavenly Father through this act of faith.

Ecclesiastes 5:4-5
>   4 When thou vowest a vow unto God, defer
> not to pay it; for he hath no pleasure in fools: pay
> that which thou hast vowed.
>   5 Better is it that thou shouldest not vow,
> than that thou shouldest vow and not pay.

It is highly recommended to ask God for His guidance in deciding if you are mentally and spiritually ready to offer this sacrifice. Also, pray to God for His acceptance and His blessing as you go on this journey.

My prayer is that God will give you the strength, motivation, and focus to get through the fast you've selected.

God bless!

Positivity

Positive thoughts are thoughts that are good, affirmative, encouraging, supporting, and reassuring. They will always reveal the good in every situation and always bring out the best in people. It creates an enthusiastic and energetic atmosphere that can light up the world, and it always reveals the most optimistic approach to happiness. You are what you think, and your thoughts make up the reality you live in. Thinking positive motivates, inspires, and always generates a constructive environment by forming a winning attitude!

> **Philippians 4:8-9**
> **8** Finally, brethren, whatsoever things are true, whatsoever things are honest, whatsoever things are just, whatsoever things are pure, whatsoever things are lovely, whatsoever things are of good report; if there be any virtue, and if there be any praise, think on these things.
> **9** Those things, which ye have both learned, and received, and heard, and seen in me, do: and the God of peace shall be with you.

Thinking positive gives its beholder a hopeful view of the life they live and the world around them. Having a positive mind-set also provides a positive perception of the history of your life up to now. It provides a positive outlook on your present circumstances and in your future as well. A positive personality is productive, and it has an attractive presence that draws all walks of life to it. That is why it is the most desired natural attribute known to humans because it is one of the few things that distinguishes humanity from every other living thing on the face of the planet.

> *Quote:* "Blessed are positive thinkers because they will have a positive influence on everything and everyone around them."

Positive thoughts can change the perception of how you look at someone or something, and that will ultimately change the way you feel about everything. Peace can exist within a positive state of mind, and developing positive thoughts will cause cohesiveness and harmony in the lives of whom it exists.

Positive Fast:

Duration: 10 Days (Beginner)
30 Days (Advance)

Instructions: Hinder and reject any and all forms of negative thinking and replace it with positive thoughts throughout the duration of the fast. It can be hard to control the way we think, and without having fully experienced control over what you think, it can seem nearly impossible to obtain control over how you think.

Doing the Negativity Fast first, before accepting the Positive Fast, will give you an advantage to controlling the way you think. It takes a lot of practice and self-awareness to address how you feel, and it takes a much greater effort to try to take control of the thoughts and ideas you have. That's why it takes a tremendous amount of patience and determination in order to complete this fast. Not only do you have to eventually create a positive mindset, you also have to limit any negative thoughts from taking over the way that you think.

As humans, we are inherently negative thinkers. By dividing the Negativity Fast and the Positivity Fast apart, it will be easier to do one fast rather than combining two fasts together. When we are strong enough to complete both fasts at the same time, we will truly experience how it feels to be entirely positive. Once you gain control over how you think and what you think, you will be so much closer to fully taking control over who you are as well.

Objective: Experience the natural effects of thinking positive. You must limit the number of negative thoughts you have during this fast. If negative thoughts are consistently occurring and become uncontrollable, try looking at things from the other person's point of view to gain another perspective. Once it's accomplished, take it one step further during the Positive Fast, and make a positive effort to make things better.

🍃 Example: Giving someone the benefit of the doubt or having thoughts that cause positive effects instead of negative ramifications will all be instances of thinking positive. Often, the people around us or the things that we are involved with can cause our feelings to get hurt or cause us to be upset. Retaliation is the most common reaction. But if we can change a vengeance into becoming an opportunity to learn something new, or if we can use it as a reason to try to understand someone better, we will have what it takes to change any negative idea into a positive state of mind.

For beginners, you may choose only to select one thing or one person to use in this fast. It will allow you to see the power of positive thoughts without having the pressure of thinking positive towards everything and everyone all at once.

Purpose: Reveal how thinking positively motivates you and influences the people around you. By creating a positive atmosphere in this exercise, it will reveal the difference between what your life was like without thinking positive and what your life is like when you have a positive outlook on life. Ultimately, by creating a clear concept of life and creating an accurate perception of the world around you and the people in it, you will see that thinking positive is the key to a productive and peaceful life.

Thoughts are everything, and ultimately you will see how your thoughts play a vital role in how you feel about a specific person or about everything in general. And one day, you will realize that your thoughts have always been the most decisive factor in how you've felt about everything and everyone throughout your entire life!

Stipulations: An outline of your fast is needed to give details of your course of action if something happens or doesn't happen.

🍃 Example: If I break my fast, I would either start over or add a certain amount of time.

State any preconditions or requests.

🍃 Example: Controlling my thoughts is hard, so I will only be required to do my best to complete this fast. Or this is a busy time for me, so I want to oppose lenience of missing one or two days of completing my fast.

State if there are going to be any other fasts that are going to be combined with the fast you've chosen. And if so, specify when any other fasts will be added to the original fast you've selected.

🍃 Example: I will include the Positivity Fast when I'm half-way through with the Negativity Fast I've selected.

Compiling two complimentary fasts together will significantly increase your results. And combining two complimentary fasts together will also improve your performance during the original fast.

🍃 Example: Adding the Meditation Fast to any of the other fasts will reveal your thoughts to help you complete the original fast of your choice more efficiently.

Recommendation: It is highly recommended that you think over these terms and conditions in prayer before accepting a fast. It is also recommended that you communicate to Yahweh the reason why you chose to fast.

🍃 Example: Spiritual growth, favor, insight, healing, etc.

It is important to know that fasting is a sacred act, and it must be sincerely done with the utmost respect. Fasting is not designed for vain reasons, and it is not meant for obtaining any form of selfish gain. It is for physical and spiritual growth and serves to offer up a pure sacrifice to God. It has the power to restore your spirit, and through the sacrifices you make, it has been known to even move the heart of our Heavenly Father through this act of faith.

Ecclesiastes 5:4-5

4 When thou vowest a vow unto God, defer not to pay it; for he hath no pleasure in fools: pay that which thou hast vowed.

5 Better is it that thou shouldest not vow, than that thou shouldest vow and not pay.

It is highly recommended to ask God for His guidance in deciding if you are mentally and spiritually ready to offer this sacrifice. Also, pray to God for His acceptance and His blessing as you go on this journey.

My prayer is that God will give you the strength, motivation, and focus to get through the fast you've selected.

God bless!

Genesis 1:26–27

26 And God said, Let us make man in our image, after our likeness: and let them have dominion over the fish of the sea, and over the fowl of the air, and over the cattle, and over all the earth, and over every creeping thing that creepeth upon the earth.

27 So God created man in his own image, in the image of God created he him; male and female created he them. (Genesis 1:26–27)

Genesis 2:7

And the LORD God formed man of the dust of the ground, and breathed into his nostrils the breath of life, and man became a living soul. (Genesis 2:7)

Genesis 2:19

19 And out of the ground the LORD God formed every beast of the field and every fowl of the air; and brought them unto Adam to see what he would call them: and whatsoever Adam called every living creature, that was the name thereof. (Genesis 2:19)

Genesis 3:1–6

3 Now the serpent was more subtil than any beast of the field which the LORD God had made. And he said unto the woman, Yea, hath God said, Ye shall not eat of every tree of the garden?

2 And the woman said unto the serpent, We may eat of the fruit of the trees of the garden:

3 But of the fruit of the tree which is in the midst of the garden, God hath said, Ye shall not eat of it, neither shall ye touch it, lest ye die.

⁴ And the serpent said unto the woman, Ye shall not surely die:

⁵ For God doth know that in the day ye eat thereof, then your eyes shall be

opened, and ye shall be as gods, knowing good and evil.

⁶ And when the woman saw that the tree was good for food, and that it was pleasant to the eyes, and a tree to be desired to make one wise, she took of the fruit thereof, and did eat, and gave also unto her husband with her; and he did eat. (Genesis 3:1–6)

Genesis 3:21–23

²¹ Unto Adam also and to his wife did the LORD God make coats of skins, and clothed them.

²² And the LORD God said, Behold, the man is become as one of us, to know good and evil: and now, lest he put forth his hand, and take also of the tree of life, and eat, and live for ever:

²³ Therefore the LORD God sent him forth from the garden of Eden, to till the ground from whence he was taken. (Genesis 3:21–23)

Deuteronomy 30:15–19

¹⁵ See, I have set before thee this day life and good, and death and evil;

¹⁶ In that I command thee this day to love the LORD thy God, to walk in his ways, and to keep his commandments and his statutes and his judgments, that thou mayest live and multiply: and the LORD thy God shall bless thee in the land whither thou goest to possess it.

¹⁷ But if thine heart turn away, so that thou wilt not hear, but shalt be drawn away, and worship other gods, and serve them;

¹⁸ I denounce unto you this day, that ye shall surely perish, and that ye shall not prolong your days upon the land, whither thou passest over Jordan to go to possess it.

¹⁹ I call heaven and earth to record this day against you, that I have set before you life and death, blessing and cursing: therefore choose life, that both thou and thy seed may live. (Deuteronomy 30:15–19)

2 Samuel 12:16–20

¹⁶ David therefore besought God for the child; and David fasted, and went in, and

lay all night upon the earth.

¹⁷ And the elders of his house arose, and went to him, to raise him up from the earth: but he would not, neither did he eat bread with them.

¹⁸ And it came to pass on the seventh day, that the child died. And the servants of David feared to tell him that the child was dead: for they said, Behold, while the child was yet alive, we spake unto him, and he would not hearken unto our voice: how will he then vex himself, if we tell him that the child is dead?

¹⁹ But when David saw that his servants whispered, David perceived that the child was dead: therefore David said unto his servants, Is the child dead? And they said, He is dead.

²⁰ Then David arose from the earth, and washed, and anointed himself, and changed his apparel, and came into the house of the LORD, and worshipped: then he came to his own house;

and when he required, they set bread before him, and he did eat. 2 (Samuel 12:16–20)

1 Samuel 16:23

23 And it came to pass, when the evil spirit from God was upon Saul, that David took an harp, and played with his hand: so Saul was refreshed, and was well, and the evil spirit departed from him. (1 Samuel 16:23)

Job 38:1–18 New King James Version (NKJV)

38 Then the LORD answered Job out of the whirlwind, and said:

2 "Who *is* this who darkens counsel By words without knowledge?

3 Now prepare yourself like a man; I will question you, and you shall answer Me.

4 "Where were you when I laid the foundations of the earth? Tell *Me,* if you have understanding.

5 Who determined its measurements? Surely you know! Or who stretched the line upon it?

6 To what were its foundations fastened? Or who laid its cornerstone,

7 When the morning stars sang together, And all the sons of God shouted for joy?

8 "Or *who* shut in the sea with doors, When it burst forth *and* issued from the womb;

9 When I made the clouds its garment, And thick darkness its swaddling band;

10 When I fixed My limit for it, 1253 And set bars and doors;

11 When I said, 'This far you may come, but no farther, And here your proud waves must stop!'

¹² "Have you commanded the morning since your days *began, And* caused the dawn to know its place,

¹³ That it might take hold of the ends of the earth, And the wicked be shaken out of it?

¹⁴ It takes on form like clay *under* a seal, And stands out like a garment.

¹⁵ From the wicked their light is withheld, And the upraised arm is broken.

¹⁶ "Have you entered the springs of the sea? Or have you walked in search of the depths?

¹⁷ Have the gates of death been revealed to you? Or have you seen the doors of the shadow of death?

¹⁸ Have you comprehended the breadth of the earth? Tell *Me,* if you know all this.

(Job 38:1–18, New King James Version - NKJV)

Psalms 139:14 I will praise thee; for I am fearfully and wonderfully made: marvelous are thy works; and that my soul knoweth right well. (Psalms 139:14)

Proverbs 1:20–22

²⁰ Wisdom crieth without; she uttereth her voice in the streets:

²¹ She crieth in the chief place of concourse, in the openings of the gates: in the city she uttereth her words, saying,

²² How long, ye simple ones, will ye love simplicity? and the scorners delight in their scorning, and fools hate knowledge? (Proverbs 1:20–22)

Proverbs 1:23–28

²³ Turn you at my reproof: behold, I will pour out my spirit unto you, I will make known my words unto you.

²⁴ Because I have called, and ye refused; I have stretched out my hand, and no man regarded;

²⁵ But ye have set at nought all my counsel, and would none of my reproof:

²⁶ I also will laugh at your calamity; I will mock when your fear cometh;

²⁷ When your fear cometh as desolation, and your destruction cometh as a whirlwind; when distress and anguish cometh upon you.

²⁸ Then shall they call upon me, but I will not answer; they shall seek me early, but they shall not find me. (Proverbs 1:23–28)

Proverbs 3:5–6

⁵ Trust in the LORD with all thine heart; and lean not unto thine own understanding.

⁶ In all thy ways acknowledge him, and he shall direct thy paths. (Proverbs 3:5–6)

Proverbs 6:6–11

⁶ Go to the ant, thou sluggard; consider her ways, and be wise:

⁷ Which having no guide, overseer, or ruler,

⁸ Provideth her meat in the summer, and gathereth her food in the harvest.

⁹ How long wilt thou sleep, O sluggard? when wilt thou arise out of thy sleep?

¹⁰ Yet a little sleep, a little slumber, a little folding of the hands to sleep:

[11] So shall thy poverty come as one that trav-elleth, and thy want as an armed man. (Proverbs 6:6–11)

Proverbs 13:12
[12] Hope deferred maketh the heart sick: but when the desire cometh, it is a tree of life. (Proverbs 13:12)

Proverbs 15:13
[13] A merry heart maketh a cheerful coun-tenance: but by sorrow of the heart the spirit is broken. (Proverbs 15:13)

Proverbs 16:18–19
[18] Pride goeth before destruction, and an haughty spirit before a fall.
[19] Better it is to be of an humble spirit with the lowly, than to divide the spoil with the proud. (Proverbs 16:18–19)

Proverbs 16:32
[32] He that is slow to anger is better than the mighty; and he that ruleth his spirit than he that taketh a city. (Proverbs 16:32)

Proverbs 17:22
[22] A merry heart doeth good like a medicine: but a broken spirit drieth the bones. (Proverbs 17:22)

Proverbs 22:6
Train up a child in the way he should go: and when he is old, he will not depart from it. (Proverbs 22:6)

Proverbs 22:24–25

24 Make no friendship with an angry man; and with a furious man thou shalt not go:

25 Lest thou learn his ways, and get a snare to thy soul. (Proverbs 22:24–25)

Proverbs 25:28

28 He that hath no rule over his own spirit is like a city that is broken down, and without walls. (Proverbs 25:28)

Proverbs 29:18

18 Where there is no vision, the people perish: but he that keepeth the law, happy is he. (Proverbs 29:18)

Ecclesiastes 2:24

24 There is nothing better for a man, than that he should eat and drink, and that he should make his soul enjoy good in his labor. This also I saw, that it was from the hand of God. (Ecclesiastes 2:24)

Ecclesiastes 3:1–8

1 To every thing there is a season, and a time to every purpose under the heaven:

2 A time to be born, and a time to die; a time to plant, and a time to pluck up that which is planted;

3 A time to kill, and a time to heal; a time to break down, and a time to build up;

4 A time to weep, and a time to laugh; a time to mourn, and a time to dance;

5 A time to cast away stones, and a time to gather stones together; a time to embrace, and a time to refrain from embracing;

⁶ A time to get, and a time to lose; a time to keep, and a time to cast away;

⁷ A time to rend, and a time to sew; a time to keep silence, and a time to speak;

⁸ A time to love, and a time to hate; a time of war, and a time of peace. (Ecclesiastes 3:1–8)

Isaiah 43:18–19

¹⁸ Remember ye not the former things, neither consider the things of old.

¹⁹ Behold, I will do a new thing; now it shall spring forth; shall ye not know it? I will even make a way in the wilderness, and rivers in the desert. (Isaiah 43:18–19)

Jeremiah 17:7–8 New International Version

⁷ "But blessed is the one who trusts in the LORD, whose confidence is in him.

⁸ They will be like a tree planted by the water that sends out its roots by the stream. It does not fear when heat comes; its leaves are always green. It has no worries in a year of drought and never fails to bear fruit." Jeremiah 17:7–8 (NIV)

Zechariah 7:13–14

¹³ Therefore it is come to pass, that as he cried, and they would not hear; so they cried, and I would not hear, saith the LORD of hosts:

¹⁴ But I scattered them with a whirlwind among all the nations whom they knew not. Thus the land was desolate after them, that no man passed through nor returned: for they laid the pleasant land desolate. (Zechariah 7:13–14)

Matthew 4:5–7

⁵ Then the devil taketh him up into the holy city, and setteth him on a pinnacle of the temple,

⁶ And saith unto him, If thou be the Son of God, cast thyself down: for it is written, He shall give his angels charge concerning thee: and in their hands they shall bear thee up, lest at any time thou dash thy foot against a stone.

⁷ Jesus said unto him, It is written again, Thou shalt not tempt the Lord thy God. (Matthew 4:5–7)

Matthew 5:13–16

¹³ Ye are the salt of the earth: but if the salt have lost his savor, wherewith shall it be salted? it is thenceforth good for nothing, but to be cast out, and to be trodden under foot of men.

¹⁴ Ye are the light of the world. A city that is set on an hill cannot be hid.

¹⁵ Neither do men light a candle, and put it under a bushel, but on a candlestick; and it giveth light unto all that are in the house.

¹⁶ Let your light so shine before men, that they may see your good works, and glorify your Father which is in heaven. (Matthew 5:13–16)

Matthew 5:43–45

⁴³ Ye have heard that it hath been said, Thou shalt love thy neighbour, and hate thine enemy.

⁴⁴ But I say unto you, Love your enemies, bless them that curse you, do good to them that hate you, and pray for them which despitefully use you, and persecute you;

⁴⁵ That ye may be the children of your Father which is in heaven: for he maketh his sun to rise

on the evil and on the good, and sendeth rain on the just and on the unjust. (Matthew 5:43–45)

Matthew 6:22–23

22 The light of the body is the eye: if therefore thine eye be single, thy whole body shall be full of light.

23 But if thine eye be evil, thy whole body shall be full of darkness. If therefore the light that is in thee be darkness, how great is that darkness! (Matthew 6:22–23)

Matthew 7:6

6 Give not that which is holy unto the dogs, neither cast ye your pearls before swine, lest they trample them under their feet, and turn again and rend you. (Matthew 7:6)

Matthew 7:15–20

15 Beware of false prophets, which come to you in sheep's clothing, but inwardly they are ravening wolves.

16 Ye shall know them by their fruits. Do men gather grapes of thorns, or figs of thistles?

17 Even so every good tree bringeth forth good fruit; but a corrupt tree bringeth forth evil fruit.

18 A good tree cannot bring forth evil fruit, neither can a corrupt tree bring forth good fruit.

19 Every tree that bringeth not forth good fruit is hewn down, and cast into the fire.

20 Wherefore by their fruits ye shall know them. (Matthew 7:15–20)

Matthew 10:32–33

32 Whosoever therefore shall confess me before men, him will I confess also before my Father which is in heaven.

33 But whosoever shall deny me before men, him will I also deny before my Father which is in heaven. (Matthew 10:32–33)

Matthew 10:39

39 He that findeth his life shall lose it: and he that loseth his life for my sake shall find it. (Matthew 10:39)

Matthew 11:28–30

28 Come unto me, all ye that labour and are heavy laden, and I will give you rest.

29 Take my yoke upon you, and learn of me; for I am meek and lowly in heart: and ye shall find rest unto your souls.

30 For my yoke is easy, and my burden is light. (Matthew 11:28–30)

Matthew 14:28–31

28 And Peter answered him and said, Lord, if it be thou, bid me come unto thee on the water.

29 And he said, Come. And when Peter was come down out of the ship, he walked on the water, to go to Jesus.

30 But when he saw the wind boisterous, he was afraid; and beginning to sink, he cried, saying, Lord, save me.

31 And immediately Jesus stretched forth his hand, and caught him, and said unto him, O thou of little faith, wherefore didst thou doubt? (Matthew 14:28–31)

Matthew 16:22–23

²² Then Peter took him, and began to rebuke him, saying, Be it far from thee, Lord: this shall not be unto thee.

²³ But he turned, and said unto Peter, Get thee behind me, Satan: thou art an offence unto me: for thou savourest not the things that be of God, but those that be of men. (Matthew 16:22–23)

Matthew 18:2–4

² And Jesus called a little child unto him, and set him in the midst of them,

³ And said, Verily I say unto you, Except ye be converted, and become as little children, ye shall not enter into the kingdom of heaven.

⁴ Whosoever therefore shall humble himself as this little child, the same is greatest in the kingdom of heaven. (Matthew 18:2–4)

Matthew 18:21–22

²¹ Then came Peter to him, and said, Lord, how oft shall my brother sin against me, and I forgive him? till seven times?

²² Jesus saith unto him, I say not unto thee, Until seven times: but, Until seventy times seven. (Matthew 18:21–22)

Matthew 21:12–13

¹² And Jesus went into the temple of God, and cast out all them that sold and bought in the temple, and overthrew the tables of the money-changers, and the seats of them that sold doves,

¹³ And said unto them, It is written, My house shall be called the house of prayer; but

ye have made it a den of thieves. (Matthew 21:12–13)

Matthew 25:40

40 And the King shall answer and say unto them, Verily I say unto you, Inasmuch as ye have done it unto one of the least of these my brethren, ye have done it unto me. (Matthew 25:40)

Matthew 27:3–5

3 Then Judas, which had betrayed him, when he saw that he was condemned, repented himself, and brought again the thirty pieces of silver to the chief priests and elders,

4 Saying, I have sinned in that I have betrayed the innocent blood. And they said, What is that to us? see thou to that.

5 And he cast down the pieces of silver in the temple, and departed, and went and hanged himself. (Matthew 27:3–5)

Mark 8:36–38

36 For what shall it profit a man, if he shall gain the whole world, and lose his own soul?

37 Or what shall a man give in exchange for his soul?

38 Whosoever therefore shall be ashamed of me and of my words in this adulterous and sinful generation; of him also shall the Son of man be ashamed, when he cometh in the glory of his Father with the holy angels. (Mark 8:36–38)

Luke 6:37

37 Judge not, and ye shall not be judged: condemn not, and ye shall not be condemned: forgive, and ye shall be forgiven. (Luke 6:37)

Luke 7:19

¹⁹ And John calling unto him two of his disciples sent them to Jesus, saying, Art thou he that should come? or look we for another? (Luke 7:19)

Luke 10:38–42

³⁸ Now it came to pass, as they went, that he entered into a certain village: and a certain woman named Martha received him into her house.

³⁹ And she had a sister called Mary, which also sat at Jesus' feet, and heard his word.

⁴⁰ But Martha was cumbered about much serving, and came to him, and said, Lord, dost thou not care that my sister hath left me to serve alone? bid her therefore that she help me.

⁴¹ And Jesus answered and said unto her, Martha, Martha, thou art careful and troubled about many things:

⁴² But one thing is needful: and Mary hath chosen that good part, which shall not be taken away from her. (Luke 10:38–42)

Luke 13:6–7

⁶ He spake also this parable; A certain man had a fig tree planted in his vineyard; and

he came and sought fruit thereon, and found none.

⁷ Then said he unto the dresser of his vineyard, Behold, these three years I come seeking fruit on this fig tree, and find none: cut it down; why cumbereth it the ground? (Luke 13:6–7)

John 1:1–9

[1] In the beginning was the Word, and the Word was with God, and the Word was God.

[2] The same was in the beginning with God.

[3] All things were made by him; and without him was not any thing made that was made.

[4] In him was life; and the life was the light of men.

[5] And the light shineth in darkness; and the darkness comprehended it not.

[6] There was a man sent from God, whose name was John.

[7] The same came for a witness, to bear witness of the Light, that all men through him might believe.

[8] He was not that Light, but was sent to bear witness of that Light.

[9] That was the true Light, which lighteth every man that cometh into the world. (John 1:1–9)

Acts 17:30

[30] And the times of this ignorance God winked at; but now commandeth all men every where to repent. (Acts 17:30)

Romans 1:21–25

[21] Because that, when they knew God, they glorified him not as God, neither were thankful; but became vain in their imaginations, and their foolish heart was darkened.

[22] Professing themselves to be wise, they became fools,

[23] And changed the glory of the uncorruptible God into an image made like to corruptible

man, and to birds, and fourfooted beasts, and creeping things.

²⁴ Wherefore God also gave them up to uncleanness through the lusts of their own hearts, to dishonour their own bodies between themselves:

²⁵ Who changed the truth of God into a lie, and worshipped and served the creature more than the Creator, who is blessed for ever. Amen. (Romans 1:21–25)

Romans 5:1–4

¹ Therefore being justified by faith, we have peace with God through our Lord Jesus Christ:

² By whom also we have access by faith into this grace wherein we stand, and rejoice in hope of the glory of God.

³ And not only so, but we glory in tribulations also: knowing that tribulation worketh patience;

⁴ And patience, experience; and experience, hope. (Romans 5:1–4:)

Romans 7:14–15

¹⁴ For we know that the law is spiritual: but I am carnal, sold under sin.

¹⁵ For that which I do I allow not: for what I would, that do I not; but what I hate, that do I. (Romans 7:14–15)

Romans 8:28

²⁸ And we know that all things work together for good to them that love God, to them who are the called according to his purpose. (Romans 8:28)

Romans 12:2

² And be not conformed to this world: but be ye transformed by the renewing of your mind, that ye may prove what is that good, and acceptable, and perfect, will of God. (Romans 12:2)

1 Corinthians 10:13

¹³ There hath no temptation taken you but such as is common to man: but God is faithful, who will not suffer you to be tempted above that ye are able; but will with the temptation also make a way to escape, that ye may be able to bear it. (1 Corinthians 10:13)

1 Corinthians 13:11

¹¹ When I was a child, I spake as a child, I understood as a child, I thought as a child: but when I became a man, I put away childish things. (1 Corinthians 13:11)

1 Corinthians 15:33

³³ Be not deceived: evil communications corrupt good manners. (1 Corinthians 15:33)

2 Corinthians 5:17

¹⁷ Therefore if any man be in Christ, he is a new creature: old things are passed away; behold, all things are become new. (2 Corinthians 5:17)

Galatians 6:7

⁷ Be not deceived; God is not mocked: for whatsoever a man soweth, that shall he also reap. (Galatians 6:7)

Ephesians 4:26–27

²⁶ Be ye angry, and sin not: let not the sun go down upon your wrath:

²⁷ Neither give place to the devil. (Ephesians 4:26–27)

Ephesians 4:29

²⁹ Let no corrupt communication proceed out of your mouth, but that which is good to the use of edifying, that it may minister grace unto the hearers. (Ephesians 4:29)

Ephesians 5:25–27

²⁵ Husbands, love your wives, even as Christ also loved the church, and gave himself

for it;

²⁶ That he might sanctify and cleanse it with the washing of water by the word,

²⁷ That he might present it to himself a glorious church, not having spot, or wrinkle, or any such thing; but that it should be holy and without blemish. (Ephesians 5:25–27)

Ephesians 6:10–18

¹⁰ Finally, my brethren, be strong in the Lord, and in the power of his might.

¹¹ Put on the whole armour of God, that ye may be able to stand against the wiles of the devil.

¹² For we wrestle not against flesh and blood, but against principalities, against powers, against the rulers of the darkness of this world, against spiritual wickedness in high places.

¹³ Wherefore take unto you the whole armour of God, that ye may be able to withstand in the evil day, and having done all, to stand.

¹⁴ Stand therefore, having your loins girt about with truth, and having on the breastplate of righteousness;

¹⁵ And your feet shod with the preparation of the gospel of peace;

¹⁶ Above all, taking the shield of faith, wherewith ye shall be able to quench all the fiery darts of the wicked.

¹⁷ And take the helmet of salvation, and the sword of the Spirit, which is the word of God:

¹⁸ Praying always with all prayer and supplication in the Spirit, and watching thereunto with all perseverance and supplication for all saints. (Ephesians 6:10–18;)

Philippians 4:6

⁶ Be careful for nothing; but in every thing by prayer and supplication with thanksgiving let your requests be made known unto God. (Philippians 4:6)

Philippians 4:8–9

⁸ Finally, brethren, whatsoever things are true, whatsoever things are honest, whatsoever things are just, whatsoever things are pure, whatsoever things are lovely, whatsoever things are of good report; if there be any virtue, and if there be any praise, think on these things.

⁹ Those things, which ye have both learned, and received, and heard, and seen in me, do: and the God of peace shall be with you. (Philippians 4:8–9)

Colossians 3:12–13

[12] Put on therefore, as the elect of God, holy and beloved, bowels of mercies, kindness, humbleness of mind, meekness, longsuffering;

[13] Forbearing one another, and forgiving one another, if any man have a quarrel against any: even as Christ forgave you, so also do ye. (Colossians 3:12–13)

1 Thessalonians 5:16–18

[16] Rejoice evermore.

[17] Pray without ceasing.

[18] In every thing give thanks: for this is the will of God in Christ Jesus concerning you. (1 Thessalonians 5:16–18)

2 Timothy 1:7

[7] 1048 For God hath not given us the spirit of fear; but of power, and of love, and of a sound mind. (2 Timothy 1:7)

Hebrews 11:1

[11] Now faith is the substance of things hoped for, the evidence of things not seen.

(Hebrews 11:1)

1 Peter 3:16

[16] Having a good conscience; that, whereas they speak evil of you, as of evildoers, they may be ashamed that falsely accuse your good conversation in Christ. (1 Peter 3:16)

Revelation 3:20

[20] Behold, I stand at the door, and knock: if any man hear my voice, and open the door, I will

come in to him, and will sup with him, and he with me. (Revelation 3:20)

Revelation 12:4

⁴ And his tail drew the third part of the stars of heaven, and did cast them to the earth: and the dragon stood before the woman which was ready to be delivered, for to devour her child as soon as it was born. (Revelation 12:4)

Revelation 12:7–9

⁷ And there was war in heaven: Michael and his angels fought against the dragon; and the dragon fought and his angels,

⁸ And prevailed not; neither was their place found any more in heaven.

⁹ And the great dragon was cast out, that old serpent, called the Devil, and Satan, which deceiveth the whole world: he was cast out into the earth, and his angels were cast out with him. (Revelation 12:7–9)

About the Author

My name is Jeremy Tolbert, and I was born on September 5 in 1977, in a city south of Atlanta, Georgia. I am the fourth of five children in my family. We were raised by my father, David Tolbert, who is a former chef, factory worker, and devoted Christian father, who was laid off from his job after his employer sold the company. He is known for his humor, patience, and hard work. Through his resilience and tenacity, he taught us what being a man means. And one of my fondest memories growing up is when he would take me on some of his many jobs to help out. My mother, Shirley Tolbert, who has always been known as a beautiful independent thinker, graduated from Mercer University, a prestigious Baptist College in our hometown. She served as a school teacher for many years, and she taught us about the Bible, how to conduct ourselves at home and in public, and to always speak when we enter a room! She also influenced us to go after our dreams, and through her willfulness, she took us out of the projects and into a middle-class community to raise her family in. I grew up thinking she was one of the smartest people in the world! And just like my other two brothers felt, we wanted to one day marry someone just like her.

My family was raised in the church, and later in life, my father eventually got the opportunity to pastor his very own church. As for myself, even though I was raised the right way, I found myself doing the wrong things in life, even at times when I didn't want to.

I had one child out of wedlock when I met my wife at Central Georgia Technical College (CGTC), a local technical school in my area. She inspired me to get to know God on a personal level, and her faith was the reason I began to study the Bible for myself. After we got married, she went on to graduate with her executive master's degree in business administration. Eventually, she went from being a student-worker to getting a position as the program specialist for Institutional Effectiveness. She also became the coordinator for REACH, a program aimed to assist minority male students while they're in school to help increase the graduation rate at the same college where we first met. I became the minister of my father's church, and we changed the name of the church to Joy in the Word Ministries! I led the charge to expand the church and started a radio broadcast called "The Spoken Word."

Outside of church, I was just a routine dad, married with three children, Jordan (boy), Jamiah (girl), and Jayden (boy); and as a family, we attended church services every Wednesday, Saturday, and Sunday. We played with the kids in the park, went to their sporting events, and went to Chuck E. Cheese's or drove to a theme park for their birthdays.

Life was mostly predictable, and just like every other suburban family, we worked, paid bills, and raised the kids. And then everything changed! One day, I left the house alone to get to church early to prepare the finishing touches for a sermon in a seminar I was conducting, and God spoke to me! It was nothing like the experiences I've felt in the past or any other experience a person of God would feel while preparing to speak. It instead was as if I was talking to Him in the flesh! His words were subtle and clearly heard. As He spoke and answered the questions I asked, I became cultivated and fascinated at these *deep simplicities*. Once I came to my senses, I looked frantically around to see who was it I was talking to and found no one was there! Little did I know, after that moment, His words had changed how I thought and what I knew forever! I've since canceled my radio broadcast, the church doors closed, and I left the ministry forever. I spent the next twelve years learning what this pure and simple message meant. I began teaching this powerful, prevailing, and life-changing message to college students, to highly educated and accomplished individuals, and even to inmates serving time in jail. And no matter their background, gender, or financial stability, it changed the lives of almost every single person who listen to the words that I spoke. Soon after I went through these experiences, I began to write. And now, I will begin to give the exact same message God gave me to you! In this powerful book entitled *Interest of Love*.